Breakthrough Language Series

FURTHER GER

Ruth Rach

Ruth Rach has taught German at Sussex and Bath Universities
and has been involved in adult education both as a teacher and
researcher. She has also worked for the BBC's German Service and
has written several language books including *Breakthrough German*.

General editor Brian Hill
Professor of Modern Languages, The University of Brighton

Series adviser
Janet Jenkins
Director of Programmes, The Open Learning Foundation

MACMILLAN

Acknowledgements

THIS BOOK IS DEDICATED TO

Dewi Jessica

Location recordings, studio recordings and tape production:
Gerald Ramshaw, Polytechnic of Central London
Acting: Andrew Sachs, Corinna Schnabel, Klaus Römer
Music: David Stoll
Book design and illustrations: Gillian Riley
Editor: Ursula Runde
Photos and visuals:
Gerald Ramshaw, pages 15, 40, 44, 46, 75, 102, 103, 104, 105, 141, 183
Presse-Bild-Poss, pages 23, 87, 142, 167, 179
Mary Glasgow Publications, pages 13, 19, 28, 70, 151
German National Tourist Office London, pages 26, 52, 89, 134
U.P. Wienke, p. 135, Hans Truöl p. 36
Brigitte, pages 116, 147, 148, 149, 152, 153, 164
Der Spiegel, Zeit, Stern, p. 106
Spielen und Lernen (Velber-Verlag), DM, hobby, p. 116
Zell Tourist Office, p. 88, Heidelberg Tourist Office, p. 56
Deutsche Bundesbahn, pages 39, 41, 43, 51

Radio programmes by courtesy of **Südwestfunk, Baden-Baden**

First published 1985 by Pan Books Ltd
First published 1988 by
THE MACMILLAN PRESS LTD
Houndmills, Basingstoke, Hampshire RG21 2XS
and London
Companies and representatives
throughout the world

ISBN 0–333–48188–7 paperback
ISBN 0–333–51047–X cassettes
ISBN 0–333–48189–5 book and cassette pack

Printed in Hong Kong

10   9   8
00   99   98   97   96   95

Contents

What this course is all about

Take your time to read through the next couple of pages, which explain the course to you. Understanding what is expected of you and how the course is built up will make learning easier.

Breakthrough Further German is the result of listening to hundreds of people telling us what they want and how they learn. It's *not* a beginner's course – the emphasis is on 'further'. You should already be beyond the 'Ein Bier bitte' stage if you want to make the most of this course. It helps you to keep your existing German on the boil and puts you in situations where you can use your language for making real and useful contacts, getting to know the Germans and their country better.

There is no specific progression, though the earlier units are generally easier than the later ones. Each unit has a carefully selected balance of the following:

Interviews/eavesdropped conversations with ordinary Germans which carry key vocabulary/idioms and structures. They are recorded on location in Germany and you practise understanding the real language right from the start. To help you there is a transcript in the book of each dialogue you'll hear on the cassette, plus essential vocabulary, explanatory notes and exercises directly associated with the text. Please note that you are *not* expected just to switch on and understand immediately. Learning comes from a combination of listening, using pause and rewind buttons as many times as necessary and of studying the text.

A list of key words and phrases follows the introductory interviews and exercises. You can use this to check that you have mastered the most important elements before going on.

Grammar is the cement of the language. It helps you to understand the way German works and in each unit we've included a short analysis of items we think you'll find useful. But *Breakthrough Further German* is *not* essentially a Grammar course. Understanding when you hear or read something and making yourself understood is more important than knowing all the troublesome intricacies, which the Germans themselves quite often get wrong. Don't get bogged down here. If you find some of the points too fiddly just move on.

A short reading section comes next. It consists of one or two exercises based on authentic examples you might see in the streets of a West German city or read in German papers and magazines.

Radio comprehensions unique to this course then give you some extended listening practice. In co-operation with **Südwestfunk Baden-Baden** we have selected and edited parts of real radio programmes to give you some more genuine listening practice and to help extend your vocabulary further *if you wish*. You can approach these in different ways. More advanced learners might just be able to listen in and complete the various listening exercises. On the other hand you might need to go through them bit by bit, helped by the transcripts which we've put at the back of the book. It's up to you to select the approach which most suits your experience and your needs.

A speaking section in which you can practise relating information to your own life concludes each unit. The tasks here are open-ended. That means there is no right and wrong, through we do give you some ideas on what to say, and on the cassette you'll find a model version spoken by our two actors, Klaus Römer and Corinna Schnabel.

At the end of the book we've put a comprehensive vocabulary (both German–English and English–German). This contains all the words in the course apart from the most obvious ones, like **der**, **die**, **das**, **eins**, **zwei**, **drei**, etc.

How to work through a unit

1 Dialoge Dialogues

In each unit four dialogues recorded on location in Germany introduce the new language material, covering different aspects of the unit theme. You are not expected to understand each dialogue first time. Just listen, then rewind and, using your pause button, study line by line and read the vocabulary and the notes. Key phrases are marked ♦ and you should try to remember them as you'll practise them in the exercises. When you think you've mastered a dialogue, rewind to the beginning and without using your book listen again right through to see if you've really understood. Zero your tape counter at the beginning of each cassette side and note the numbers for each dialogue in the ☐ as you go along.

2 Übungen Exercises

There are two or three exercises linked to each dialogue, the first two practise listening and vocabulary reinforcement, the last one gives you an opportunity to speak. In most speaking exercises in this section you're given a prompt in English by our presenter Andrew Sachs. Stop the tape, say your part aloud in German, then start the tape again and listen to the correct version which will be given by either Klaus Römer or Corinna Schnabel. You will probably need to go over the speaking exercises a few times until you are familiar with the pattern. Before you start speaking, read the instruction to each exercise carefully in your book.

3 Wörter und Wendungen Key words and phrases

This is a list of the most important words and phrases from all four dialogues which were marked ♦ in the notes. Try to learn this page by heart.

4 Grammatik Grammar

As this is *not* a grammar course, the selections and explanations on these two pages are not exhaustive; we are just highlighting some of the key elements of the German language. Skip this section if you really don't like grammar, but give it a try first. The grammar section is interspersed with short exercises, so that you can test yourself.

5 Übungen: Lesen Reading exercises

This section is based on passages taken from original German brochures, newspapers or magazines. Some of it might seem quite difficult, but we have given you some extra vocabulary to help you understand the extracts. Make sure you've really understood the gist of each passage before doing the exercises linked to it.

6 Übungen: Radio Radio section

These authentic excerpts from German radio are, of course, spoken at normal speed. The first time you hear them you may not understand very much at all. But this is a useful way of sharpening your listening skills. If you persevere you will find that, by the time you get to the later units, you will be able to tune in to real German much more easily. Included as part of this section are some listening tasks, often general questions to be answered. Working on these will help you to understand what is said – as will the vocabulary below.

There is also a transcript of the recordings (see p.208). Depending on how difficult you find the excerpts, you can use the transcripts in different ways. If you do understand fairly easily then it is probably best not to look at the transcripts until after you have done the exercises. To make it easier you could, however, read the transcripts through before listening and/or listen and read at the same time. You will have to decide what suits you best. In later units try to reduce your reliance on the transcripts.

7 Sprechen Sie selbst Open-ended speaking exercises

The last section in each unit gives you opportunity to speak again, but much more freely than in the exercises linked to the dialogues. You can adapt the exercise to your own situation. We'll only give you some guidelines or some phrases you should try to use with the instruction to each exercise in your book. On the cassette Klaus or Corinna will speak a model version for you, but your version can be quite different without being wrong.

8 Study guide

At the beginning of each unit you'll find a grid which shows you on what page you'll find the individual sections. Use this as a check list to cross off the tasks you have completed.

Making the most of this course

- There is a lot of material, so decide what you want most from the course and allocate your time accordingly between the sections.

- We've tried to make the course as interesting and enjoyable as possible, but language learning is not a piece of cake. So, be patient, and above all don't get angry with yourself if you find you're progressing too slowly.

- Have confidence in us. Real language is complex and you won't understand everything first time. Treat it as a game and we will build up your knowledge slowly, selecting what is important at each stage.

- Try to study regularly but in short periods. Thirty minutes a day is usually better than a block of three and a half hours a week.

- It helps to articulate, to speak the words out loud. This may seem strange at first, but actually using the words with a friend or to yourself, is a good way of practising and remembering.

- Don't be afraid to write in the book and make your own notes. With most exercises which need writing or filling in we've provided the necessary space, but if there isn't enough room just use an extra bit of paper, or, better still, have your own special course exercise book for these tasks and extended notes. (We've also left some blank pages for extra notes at the back of the book.)

Abbreviations

m. = masculine
f. = feminine
n. = neuter
pl. = plural
sing. = singular
lit. = literally
sep. = separable

 This symbol indicates a speaking exercise

1 Am liebsten Frankenwein

You will learn

- to describe your favourite food and drink/beverage
- to talk about good and bad restaurants
- to talk about shopping

... and you'll get a chance to try out a recipe

To keep track, mark off the tasks below as you complete them.

Study guide

		Seite
	Dialog 1 + Übungen	8
	Dialog 2 + Übungen	10
	Dialog 3 + Übungen	12
	Dialog 4 + Übungen	14
	Wörter und Wendungen	16
	Grammatik	17
	Lesen	19
	Radio	21
	Sprechen Sie selbst	22

Dialog 1: Eine Meinungsumfrage

*The dialogues (**Dialoge**) present the new material. Work on them until you can understand them and pay special attention to the phrases and words marked ◗ in the vocabulary and the notes.*

Biba	Was essen Sie am liebsten?
Ingrid	Mmm – Schokoladeneis mit Schlagsahne.
Biba	Und was trinken Sie am liebsten?
Ingrid	Ah – 'n guten Wein, 'n herben Frankenwein.
Biba	Un was essen Sie am wenigsten gern?
Ingrid	Ah – so'n – so'n widerlich faden Haferschleim.
Biba	Und das Getränk, das Sie am wenigsten mögen?
Ingrid	Hm – widerlich süßer Mokkalikör.

Biba	Was essen Sie am liebsten?
Silke	Eingelegte Heringe und Gemüse.
Biba	Und was trinken Sie am liebsten?
Silke	Ostfriesentee, das ist schwarzer Tee mit Sahne und Kandiszucker.
Biba	Und was essen Sie am wenigsten gern?
Silke	Graupensuppe.
Biba	Und was trinken Sie am wenigsten gern?
Silke	Lauwarme Milch.

Biba	Was ißt du am liebsten?
Henning	Rehrücken mit Knödeln und Schwarzwälder Kirschtorte.
Biba	Und was trinkst du am liebsten?
Henning	Coca Cola.
Biba	Und was ißt du am wenigsten gern?
Henning	Weiche Eier mag ich überhaupt nicht, und harte Eier schmecken auch nicht besonders.
Biba	Und was trinkst du am wenigsten gern?
Henning	Ganz süße Limonade – das schmeckt scheußlich.

die Meinungsumfrage opinion poll
der Mokkalikör Mocha liqueur
◗ **das Getränk** drink, beverage
die Graupensuppe barley soup
lauwarm lukewarm
der Rehrücken saddle of venison
der Knödel dumpling

◗ **was essen Sie am liebsten?** what's your favourite food? (lit. what do you most like eating?)

◗ **was trinken Sie am liebsten?** what's your favourite drink?

'n herben Frankenwein short for **einen herben Frankenwein** a dry Franconian wine; in colloquial German **einen** is often shortened to **'n** or **'nen**, **eine** to **'ne**, **ein** to **'n**.

◗ **was essen Sie am wenigsten gern?** what's your least favourite food? (lit. what do you least like eating?).

eingelegte Heringe pickled herring; similar: **eingelegte Gurken** pickled gherkins.

◗ **das Gemüse** vegetables; **das Gemüse** is always singular in German: **wo ist das Gemüse?** where are the vegetables?

der Ostfriesentee lit. East Frisian tea; you serve **Ostfriesentee** by pouring it over rock candy, then cream is added.

Übungen

Before you start the first exercise, read the paragraph on exercises in the introduction on p.5.

1 Schmeckt's gut oder scheußlich? Have a look at the food and drink items below. Which ones were liked by Ingrid, Silke and Henning and which were not? Complete the list below. (Answers p.199)

süße Limonade   weiche Eier   Ostfriesentee   eingelegte Heringe Frankenwein   Schokoladeneis   Graupensuppe   Mokkalikör lauwarme Milch   Rehrücken   Schwarzwälder Kirschtorte   Coca Cola

😊 gut	😠 scheußlich

2 A lot of complaints! What's wrong with the foods and beverages below? Fill in the squares as we did in **a**. (Answers p.199)

a. Der Haferschleim ist viel zu | F | A | D | E |

b. Der Frankenwein ist viel zu | H | | |

c. Die Limonade ist viel zu | S | |

d. Diese Eier sind viel zu | W | | |

e. Diese Eier sind viel zu | H | | |

f. Der Ostfriesentee ist viel zu | S | C | H | | | | |

3 Your turn to speak. On the cassette you'll be asked to take part in a conversation. Corinna will ask you questions about your favourite foods and drinks. Andrew will whisper what you should answer in English. Say your answers aloud in German, then listen to the correct version given by Klaus, then go on to answer the next question in the same way.

◆ **'n widerlich faden Haferschleim** some disgustingly bland porridge; **widerlich** disgusting, revolting, see also above: **widerlich süß** disgustingly sweet; **fade** bland, **der Haferschleim** porridge.

◆ **weiche Eier mag ich überhaupt nicht** soft-boiled eggs I don't like at all; **ich mag** from **mögen** to like.

◆ **das schmeckt scheußlich** that tastes horrible; **das schmeckt gut** that tastes good.

Dialog 2: Im 'Weißen Bock'

Gabi	Guten Tag.
Ruth	Guten Tag. Ich möchte gerne was zu essen, bitte.
Gabi	Ja, hier ist die Tageskarte.
Ruth	Können Sie mir etwas empfehlen?
Gabi	Wir haben hier Fisch, er ist aber nicht frisch, er ist gefroren.
Ruth	Ach nee, das mag ich nicht so gern.
Gabi	Vielleicht das Jägerschnitzel?
Ruth	Hm – ist das sehr scharf?
Gabi	Nein, das ist nicht scharf.
Ruth	Und ist das mit Knoblauch?
Gabi	Ein wenig, ja.
Ruth	Ach nein – lieber nicht.
Gabi	Vielleicht das Rumpsteak mit Zwiebeln?
Ruth	Ja, hier steht 'englisch' – was heißt das denn?
Gabi	Das ist blutig.
Ruth	Das mag ich nicht so gern. Aber vielleicht können Sie in der Küche sagen, ich möchte das gut durch?
Gabi	Ja ... Wir haben dazu grüne Bohnen, die sind frisch.
Ruth	Gut, und ich möchte auch ganz gern 'nen Salat dazu noch, ja.
Gabi	Möchten Sie etwas trinken?
Ruth	Ja, gerne, ich möchte gerne ein kleines Bier.
Gabi	Danke.

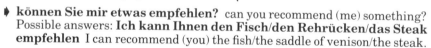

der 'Weiße Bock' restaurant in Heidelberg
- **die Kellnerin** waitress
- **der Kellner** waiter
  die Tageskarte today's menu
  der Knoblauch garlic
  grüne Bohnen green beans
- **scharf** here: hot, spicy

- **können Sie mir etwas empfehlen?** can you recommend (me) something?
  Possible answers: **Ich kann Ihnen den Fisch/den Rehrücken/das Steak empfehlen** I can recommend (you) the fish/the saddle of venison/the steak.

- **das Jägerschnitzel** a piece of meat (**Schnitzel**) fried in mushroom sauce; **der Jäger** hunter.

  ach nee oh no; **nee** is colloquial for **nein** (no).

- **lieber nicht** (I'd) rather not.

  was heißt das (denn)? what's that (then)?

- **das ist blutig** that's rare (lit. bloody); similar: **das ist medium** that's medium, **das ist gut durch** that's well done (of steaks).

- **ich möchte auch ganz gern 'nen Salat dazu** I'd quite like a salad with it as well.

Übungen *Exercises*

4 Here are a few statements in German about Dialogue 2, but a few words are missing. Write them in the blanks. (Answers p.199)

a. Ruth ist im 'Weißen Bock' und möchte etwas ....

b. Sie mag den Fisch nicht, weil er .... ist.

c. Sie mag das Jägerschnitzel nicht, weil es mit .... ist.

d. Sie möchte das Rumpsteak ....

e. Sie möchte auch ein .... Bier trinken.

5 Have a look at the menu Ruth has chosen her meal from, then answer the questions below. (Answers p.199)

Vocabulary:
mit Pilzen with mushrooms
die Scholle plaice
gebraten fried

die Kalbsleber calf's liver
die Pommes Frites (pl.) chips, French fries

Tageskarte

1	Großer Salatteller	**DM 5.80**
2	Omelette mit Pilzen und Salat	**DM 7.50**
3	Nordsee-Scholle, gebraten, mit großem Salatteller	**DM 9.50**
4	Kalbsleber mit Zwiebeln, Kartoffeln, grünem Salat	**DM 11.00**
5	Jägerschnitzel mit Pommes Frites, Salat und grünen Bohnen	**DM 13.50**
6	Rumpsteak mit Zwiebeln, Pommes Frites, Salat	**DM 17.50**

What would you order if you wanted . . .

a. . . . something hot but no fish and no meat   No. ....

b. . . . a fish dish   No. ....

c. . . . a cold, non-fattening snack   No. ....

d. . . . a meat dish without onions   No. ....

e. . . . a meat dish with green beans and a salad?   No. ....

6 You're in a restaurant, looking at the menu from Exercise 5. The waitress is coming to take your order. On the cassette Andrew will prompt you again in English. Say your order in German, then listen to Klaus. You'll practise:

ich möchte . . .   **lieber nicht**
Was können Sie empfehlen?

11

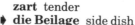

Dialog 3: Ein Reinfall

Herr
Frauenfeld

Wenn Sie einmal gut essen gehen wollen, müssen Sie schon in ein teures Restaurant gehen. Aber auch da haben wir kürzlich einen ziemlichen Reinfall erlebt. Ich hatte meine Frau zum Geburtstag eingeladen, und wir wollten gut essen. Also gingen wir in ein teures Restaurant.

Aber das Fleisch, was sie uns brachten, war nicht zart! Es war zäh wie Leder, und ich hätte mir beinahe die Zähne ausgebissen daran. Auch die Beilagen waren nicht besonders gut. Ich hatte den Verdacht, daß die Bohnen aus der Dose kamen. Und die Kartoffeln waren sehr matschig. Das einzige, was gut schmeckte, war der Salat. Aber sagen Sie doch selbst, gehen Sie nur wegen eines guten Salats in ein teures Restaurant und legen eine ganze Stange Geld hin?

♦ **der Reinfall** disaster, flop
kürzlich recently
erleben to experience

zart tender
♦ **die Beilage** side dish
♦ **matschig** soggy

ich hatte meine Frau zum Geburtstag eingeladen I had invited my wife out for her birthday (i.e. for a meal); **einladen** (sep.) to invite: **ich lade ihn zum Essen ein** I'm inviting him for dinner.

wir wollten gut essen we wanted to have a nice meal out (lit. we wanted to eat well).

♦ **es war zäh wie Leder** it was as tough as old boots (lit. tough as leather).

ich hätte mir beinahe die Zähne ausgebissen (daran) I nearly lost my teeth trying to get a chunk out of it (lit. I nearly had bitten my teeth out).

ich hatte den Verdacht I suspected (lit. I had the suspicion).

wegen eines Salats because of a salad.

eine ganze Stange (coll.) a lot of money; **die Stange** (lit.) pole.

hinlegen (sep.) to lay down, put down, here: to pay.

Note: There are quite a few verbs in the past tense here, e.g. **hatte ... eingeladen, haben ... erlebt, wollten, brachten, kamen, waren, schmeckte** etc. See **Grammatik** Unit 5 and Unit 8 for details about talking in the past.

Übungen *Exercises*
7 Not quite the same! Have a look at the expressions in here and find the bits with a similar meaning in Dialogue 3. Underline them in the dialogue. (Answers p.199)

Example: Das Fleisch war sehr *hart* = das Fleisch war <u>zäh wie Leder</u>.

a. Da haben wir *vor kurzem eine ziemlich schlechte Erfahrung gemacht*.

b. Das Fleisch, das sie uns brachten, war *nicht weich*.

c. Auch das *Gemüse* war nicht besonders gut.

d. Die Kartoffeln waren *überhaupt nicht fest*.

e. Das einzige, das ich *gerne aß*, war der Salat.

f. Legen Sie wegen eines Salats eine *große Summe* Geld hin?

8 Im Gegenteil! Pick the opposites to the words in italics from the box below and fill them in. (Answers p.199)

a. Das Fleisch ist nicht *zart*, es ist ....

b. Die Bohnen sind nicht *aus der Dose*, sie sind ....

c. Das Restaurant ist nicht *billig*, es ist ....

d. Der Wein ist nicht *süß*, er ist ....

f. Die Limonade schmeckt nicht *gut*, sie schmeckt ....

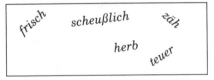

frisch   scheußlich   zäh

herb   teuer

9 Your turn to speak. Tell Corinna about a nice meal out which turned out to be a disaster. Andrew will prompt you as usual.

Dialog 4: Wo kaufen Sie ein?

Ruth   Wo kaufen Sie normalerweise ein?

Biba   Lebensmittel kaufe ich normalerweise im Supermarkt, und das Fleisch kaufe ich frisch, beim Metzger um die Ecke.

Ruth   Und wo kaufen Sie das Gemüse?

Biba   Entweder auch im Supermarkt, oder am Samstag dann auf dem Markt. Dort gibt es eine gute Auswahl und auch mal was ganz Besonderes, wie Mangos, oder Eissalat, oder irgendwelche Pilze. Heute zum Beispiel habe ich das hier gekauft...

Ruth   Ja, was ist das denn? Das sieht ja ganz komisch aus.

Biba   Ach, das sind so Pilze, die hab' ich heute auch das erste Mal gesehen. Sie sollen aus China kommen.

Ruth   Und wie werden die gekocht?

Biba   Die Verkäuferin am Markt hat mir erklärt, ich soll sie einfach in Butter dünsten, wie Champignons auch.

Ruth   Halten die sich im Kühlschrank?

Biba   Nein, das glaube ich nicht. Pilze soll man gleich essen.

---

normalerweise usually, normally
♦ **die Lebensmittel** (pl.) groceries
der Eissalat iceberg lettuce

komisch here: strange, exotic
die Champignons (pl.) button mushrooms

♦ **Lebensmittel kaufe ich... Fleisch kaufe ich...** groceries I buy... meat I buy... Note the inverted word order: The verb (**kaufen**) comes *after* the subject (**ich**). The emphasis is on **Lebensmittel** and **Fleisch**, therefore they have been put in front of the sentence. If she *hadn't* wanted the stress Biba would have said: **ich kaufe Lebensmittel/Fleisch im Supermarkt/beim Metzger.**

♦ **beim Metzger um die Ecke** at the butcher shop around the corner;
♦ similar: **beim Bäcker/Schuster um die Ecke** at the bakery/shoe-repair shop around the corner.

entweder... oder... either... or...: **Fisch gibt es entweder auf dem Markt oder im Fischgeschäft** you can buy fish either in the market or at the fishmonger's.

♦ **dort gibt es eine gute Auswahl** there is a good choice there.

was ganz Besonderes something really special.

irgendwelche Pilze mushrooms of some kind.

die sollen aus China kommen they are supposed to come from China.

♦ **wie werden die gekocht?** how are they prepared (lit. cooked)?

ich soll sie einfach in Butter dünsten I'm supposed to just sauté them in butter; remember **braten** to fry, **grillen** to grill, **backen** to bake.

♦ **halten die sich im Kühlschrank?** do they keep in the fridge?
sich halten to keep: **die Blumen halten sich gut** the flowers are keeping well.

Übungen *Exercises*

10 Try this word puzzle by filling in the squares. The letters numbered 1–10 will give you a famous German 'institution'. (Answers p.199)

a. Auf dem Markt gibt es manchmal auch was ganz →

b. Diese Pilze kommen aus →

c. Das Fleisch kaufe ich gleich um die →

d. Ich kaufe die Lebensmittel im →

e. Der .... hat frisches Fleisch →

f. Auf dem Markt gibt es eine gute →

g. Die Pilze halten sich nicht im →

h. Am Samstag kaufe ich das Gemüse auf dem →

i. Die Pilze kann man in .... dünsten, →

j. genauso wie .... →

1	2	3	4	5	6	7	8	9	10

11 There are two speaking exercises this time. First, Klaus is asking you about your shopping habits. As usual, Andrew will prompt you by whispering your answers in English. Some phrases you'll use are:

im Supermarkt   **eine gute Auswahl**
beim Metzger   **etwas Besonderes**
beim Bäcker   **am Samstag**

12 In the second speaking exercise for Dialogue 4 it's your turn to ask Corinna some questions on something she's bought in the market. Use your pause button to give yourself time to think after Andrew's prompts.

Wörter und Wendungen   *Key words and phrases*

*Each Unit has a **key words and phrases** section. Make sure you really know these before you go on.*

Likes and dislikes

Was essen/trinken Sie gern?	What do you like to eat/drink?
Was essen/trinken Sie ...	What do you like to eat/drink ...
am liebsten?	most of all?
am wenigsten gern?	least of all?
Ich esse/trinke gern ...	I like to eat/drink ...
Am liebsten esse/trinke ich ...	I like to eat/drink most of all ...
Fisch	fish
Fleisch	meat
Gemüse	vegetables
Bier	beer
Wein	wine
Tee	tea
Weiche Eier/süße Limonade mag ich überhaupt nicht	I don't like soft-boiled eggs/sweet lemonade at all
Das schmeckt gut/nicht gut/ scheußlich/widerlich/fade	That tastes good/does not taste good/tastes disgusting/revolting/ bland

In a restaurant

Ich möchte gerne etwas (zu) essen/trinken	I'd like something to eat/drink
Was können Sie empfehlen?	What can you recommend?
Wir haben ...	We have ...
Fisch	fish
Rumpsteak	rumpsteak
Jägerschnitzel	schnitzel
Salat	salad
Das ist ...	That's ...
scharf	spicy
blutig	rare
medium	medium
gut durch	well done
gefroren	frozen
frisch	fresh
aus der Dose	canned
mit Zwiebeln	with onions
mit Knoblauch	with garlic

Shops and markets

Lebensmittel/Gemüse/Brot/Fleisch kaufe ich ...	I buy groceries/vegetables/bread/ meat ...
im Supermarkt	at the supermarket
auf dem Markt	at the market
beim Bäcker	at the bakery
beim Metzger	at the butcher shop
Da gibt es eine gute Auswahl	There's a good choice there

Grammatik   *Grammar*

This book is <u>not</u> intended to be a comprehensive grammar course. If 'grammar' really puts you off you can probably get by without studying these sections.
However, understanding the structure of a language and seeing how it is put together can be fascinating and useful. Don't expect to grasp all the grammar at once. It needs patience, and even native German speakers make 'mistakes'. We'll try to present the most important grammar in digestible portions.

Adverbs and adjectives

These are words which tell you more about a verb:

Concorde flies   Concorde flies <u>fast</u> (adverb)

or noun:
It's a book   It's a <u>good</u> book (adjective)

Adverbs often behave similarly in German and English, i.e. if you make a comparison they add **-er** or **-(e)st**:

Sie läuft	**schnell**	**schneller**	**am schnell<u>sten</u>**
She runs	fast	fast<u>er</u>	the fast<u>est</u>
Es riecht	**frisch**	**frisch<u>er</u>**	**am frischesten**
It smells	fresh	fresh<u>er</u>	the fresh<u>est</u>

The form of the adverb with **-er** is called comparative, the form with **-(e)st** is called superlative. Here are some examples of common comparative and superlative adverbs:

zart	**zarter**	**am zartesten**
tender	more tender	most tender
wenig	**weniger**	**am wenigsten**
little	less	least
laut	**lauter**	**am lautesten**
loud	louder	loudest
schnell	**schneller**	**am schnellsten**
fast	faster	fastest
glücklich	**glücklicher**	**am glücklichsten**
happy	happier	happiest

13 Try this exercise. Write out the comparative and superlative forms of the words below. (Answers p.199)

a. zäh   ....

b. weich   ....

c. matschig   ....

d. klein   ....

e. herb   ....

Adjectives do not add information to a verb (like adverbs), but to a noun: **der gute Wein** the good wine, **das zarte Fleisch** the tender meat. The most difficult thing about adjectives in German is that – unlike adverbs – they have endings, and on top of that the endings change before a noun. The rules for this are very complex, so don't attempt to learn them all at once. Basically there are two things which decide the ending of an adjective:

a. the word preceding the adjective, e.g. **der** or **ein** (**der alte Mann, ein alter Mann**).

b. the function of the phrase (adjective + noun) in a sentence, e.g. is it subject or object:
Der alte Mann ist krank. (Subject) The old man is sick.
Ich sehe den alten Mann. (Object) I see the old man.

Here is what happens to adjectives when they follow a word of the so-called 'der' group. (The 'ein' group are dealt with in Unit 2.) By 'der' group we mean any of the words for 'the' (i.e. **der**, **die**, **das**) plus any of the variations of **dieser** (this), **jener** (that) and **jeder** (each). Here are some examples:

Der frische Fisch schmeckt gut.	The fresh fish tastes good.
Die kalte Milch ist gut.	The cold milk is good.
Das deutsche Bier ist wunderbar.	German beer is wonderful.
Ich esse den frischen Fisch.	I'm eating fresh fish.
Ich trinke die kalte Milch.	I'm drinking cold milk.
Ich trinke das deutsche Bier.	I'm drinking German beer.
Ich trinke die deutschen Weine.	I drink the German wines.
mit der frischen Milch.	with fresh milk.
bei dem schlechten Wetter.	in bad weather.

As you can see from the above examples, the ending of the adjective is sometimes **-e**, sometimes **-en**. Whenever the adjective is part of the *subject* (nominative) it always has **-e**: **Der frische Fisch schmeckt gut.** When it is part of the direct *object* (accusative) the ending is **-e** with **die** or **das** words: **Ich trinke die kalte Milch/das deutsche Bier,** but **-en** after **der** (masculine) which itself changes to **den**: **Ich esse den frischen Fisch.** In all other cases the adjective ending is **-en**: **bei dem schlechten Wetter, die deutschen Weine.**

Adjective endings	Masculine (**der**)	Feminine (**die**)	Neuter (**das**)
Subject (nominative)	**-e**	**-e**	**-e**
Object (accusative)	**-en**	**-e**	**-e**
All others:	**-en**		

14 Fill in the right adjective endings as we have done for **a**. (Answers p.199)

a. Die lauwarme Milch schmeckt scheußlich.

b. Ich habe das klein............. Glas kaputt gemacht.

c. Er hat den alt............ Mann besucht.

d. Die grün............. Bohnen schmecken herrlich.

e. Der französisch............. Wein ist teuer.

Übungen: Lesen

15 Nearly all German towns have a **Wochenmarkt**, i.e. a market that takes place on a certain day of the week (often on Saturdays). You can buy all sorts of things there, from fresh fruits and vegetables to pottery, junk, plants, household goods, kitchenware, etc. If you wanted to be informed on what's offered or what prices are like, you can have a look at the **Marktbericht** (market report) in the local paper. Here is an extract of the **Mittwochsmarkt** (Wednesday market) in the city of Ulm. Study it, then answer the questions below. (Answers p.199)

Mittwochsmarkt

Auf dem Ulmer Markt gab es gestern eine gute Auswahl an italienischen Trauben und Williams-Birnen. Auch Pfirsiche aus Griechenland wurden billig verkauft. Relativ teuer sind jetzt die Erdbeeren. Es gab sehr schöne Tomaten, grüne Bohnen und billige Gurken. Sehr teuer aber ist zur Zeit der Blumenkohl.

Die Preise für Gemüse (per Kilo): Spinat 3,– bis 3,60 DM; Tomaten 1,60; Kartoffeln 1,–; Blumenkohl 2,– bis 3,50; rote Zwiebeln 2,40 bis 2,80; gelbe Zwiebeln 1,50 bis 2,–; Gurken 0,50 bis 1,20 (per Stück).

Die Preise für Obst (per Kilo): Trauben 2,50 bis 2,80; Birnen 2,– bis 2,80; Pfirsiche 2,50 bis 2,80; Erdbeeren 4,– bis 4,50; Zitronen 2 bis 3 Stück 1,– DM.

Vocabulary:
die Traube grape
die Birne pear
der Pfirsich peach
die Erdbeere strawberry

der Blumenkohl cauliflower
der Spinat spinach
die Zitrone lemon

a. Where do the peaches come from? ....

b. Which fruits come from Italy? ....

c. Which fruit is comparatively expensive? ....

d. What would you pay for a cucumber? ....

e. Which kind of onion is the cheapest? ....

f. How much are the lemons? ....

16 Try to understand this recipe – you'll find some extra vocabulary below, then mark the correct boxes. (Answers p.199)

Das schnelle Rezept

Schweineschnitzel mit Senfsoße

(zwei Portionen)

2 Schweineschnitzel
30 Gramm Margarine
Salz
Pfeffer
Crème Fraîche
1 Löffel Senf

Schnitzel in heißer Margarine von jeder Seite etwa 7 Minuten braten. Herausnehmen, salzen und pfeffern. Crème Fraîche zum Bratensatz geben. Die Soße dann mit Salz, Pfeffer und Senf abschmecken und über die Schnitzel gießen.
Beilagen: Salzkartoffeln und Bohnen.

Vocabulary:
die Senfsoße mustard sauce
der Löffel spoon
der Bratensatz meat juice

abschmecken to flavour
gießen to pour

a. Would the recipe appeal to a vegetarian?
☐ yes
☐ no

b. Do you need herbs for this dish?
☐ yes
☐ no

c. Do you leave the Schnitzel in the pan all the time?
☐ yes
☐ no

d. Do you have the Schnitzel with rice and beans?
☐ yes
☐ no

e. Is the dish for one person only?
☐ yes
☐ no

Übungen: Radio

For these exercises you will always hear authentic radio material recorded from **Südwestfunk**, a radio station in Baden-Baden in southwest Germany. The extracts we have chosen are intended to give you practice at listening to spoken German, but you are not expected to understand every word. Just try to get the gist of each item by listening several times and using the extra vocabulary supplied in the book. Complete transcripts of all radio sections can be found at the back of the book starting on p.208.

17 The first recordings in this section are two commercials advertising a snack and a drink. Listen, refer to the vocabulary if you have to, then mark the right boxes below. (Answers p.199)

Vocabulary (**Deit**):
dieser Stau! what a jam!
sein Lieblings- his favourite
in Form bleiben to stay in shape
die schlanke Linie slimline
der Durst thirst
dick fat

Vocabulary (**Chips-frisch**):
mein liebendes Weib my loving spouse
probieren to try
lecker delicious
die Chips (pl.) crisps, potato chips
fabelhaft fantastic, great
der Schatz treasure
knusper-knabber-knackig-frisch crispy-crunchy-crackling fresh

a. Deit is
  ☐ a chocolate bar
  ☐ a drink
  ☐ a special kind of fruit

b. Chips-frisch is
  ☐ a packet of crisps/potato chips
  ☐ a sandwich
  ☐ chocolate with nuts

c. Which product would appeal to slimmers?
  ☐ Deit
  ☐ Chips-frisch

d. Deit has
  ☐ chocolate flavour
  ☐ fruit flavour
  ☐ vanilla flavour

e. Above all, **Chips-frisch** tastes
  ☐ sweet
  ☐ bitter
  ☐ fresh

18 Write down all the adjectives you've heard in the two commercials, e.g. **dick**, **schlank**, etc. (Answers p.199)

....

....

....

19 Another commercial advertising food – baby food. **Milupa** is a famous baby food brand in West Germany. Listen to the advertisement, then fill in the missing words in the transcript below. (Answers p.208 in complete transcript)

Vocabulary:

die Mütterberatung mothers' counseling service	**die Rezeptur** recipe
brauchen to need	**ausreichend** sufficient
das Getränk drink, beverage	**gesüßt** sweetened

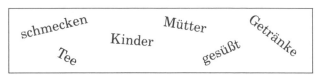

Die Milupa-.. beratung informiert:

.... haben oft Durst, das wissen wir, und sie

brauchen die richtigen Getränke. Milupa hat jetzt ....

......................-Getränke mit neuer Rezeptur. Sie sind leicht, aber

ausreichend ...., und sie ....

.... kleinen und großen Kindern.

Übungen: Sprechen Sie selbst

Open-ended speaking exercises

In this section it's your turn to speak again, but the exercises here are 'open-ended', i.e. you can adapt the exercise to cover your own situation – there is no 'right' and 'wrong'. We'll only give you some guidelines or some phrases you should try to use. On the cassette there'll always be a 'model' version, spoken by Klaus or Corinna of what you could have said, but these are just suggestions – your version might be quite different. Here's just one exercise to start with.

20 Here are some key words and phrases you have come across in this unit. Try to make up a sentence with each of them. Check **Wörter und Wendungen** on p.16 if you're not sure what a phrase means. There are sample sentences on the cassette for comparison.

das schmeckt	**am liebsten**
überhaupt nicht	**empfehlen**
ich mag	**eine gute Auswahl**
frisch	

2 Mein Traumurlaub

You will learn

- to talk about your dream holiday/vacation
- to say what you do at Christmas
- to understand the weather report

... and you'll get a chance to sample German holiday brochures

Study guide

Dialog 1: Mein Traumurlaub

Biba Wie stellen Sie sich Ihren Traumurlaub vor?

Silke Am liebsten würde ich den ganzen Tag lang nichts tun – am Strand liegen, mich von der Sonne rösten lassen, abends schön essen gehen, tanzen, vielleicht in die Disko gehen.

Amin Ja, wissen Sie, mein Traumurlaub – das wäre, mit einem guten Freund in einem Jeep durch die Rocky Mountains zu fahren, in Amerika; abends am Lagerfeuer zu sitzen, ganz alleine, tagelang, wochenlang niemanden zu sehen. Und eine andere Möglichkeit wäre, mit der transsibirischen Eisenbahn von Moskau quer nach Peking – nicht mit dem Flugzeug, das fände ich langweilig.

Ingrid Oh – ich würde gern einen Bildungsurlaub machen: Griechenland, Ägypten, vielleicht sogar Indien, und dort die ganzen Kunstschätze besichtigen. Vielleicht mit einem Reiseführer, der alles genau erklären kann. Also das stelle ich mir ganz toll vor, so über die Geschichte dort etwas zu erfahren, und so über die Hintergründe, wie die Menschen dort gelebt haben.

▶ **der Strand** beach
▶ **das Lagerfeuer** camp fire
allein(e) alone
niemand nobody

die Möglichkeit possibility
▶ **das Flugzeug** aeroplane
Griechenland Greece
Ägypten Egypt
Indien India

▶ **wie stellen Sie sich Ihren Traumurlaub vor?** how do you see (lit. imagine) your dream holiday/vacation? **sich vorstellen** (to imagine) is a reflexive verb and also separable. This means that the prefix **vor** splits from the verb **stellen** in certain cases (see **Grammatik**).

... mich von der Sonne rösten lassen let myself be roasted by the sun.

das wäre ... that would be ...

▶ **mit der transsibirischen Eisenbahn ... quer nach Peking** by Trans-Siberian Railway right through to Peking.

▶ **der Bildungsurlaub** special trip where you combine fun with education, increasingly popular in Germany; **die Bildung** education, **der Urlaub** holiday, vacation. Note that such compound nouns (words consisting of two separate nouns) will take the gender of the second word: <u>der</u> **Bildungsurlaub**. Similarly: <u>der</u> **Reiseführer** (= **die Reise, der Führer**) tour guide.

▶ **der Kunstschatz** (= **die Kunst, der Schatz**) art treasure; **besichtigen** to see, have a look at.

ganz toll (coll.) really exciting

(so) über die Geschichte dort etwas zu erfahren to learn something about the history there; **erfahren** to learn, to experience.

wie die Menschen dort gelebt haben how people used to live there.

der Hintergrund, die Hintergründe background(s)

Übungen

1 Who says what? Play through the dialogue without looking at the text. <u>S</u>ilke is the first person interviewed, <u>A</u>min the second, <u>I</u>ngrid the third. (Answers p.199)

My dream holiday/vacation is to ...

a. go to Greece or Egypt, or even India   S   A   I

b. go to a disco in the evening   S   A   I

c. take a trip on the Trans-Siberian Railway   S   A   I

d. do nothing at all   S   A   I

e. drive through the Rocky Mountains in a jeep   S   A   I

f. roast in the sun on the beach   S   A   I

g. learn more about the culture and history of a country
  S   A   I

h. sit by a camp fire in the evening   S   A   I

2 What would you like to do on holiday? Have a look at the drawings and write down what the people in the pictures are dreaming about. (Answers p.199)

a. am Strand liegen   **b.** ....   **c.** ....

d. ....   **e.** ....   **f.** ....

3 Your turn to speak. Andrew will whisper what you should say – say it, then listen to the correct version and go on to the next sentence. Start each sentence with **am liebsten**. You'll practice the phrases below, but watch out, they are not in the right order.

Am liebsten würde ich ...

... durch die Rocky Mountains fahren
... am Strand liegen
... in die Disko gehen

Dialog 2: Sommerferien

Der Bayrische Wald

Ruth Wann machen Sie Sommerferien?

Heide Na ja, wir haben zwei Kinder – eins ist in der Schule und das andere ist im Kindergarten, und das müssen wir beachten.

Ruth Ja, fahren Sie dann überhaupt weg?

Heide Ja, ja, das schon, aber wir fahren genau dann weg, wenn die Kinder Ferien haben, also so im Juli oder August.

Ruth Ja, und wohin fahren Sie denn da?

Heide Wir fahren in den Bayrischen Wald. Wir machen Urlaub auf einem Bauernhof. Das ist nicht allzu teuer, die Leute sind freundlich zu den Kindern, die Luft ist gesund, das Essen ist gut, und wir können Ausflüge machen. Außerdem gibt's Ermäßigungen für die Kinder, und das brauchen wir.

die Schule school
allzu teuer all that expensive
die Leute (pl.) people
die Urlaubspläne (pl.) holiday plans
♦ **die Sommerferien** (pl.) summer holidays/vacation

♦ **der Bauernhof** farm
die Luft air
gesund healthy, good for you
♦ **der Ausflug** excursion, trip
♦ **die Ermäßigung** reduction
brauchen to need

♦ **wann machen Sie Ferien?** when do you go on holiday/vacation? **Ferien/Urlaub** both mean holiday or vacation, but note that **die Ferien** is always used in the plural and **der Urlaub** in the singular: **meine Ferien sind im August** but **mein Urlaub ist im August**.

das müssen wir beachten we have to take that into account. Heide is using the inverted word order here. Because she wants to stress **das** she puts it at the front of the sentence. Had she not wanted the stress she would have said **wir müssen das beachten**.

♦ **fahren Sie dann überhaupt weg?** do you go away at all? **wegfahren** is another separable verb.

wohin fahren Sie denn da? **denn, da** are just 'fillers'. Such words carry no special meaning, but are often used in German to give a sentence a certain intonation or flavour. Here you might translate: where are you going to go, then?

wir fahren in den Bayrischen Wald we'll go to the Bavarian Forest (a large forest region in south-east Bavaria, near the border with Czechoslovakia).

Übungen

4 After listening to Dialogue 2, complete these sentences in English.
(Answers p.199)

a. Heide has two children, one is at ...., and the

other one is at ....

b. They can only go on holiday in the months of

.... or ....

c. This year they'll go to ....

d. They'll be spending their holiday on ....

e. It's not too ...., the people are

......................................, the air is ...., and they

can go on ....

f. There are also special .... for the children.

5 Read what Wanda has to say about her holiday/
vacation and answer the questions below with
either 'yes' or 'no'. (Answers p.199)

Wanda   Wir machen im Sommer Ferien, wenn mein Mann Urlaub hat.
Leider müssen wir in den nächsten Jahren zu Hause bleiben, weil
wir ein Baby haben. Wir haben auch zu wenig Geld, um weg-
zufahren. Aber man kann auch zu Hause viel machen: Wir machen
Tagesausflüge, gehen im Wald spazieren, gehen schwimmen, besuchen Freunde. Manchmal kommen meine Eltern zu Besuch. Sie sind
gute Babysitter, und so können wir – mein Mann und ich – auch mal
allein ausgehen.

a. Does Wanda's husband take his holidays in the summer? ....

b. Will they be able to go away every year from now on? ....

c. Do they have a teenage daughter? ....

d. Will they be completely housebound? ....

e. Will they sometimes be able to go out alone? ....

6 Pretend you're Wanda (Exercise 5) and answer the questions Klaus will ask
you on the cassette about your holiday. Corinna will give the correct version
for you to check.

Dialog 3: Weihnachten

Silke Eigentlich ist Weihnachten ein Familienfest. Da sitzt die ganze Familie zusammen, unterm Weihnachtsbaum. Die Mutter hat was Gutes gekocht, die Kerzen brennen, die Kinder singen Lieder – Weihnachtslieder, und meist wird auch Hausmusik gemacht. Es ist eigentlich sehr gemütlich. Vor allen Dingen: Geschenke zu bekommen, ist eine spannende Sache.

Irgendwie hat sich aber die Bedeutung von dem Fest für mich geändert, seitdem die Familie nicht mehr so wichtig ist für mich. Ich sitze heute am liebsten in der Wohngemeinschaft. Wir kochen was sehr Schönes, zünden Kerzen an, unterhalten uns, und machen uns einen sehr schönen gemütlichen Abend.

- **das Weihnachtsfest** ⎫
- **(die) Weihnachten** ⎬ Christmas
  eigentlich actually ⎭
- **der Weihnachtsbaum** Christmas tree
- **das Familienfest** family occasion

- **das Weihnachtslied** Christmas carol
  meist in most cases
- **brennen** to burn
- **die Kerze** candle

die Mutter hat was Gutes gekocht Mother has cooked something nice. The traditional Christmas dish for Christmas day (**der Weihnachtstag**) is a goose – **die Weihnachtsgans**.

meist wird auch Hausmusik gemacht often we play music (i.e. everybody plays his or her musical instrument); **die Hausmusik** (lit. house music) has quite a tradition in Germany and Austria.

vor allen Dingen above all things.

- **Geschenke zu bekommen, ist eine spannende Sache** it's exciting to get presents. Presents are usually handed out on Christmas Eve –
- **am Heiligen Abend**.

- **gemütlich** cosy, comfortable; **die Gemütlichkeit** cosiness.

irgendwie hat sich die Bedeutung ... für mich geändert somehow the meaning ... has changed for me.

die Wohngemeinschaft group of people living communally, sharing a house or an apartment.

anzünden (sep.) to light: **wir zünden die Kerzen an** we light the candles.

- **wir unterhalten uns** we talk (to each other).

Übungen

7 Find shorter expressions for the phrases in italics, as Silke did in Dialogue 3. (Answers p.199)

Example: Weihnachten ist ein *Fest für die ganze Familie*.

Weihnachten ist ein **Familienfest**...

a. Wir singen *Lieder für Weihnachten*.

Wir singen ....

b. Wir machen *zu Hause Musik*.

Wir machen ....

c. Heute sitze ich am liebsten in unserer *Wohnung mit Freunden zusammen*.

Heute sitze ich am liebsten in der ....

d. Wir machen uns einen *schönen, romantischen* Abend.

Wir machen uns einen .... Abend.

8 Read through the passage below and see what Ingrid, a friend of Silke's, has to say about Christmas. Then decide whether the statements underneath are True or False (**Richtig oder Falsch**). (Answers p.199)

kommerzialisiert commercialized **Geld ausgeben** (sep.) to spend
sich freuen to enjoy s.th. money
 die Kirche church

> Früher, als ich noch ein Kind war, war Weihnachten viel schöner. Ich freute mich schon wochenlang auf den 24. Dezember. Ich machte eine Liste mit Geschenken. Und dann, am Heiligen Abend, gab es endlich die Geschenke. Wir sangen Weihnachtslieder und gingen in die Kirche. Alles war sehr romantisch und gemütlich. Heute ist alles so laut, so kommerzialisiert. Jeder kauft zuviel, gibt zuviel Geld aus, und niemand kann sich so richtig über das Fest freuen.

a. Christmas is much nicer today than it used to be **R** **F**
b. Ingrid always used to look forward to Christmas Eve **R** **F**
c. Christmas presents were handed out on Christmas Day **R** **F**
d. Ingrid's family sang Christmas songs and went to church **R** **F**
e. Today nobody spends any money on Christmas presents **R** **F**

 **9** Join in on the conversation on the cassette. Klaus will ask a few questions about your Christmas. Andrew will prompt you as usual.

Dialog 4: Wintersport

Dorothee   Also, im letzten Winter war ich zum ersten Mal skifahren. Zuerst habe ich auf einem Idiotenhügel wirklich einen Anfängerkurs besuchen müssen. Na ja, und nach ein paar Stunden ist es mir wirklich schon ganz gut geglückt. Morgens zwei Stunden, mittags mal zwei – und hin und wieder hingeflogen. Wie gesagt, am Schluß ist es doch ganz gut gegangen.

Ruth   Hm – und wie waren denn die anderen Leute?

Dorothee   Na ja, es war sehr interessant. Besonders, wenn du zum Après-Ski gegangen bist. Du hast verrückte Leute gesehen, man konnte viel unternehmen, einfach toll.

Ruth   Hmm – was hast du denn alles gemacht? Beim Après-Ski?

Dorothee   Hmm – Ginfizz getrunken, tanzen gegangen, essen gegangen – alles Mögliche.

Ruth   Und wie war das Wetter?

Dorothee   Einfach toll. Ich hab' mir sogar noch einen kleinen Sonnenbrand geholt.

vorher before   **einfach toll** simply great
am Schluß in the end   **der Sonnenbrand** sunburn
verrückt crazy

♦ **skifahren** (sep.) to ski; see also **der Skikurs** skiing lessons; **der Skilehrer** skiing instructor; **der Skiurlaub** skiing trip.

der Idiotenhügel (coll.) ski slope for beginners; **der Idiot** idiot.

ich habe ... einen Anfängerkurs besuchen müssen I had to attend a beginner's course; **der Anfänger** beginner, **anfangen** (sep.) to begin.

est ist mir ... geglückt it turned out all right (for me); **glücken** to turn out well, to work well, i.e. **diese Übung ist mir gut geglückt** this exercise worked well (for me), **das Glück** luck.

♦ **morgens** in the morning; **mittags** at lunch time, also: in the afternoon; **abends** in the evening; **nachts** at night.

(Ich bin) hin und wieder hingeflogen I took a fall every now and then; **hinfliegen** (sep.) (lit. to fly down) is colloquial for **hinfallen** (to fall).

♦ **man konnte viel unternehmen** you could do a lot.

alles Mögliche all kinds of things.

ich hab mir ... geholt I got; **holen** to fetch, to get.

Übungen

10 Here is a questionnaire which Dorothee is asked to fill in after returning from her skiing trip. Could you do it for her? (Answers p.199)

a. Wie war der Skiurlaub?	☐ gut	☐ schlecht
b. Waren Sie Anfänger?	☐ ja	☐ nein
c. Wie viele Stunden pro Tag sind Sie skigefahren?	☐ zwei Stunden	☐ mehr als zwei Stunden
d. Wie war das Après-Ski?	☐ interessant	☐ langweilig
e. Wie war das Wetter?	☐ gut	☐ schlecht

11 There were quite a few compound nouns in the dialogue, i.e. words consisting of two separate words, like **Ski|urlaub**. Below you'll find six words. Match them up to form three compound nouns, then write each new word under the appropriate picture. (Answers p.199)

Brand   Ski   Idioten   Kurs   Hügel   Sonnen

a. ....

b. ....

c. ....

12 On the cassette Klaus and Corinna will act out a shorter version of Dialogue 4. Just repeat Corinna's answers in the pauses.

Wörter und Wendungen

Remember that you should know these *key words and phrases* before going on.

Holidays, vacation: What kind?

der Traumurlaub	dream holiday/vacation
der Bildungsurlaub	educational holiday/vacation
der Skiurlaub	skiing holiday/vacation
die Sommerferien	summer holidays/vacation
die Winterferien	winter holidays/vacation
der Ausflug	excursion, trip
Ferien auf dem Bauernhof	farm holidays/vacation

What to do

am Strand liegen	lie on the beach
nichts tun	do nothing
essen/tanzen/in die Disko gehen	go out to eat/go dancing/to the disco
durch die Rocky Mountains/in den Bayrischen Wald fahren	drive through the Rocky Mountains/go to the Bavarian Forest
am Lagerfeuer sitzen	sit round the camp fire
Kunstschätze besichtigen	to look at art treasures
skifahren	to ski
viel unternehmen	to do a lot
Ferien/Urlaub machen	to go on holiday/vacation
wegfahren	to go away

How to get somewhere

mit dem Flugzeug	by plane
mit dem Jeep/Auto	by jeep/car
mit der Eisenbahn	by train

Christmas

Weihnachten, das Weihnachtsfest	Christmas
der Weihnachtsbaum	Christmas tree
das Weihnachtslied	Christmas carol
der Heilige Abend	Christmas Eve
das Familienfest	family occasion
Geschenke bekommen	to receive presents
die Kerzen brennen	the candles are burning
wir unterhalten uns	we talk
wir machen uns einen gemütlichen Abend	we have a nice cosy evening

Grammatik

Verb prefixes

In English many verbs have prefixes, i.e. syllables like un-, pre-, de- in front of a verb: <u>un</u>load, <u>pre</u>determine, <u>de</u>stroy. But we tend not to notice them as a special type of verb. In German prefixes can cause more of a problem. Let's take, for example, the verbs **vorstellen** (to imagine), **wegfahren** (to go away), **anzünden** (to light):

Wie stellen Sie sich Ihren Traumurlaub vor? How do you imagine your dream holiday/vacation?
Wann fahren Sie weg? When are you going away?
Wir zünden Kerzen an. We light candles.

You can see that in the examples above the prefixes separate from the main stem of the verb and go to the end of the sentence. Other common separable verbs are **mitnehmen** (to take along), **hinfahren** (to go somewhere), **ausgeben** (to spend, e.g. money), **anfangen** (to begin), **aufhören** (to stop), **einladen** (to invite), and many others.

There are, however, verbs with prefixes which do not separate. The most common of these prefixes are **be-, ge-, emp-, ent-, zer-, er-, ver-**, e.g.

beginnen: die Vorstellung beginnt um neun Uhr.
to begin: the performance begins at nine o'clock.

empfehlen: Ich empfehle das Rindfleisch.
to recommend: I recommend the beef.

verstehen: Ich verstehe überhaupt nichts.
to understand: I don't understand anything at all.

During the course you will come across many examples of both separable and inseparable prefixes. To help you to distinguish them, verbs with separable prefixes will have (sep.) after them, e.g. **vorstellen** (sep.).

13 Translate the following phrases. There are examples of both separable and inseparable prefixes. You'll need the following verbs: **ausgeben, verstehen, erklären, wegfahren, zumachen, aufmachen.** (Answers p.199)

a. We'll go away tomorrow. ....
....

b. I'm spending a lot of money. ....
....

c. The restaurant opens at 12 o'clock. ....
....

d. I don't understand what you're saying. ....
....

e. Please shut the door! ....
....

f. The guide explains everything. ....
....

Adjective endings

In Unit 1 the endings after the so-called '**der**' group were listed. Now it is the turn of the '**ein**' group. If necessary just refresh your memory by looking at p.18. The '**ein**' group comprises all words incorporating '**ein**', including **kein**, plus all the 'possessives' such as **mein, dein, sein, ihr, unser**. Remember that the function in the sentence is also important. See how the endings for this group work by looking at the following examples.

Ein langer Urlaub wäre schön. (1) A long holiday would be nice.
Das ist eine ganz andere Sache. (2) That's a completely different matter.
Ein kaltes Bier ist immer gut. (3) A cold beer is always good.
Wir haben einen schönen Urlaub gehabt. (4) We had a nice trip.
Sie sah keine andere Möglichkeit. (5) She didn't see any other
    possibility.
Wir haben ein kaltes Bier getrunken. (6) We drank a cold beer.
Ich habe deine beiden kleinen Schwestern gesehen. (7) I saw your two
    young sisters.

So from the examples (1)–(7) above you can see that when the adjective is part of the subject, the ending is **-er** with a singular masculine noun (1), **-e** with a singular feminine (2) and **-es** with a singular neuter noun (3). When the word is part of the direct object of the sentence, it is **-en** with masculine nouns (4), **-e** again with feminine nouns (5) and **-es** again with neuter nouns (6). In all other cases including plurals the ending is **-en** (7):

	masculine	feminine	neuter
Subject (nominative)	**-er**	**-e**	**-es**
Object (accusative)	**-en**	**-e**	**-es**
All others	**-en**		

14 Try to fill in the right endings. (Answers p.199)

a. Ein gut............ Reiseführer ist wichtig.

b. Ein kalt............ Bier schmeckt besser als ein warm............

c. Ich habe einen alt............ Freund getroffen.

d. Wir haben einen sehr gemütlich............ Abend gehabt.

e. Ich möchte mit meiner deutsch............ Freundin auf Urlaub fahren.

f. Eine gut............ Geschichte höre ich immer gern.

Übungen: Lesen

15 Urlaub, Urlaub ... Study the travel advertisements we have taken from West German newspapers. Which of the captions below would fit which ad? (Asnwers p.199)

Traumurlaub   Kreativurlaub   Bildungsurlaub

Ferien auf dem Bauernhof   Abenteuerurlaub

ZYPERN
ein Urlaub, von dem
Sie noch lange
träumen werden.

a. ....

TOSCANA

TÖPFERN, MALEN,
SCHREIBEN —
entdecken Sie Ihre
Kreativät wieder!

3 Wochen ab DM 900

c. ....

Ägypten

10 Tage klassische
Rundreise – ab DM 1999

Erfahrene Reiseführer
informieren Sie über Land
und Leute, Geschichte und Kultur.

b. ....

Zurück zur Natur –
kommen Sie auf
unseren Hof in Oberbayern!
Kinder und Tiere sind bei
uns willkommen!

d. ....

Abenteuer Kanada
im Kanu durch das
Yukon-Territorium, oder
Trail-Wandern in British Columbia
in den schönsten Nationalparks.

e. ....

Vocabulary:
die Götter (pl.) the gods
erfahren experienced
die Rundreise tour
die Kreativität creativity
das Kanu canoe
zurück zur Natur back to nature

töpfern to do pottery
malen to paint
entdecken to discover
das Abenteuer adventure
Zypern Cyprus

16 Three friends – Anne, Claudia, and Elke – are away on a skiing trip over Christmas. Read the postcard Anne has written to another friend, then answer the questions below. (Answers p.199)

> Liebe Margot,
> Viele Grüße aus unserem Skiurlaub. Gut, daß wir Skigymnastik gemacht haben: wir sind sehr fit. Nur Elke fährt noch auf dem Idiotenhügel, Claudia und ich sind schon keine Anfänger mehr. Weihnachten ohne Familie ist viel schöner! Wir haben am Heiligen Abend in der Skihütte zusammen gesessen und uns einen gemütlichen Abend gemacht. Leider gab es keine Geschenke, dafür aber viel Après-Ski.
> Bis bald,
> Deine Anne

die Skigymnastik exercises to prepare you for skiing

a. Are the three girls fit?

....

b. Are they all past beginner's level?

....

c. Are they missing their families at Christmas?

....

d. What did they do on Christmas Eve?

....

e. What was there instead of presents?

....

Übungen: Radio

17 On the cassette you'll hear a commercial by a travel agent called **Neckermann-Reisen**. Listen a few times, then write down what you hear using your pause and rewind button as often as necessary. It's a sort of dictation. (Answers p.208 in transcript)

Vocabulary:
gebucht booked
dicht close
der Apparat here: radio
der Geheimtip hot tip
mittendrin in the middle

Süd-Dalmatien Southern Dalmatia
die Klubanlage holiday/vacation camp, compound
die Halbpension half board, i.e. breakfast and supper
das Reisebüro travel agency

18 Listen to the weather report – first for North and South Germany, then for Austria and Switzerland. Where and when will it be sunny, rainy, windy or cloudy? Mark the chart under the appropriate symbol and fill in the temperatures. (Answers p.199).

	Sonne	Regen	Wolken	Wind	Temperaturen
Norddeutschland morgen: Mittwoch: Donnerstag:					
Süddeutschland zuerst: später:					

19 Now for the second part of the weather report, which is for Austria and Switzerland. Fill in the grid as for **Übung 18**. (Answers p.199)

Österreich/Schweiz erst: dann:					

Vocabulary:
heiter fair
bewölkt, wolkig cloudy
überwiegend veränderlich mostly changeable
aufgelockerte Bewölkung intermittent clouds
die Alpennordseite north side of the Alps
zeitweise at times

20 Imagine you've written a postcard while on holiday in Spain and are reading it out aloud to someone. Say that the weather is fine, that you're lying on the beach doing nothing all day and that the food is wonderful. In the evenings you often go dancing at the disco. On the cassette you can hear a version of what you could have said.

21 Try to give a short definition of the following words:

Anfängerkurs Familienfest Hausmusik Reiseführer Weihnachtsbaum

First listen to the cassette, where Corinna defines **Traumurlaub**. Then define the above words in a similar way before checking on the cassette.

3 Erster oder zweiter Klasse?

You will learn

- to buy a ticket and enquire about trains
- to rent a car and understand directions
- to understand travel news on the radio

... and you'll find out what pink elephants have to do with the German Federal Railway

Study guide

Dialog 1: Einfach bitte!

Ruth	Ich möchte eine Karte nach Garmisch bitte.
Beamtin	Einfach – oder hin und zurück?
Ruth	Einfach bitte.
Beamtin	Erster oder zweiter Klasse?
Ruth	Zweiter Klasse.
Beamtin	Möchten Sie einen Intercity-Zuschlag?
Ruth	Ja, bitte.
Beamtin	Vierundachtzig Mark bitte.
Ruth	Vierundachtzig Mark – hier sind hundert Mark.
Beamtin	Neunzig, einhundert ... Danke.

♦ **der Hauptbahnhof** main station ♦ **der Zuschlag** surcharge
die Beamtin clerk (f.) ♦ **einfach** single/one-way (ticket)
der Beamte clerk (m.)

♦ **der Fahrkartenschalter** ticket office; **die Fahrkarte** or **die Karte** ticket.

♦ **hin und zurück** return (ticket), lit. to ... and back; Ruth could also have asked for a **Rückfahrkarte** return ticket, round trip.

♦ **Erster oder zweiter Klasse?** first or second class?

vierundachtzig Mark bitte eighty-four marks please; **neunzig** ninety, **(ein)hundert** one hundred. More about numbers in **Grammatik**.

Übungen

1 What's Ruth's ticket? Listen to Dialogue 1, then mark the right boxes below. (Answers p.200)

a. What kind of ticket does she ask for?

☐ single/one-way   ☐ return/round trip

b. Which class does she want to travel in?

☐ first   ☐ second

c. What train does she want to travel on?

☐ Ordinary train   ☐ Intercity train

d. How much is her ticket?

☐ DM 84.–   ☐ DM 90.–

IC 599 Ludwig Uhland

Hamburg=Altona–
Hannover-Frankfurt (M)–
Mannheim-Stuttgart–
München

DB Bw Hmb2 01202

2 **Und nun nach Wien!** Someone is buying a ticket to Vienna – **Wien.** Complete the dialogue at the ticket office below by translating the English phrases into German. (Answers p.200)

Guten Tag.

a. Good day ....

Sie wünschen?

b. A ticket to Vienna, please ....

Einfach?

c. No, return (round trip) please ....

Und möchten Sie einen Intercity-Zuschlag?

d. Yes, please ....

Möchten Sie erster oder zweiter Klasse fahren?

e. First class, please ....

3 Your turn to speak. Switch on your cassette, where *you'll* be asked to buy a ticket to Vienna. Make sure you've done Exercise 2 first.

Dialog 2: Am Informationsschalter

Ruth	Ich möchte nach Garmisch fahren, bitte.
Beamter	Möchten Sie heute fahren?
Ruth	Nein, ich möchte morgen vormittag fahren.
Beamter	Morgen vormittag fährt ein Intercity-Zug in Heidelberg ab um 9.41 Uhr. Dort müßten Sie in München umsteigen und wären in Garmisch-Partenkirchen um 15.20 Uhr.
Ruth	Gut – und – eh – ist der teurer, der Intercity-Zug?
Beamter	Der Intercity-Zug kostet einen Zuschlag von fünf DM in der zweiten Klasse, und zehn DM in der ersten Klasse.
Ruth	Und gibt's auch normale Züge?
Beamter	Ja, es gibt einen Schnellzug, allerdings fährt dieser Zug eine Stunde länger bis Garmisch-Partenkirchen.
Ruth	Ach, ja. Und haben Sie Ermäßigung für Kinder?
Beamter	Die Ermäßigung für Kinder ist von vier bis elf Jahren der halbe Fahrpreis.
Ruth	Und gibt's auch andere Ermäßigungen?
Beamter	Es gibt eine Vorzugskarte – diese Karte ist 20 Prozent ermäßigt, und es müßte bei der Rückfahrt ein Wochenende dazwischen sein.

▶ **der Zug** train   **allerdings** but
normal ordinary, normal   **die Vorzugskarte** cheap special (ticket)

▶ **morgen vormittag** tomorrow morning; similar: **morgen nachmittag** tomorrow afternoon, **gestern abend** yesterday evening or last night, **heute abend** tonight, etc.

▶ **möchten Sie heute fahren?** would you like to go today?
fahren can mean to go, to travel, to drive, to (take a) ride, depending on the context: **ich fahre am liebsten mit dem Zug** I like travelling by train best; **ich fahre gern Auto** I like driving (a car); **die Kinder möchten gern in deinem Auto fahren** the children would like to ride in your car.

▶ **(der Zug) fährt um 9.41 Uhr in Heidelberg ab** the train leaves Heidelberg at 9.41; **abfahren** (sep.) to leave, to depart, **die Abfahrt** departure; **ankommen** (sep.) to arrive, **die Ankunft** arrival. *Note:* **9.41 Uhr** is spoken **9 Uhr 41** (neun Uhr einundvierzig), similar: **10.20 Uhr = zehn Uhr zwanzig, 13.12 Uhr = dreizehn Uhr zwölf**, etc.

▶ **dort müßten Sie in München umsteigen** you'd have to change at Munich; **umsteigen** (sep.) to change (trains): **ich steige in Wien um** I'll change in Vienna, but if there is another verb in the sentence (like **müßten** here) it is not split.

... und wären in Garmisch-Partenkirchen um 15.20 Uhr ... and you'd be in Garmisch-Partenkirchen at 15.20; **müßten** (above) and **wären** are subjunctive forms of **müssen** and **sein** and are used in polite speech. More about the subjunctive in Unit 12.

es gibt einen Schnellzug there is a fast train. **Schnellzüge** are express trains, but they are not as fast as Intercity trains for which you have to pay a surcharge – **einen Zuschlag**.

▶ **und haben Sie Ermäßigung für Kinder?** and do you have (any) reduction for children?

▶ **der halbe Fahrpreis** half the fare; **der ganze Fahrpreis** the full fare.

es müßte bei der Rückfahrt ein Wochenende dazwischen sein there must be a weekend in between (the outward and the return journey).

Übungen

4 Nach Garmisch! Listen to Dialogue 2 again and complete the notes below. (Answers p.200)

Heidelberg–Garmisch

a. Abfahrt: vormittags um .... Uhr.

b. Umsteigen in ....

c. Ankunft in Garmisch um .... Uhr

d. Intercity-Zuschlag: 1. Klasse .... DM

　　　　　　　　　　　 2. Klasse .... DM

e. Schnellzug: fährt .... länger

f. Ermäßigung für Kinder: .... Prozent

g. Vorzugskarte: Ermäßigung .... Prozent

5 Fill in the appropriate words. (Answers p.200)

Zuschlag　umsteigen　Ermäßigung

a. Es gibt keinen direkten Zug nach Garmisch. Sie müssen einmal

....

b. Kinder bezahlen nicht den vollen Preis. Sie bekommen eine

....

c. Der Intercity ist schneller, aber er kostet auch einen ....

 6 Now it's your turn to ask for some information at a railway station. You want to go to Cologne. Andrew will prompt you on the cassette as usual.

Dialog 3: Vielleicht einen VW Golf

Horst	Guten Tag! Ich möchte gern ein Auto mieten. Welche Typen haben Sie?
H. Wallenwein	PKW, LKW, Wohnmobile . . .
Horst	Ich suche einen PKW. Vielleicht einen VW Golf – was würde der denn kosten?
H. Wallenwein	Der Tagespreis liegt bei achtundfünfzig Mark plus Kilometergeld.
Horst	Gut. Haben Sie auch einen Wochenpreis?
H. Wallenwein	Wochenpauschalen gibt es – die sehr günstig sind zu 380 Mark.
Horst	Ah, ja. Was würde denn ein Diesel kosten, zum Beispiel?
H. Wallenwein	Der Diesel – eh – ist in der Regel zehn Mark teurer pro Tag.
Horst	Pro Tag zehn Mark teurer. Haben Sie auch Automatik?
H. Wallenwein	Automatik gibt es auch.
Horst	Wie kann ich denn bezahlen? Muß ich bar bezahlen, oder kann ich auch mit einer Kreditkarte bezahlen?
H. Wallenwein	Sie können mit Kreditkarte bezahlen. American Express oder Eurocard ist möglich.
Horst	Ja gut, vielen Dank.
H. Wallenwein	Danke schön.

- **die Autovermietung** car rental
- **mieten** to rent, to hire
  das Wohnmobil mobile home
  vielleicht perhaps, maybe
- **bar** cash
- **die Kreditkarte** credit card
  möglich possible

- **welche Typen haben Sie?** what (car) makes do you have?
  der Typ brand, make

- **der PKW** – short for **der Personenkraftwagen** – car; **PKW** is more official than **Auto** (car), and used here in contrast to **LKW** – **der Lastkraftwagen** lorry, truck.

- **ich suche . . . einen VW Golf** I'm looking for a Volkswagen Golf. Similar: **ich suche einen Ford/Opel/Fiat/Mercedes** I'm looking for a Ford/Opel/Fiat/Mercedes.

- **der Tagespreis liegt bei 58 Mark** the daily rate comes to 58 Marks.

- **plus Kilometergeld** plus mileage (i.e. rate per kilometre)

- **die Wochenpauschale** weekly rate; **die Wochenpauschalen sind sehr günstig** the weekly rates are very good value/a bargain.

  in der Regel as a rule.

  haben Sie auch Automatik? do you also have any automatic (cars)?

- **wie kann ich bezahlen?** how can I pay?

Übungen

7 Mark the correct boxes after listening to the dialogue. (Answers p.200)

a. Horst sucht
- ☐ einen PKW
- ☐ einen LKW
- ☐ ein Wohnmobil

b. Der Tagessatz für einen PKW ist
- ☐ 68 Mark
- ☐ 57 Mark
- ☐ 58 Mark

c. Die Wochenpauschale für einen PKW ist
- ☐ günstig
- ☐ nicht günstig

d. Ein Diesel ist
- ☐ billiger als ein normaler PKW
- ☐ teurer als ein normaler PKW

e. Horst fragt: 'Kann ich ...
- ☐ bar
- ☐ mit Kreditkarte
- ☐ mit Scheck
... bezahlen?'

8 In der Autovermietung. Translate the sentences below into German. (Answers p.200)

a. I want to rent a car. ....

....

b. What types have you got? ....

....

c. How much would a Ford Escort be? ....

....

d. Is there a weekly rate? ....

....

e. Have you also got any automatics? ....

....

f. How can I pay? ....

....

g. Can I pay by credit card? ....

....

9 Your turn to speak again. Switch on the cassette and listen to Andrew's prompts. You're supposed to rent a car, for which Exercise 8 will have prepared you.

Dialog 4: Wie komme ich da hin?

Horst Ich möchte jetzt gerne nach Basel fahren. Wie komme ich da am besten hin?

Herr Wallenwein Der schnellste Weg von uns hier ist Richtung Innenstadt über die – eh – Neckarbrücke bis zum Römerkreis. Sie fahren dann rechts ab, dem Schild nach: Autobahn Basel. Sie fahren dann auf der Autobahn zirka 260 Kilometer. Ich hoffe nur, daß Sie nicht in einen Stau reinkommen. Sollte dies passieren, empfehle ich Ihnen, bis Baden-Baden zu fahren und dann über die Schwarzwaldhochstraße Richtung Basel. Das ist eine sehr interessante Strecke.

Biba Wie komme ich am besten zum Heidelberger Schloß?

Gabi Mit dem Bus kommen Sie am besten hin.

Biba Und wo fährt der Bus ab?

Gabi Hier. Die nächste Haltestelle ist hier über die Straße.

Biba Und wann fährt der nächste Bus?

Gabi Die fahren alle zehn Minuten ab.

▶ **wie komme ich am besten nach Basel/zum Schloß/zur Autobahn?** what's the best way to Basle/the castle/the motorway (expressway)?

▶ **der schnellste Weg von hier ist Richtung Innenstadt** the quickest way from here is towards the town centre; **die Richtung** (lit. direction): **fahren Sie Richtung Autobahn** go towards the motorway (expressway).

über die Neckarbrücke bis zum Römerkreis across the Neckar bridge up to the Römerkreis (a roundabout/traffic circle in Heidelberg).

▶ **Sie fahren rechts ab** turn right; or **Sie fahren links ab** turn left; **geradeaus** straight ahead.

dem Schild nach following the sign.

▶ **... daß Sie nicht in einen Stau reinkommen** ... that you won't get stuck in a (traffic) jam; **der Verkehrsstau** (short **der Stau**) traffic jam.

sollte dies passieren should this happen

über die Schwarzwaldhochstraße via the Black Forest Route; **die Hochstraße** (lit. high road) mountain road.

eine interessante Strecke an interesting route

▶ **mit dem Bus** by bus; similar: **mit dem Zug** by train, **mit dem Auto** by car.

▶ **die nächste Haltestelle** the nearest (bus) stop

▶ **der nächste Bus** the next bus; note that **nächste** means both 'next' and 'near/est'.

▶ **alle zehn Minuten** every ten minutes; **alle zwei Tage** every two days; *but* **jede Stunde** every hour, **jede Woche** every week, weekly.

Übungen

10 Der schnellste Weg nach Basel. Fill in the gaps after you have listened to Dialogue 4. Try not to look at the text on the opposite page, only use it to check when you've completed the exercise.

Der schnellste Weg von hier ist Richtung ....

über die .... bis zum Römerkreis. Sie fahren

dann .... ab, dem Schild nach:

.... Sie fahren dann auf der Autobahn zirka

.... Kilometer. Ich hoffe nur, daß Sie nicht in einen

.... reinkommen. Sollte dies passieren,

empfehle ich Ihnen, bis .... zu fahren und

dann über die Schwarzwaldhochstraße ....

Basel. Das ist eine sehr interessante ....

11 Wohin möchte Biba? Answer the questions below. (Answers p.200)

a. Where does Biba want to go?

....

b. What should she use in order to get there?

....

c. What's the German word for bus stop?

....

d. Is the nearest bus stop far away?

....

e. How frequent are the buses?

....

12 It's your turn to ask for directions now. You want to go to the station – **zum Bahnhof**. Andrew will prompt you on the cassette.

Wörter und Wendungen

At the railway station

Ich möchte ...
    eine Fahrkarte nach Garmisch
    eine Rückfahrkarte nach Wien

    heute/morgen/am Sonntag fahren
    erster/zweiter Klasse fahren
    einen Intercity-Zuschlag
    mit dem Schnellzug fahren
der Hauptbahnhof
einfach nach Heidelberg

hin und zurück nach Baden-Baden
die Abfahrt
die Ankunft
Der Zug fährt ab/kommt an um ...
Gibt es Ermäßigung?
Muß ich umsteigen?
der halbe/volle Fahrpreis

I would like ...
    a ticket to Garmisch
    a return/round trip ticket to Vienna

    to go today/tomorrow/on Sunday

    to go first/second class
    an Intercity surcharge
    to go by express train
main station
single/one-way (ticket) to Heidelberg
return/round trip to Baden-Baden

departure
arrival
The train departs/arrives at ...

Is there a reduction?
Do I have to change?
half the fare/the full fare

Renting a car

Ich möchte gern ...
    ein Auto/einen PKW mieten
Was kostet ein Fiat/Ford/VW Golf?

mit Automatik
der Tagespreis
Die Wochenpauschale ist sehr günstig
Kann ich bar/mit Kreditkarte bezahlen?

I would like to rent ...
    a car
How much is a Fiat/Ford/VW Golf?

with automatic (transmission)
daily rate
The weekly rate is very good value/a bargain
Can I pay cash/by credit card?

Directions

Wie komme ich am besten ...
    nach Basel?
    zur Autobahn?
    zum Schloß?
    zur Haltestelle?
mit dem Bus/Zug/Auto
Wann fährt der nächste Bus/Zug ab?
Wo ist die nächste Haltestelle?
Fahren Sie ...
    nach rechts/links
    geradeaus
    bis zum Bahnhof
der Stau
das Schild
die Strecke

What's the best way ...
    to Basle?
    to the motorway/expressway?
    to the castle?
    to the (bus) stop?
by bus/train/car
When does the next bus/train leave?

Where is the nearest stop?
Go ...
    right/left
    straight on
    until you get to the station
(traffic) jam
sign
route

Grammatik

Numbers and dates

Check your numbers

13 Write out the figures below. Remember that in German you say the ones before the tens, e.g. 39 = **neununddreißig**. (Answers p.200)

a. 9 ....
b. 19 ....
c. 44 ....
d. 71 ....

e. 17 ....
f. 50 ....
g. 33 ....
f. 62 ....

14 And now write down the numbers. (Answers p.200)

a. siebenundachtzig ....
b. dreiundneunzig ....
c. zweihundertdreißig ....
d. dreizehn ....

e. vierhundertzweiundzwanzig ....
....
f. sechshundertsechsundsechzig
....

Don't forget:

1000 = **(ein)tausend**
2000 = **zweitausend**
10 000 = **zehntausend**
100 000 = **hunderttausend**
1 000 000 = **eine Million**
2 564 359 = **zwei Millionen fünfhundertvierundsechzigtausend-dreihundertneunundfünfzig**. (Note that there is a space but no comma between figures.)

15 Write out in figures: (Answers p.200)

a. tausenddreihundertundeins ....
b. fünftausendsechshundertachtzig ....
c. zehntausendachthundertvierundvierzig ....
d. dreiundfünfzigtausendzwanzig ....
e. siebzig Millionen ....
f. sieben Millionen achthunderttausend ....

The date
For dates you need ordinal numbers, i.e. **der erste** (the first), **der zweite** (the second), **der dritte** (the third). These three are the only irregular ordinal numbers, after that you just add **-te** to numbers up to 19:
der vierte, der fünfte, der elfte, der achtzehnte, etc.
And you add **-ste** to numbers after 19:
der zwanzigste, der einundfünfzigste, der dreihundertste, etc.
Sieben (7) is shortened to **sieb-**: der siebte, **siebzehnte, siebzigste.**

The short way of saying the date is:
Heute ist der ...
7.9.85   (**siebte neunte fünfundachtzig**)
11.12.71   (**elfte zwölfte einundsiebzig**)
but: **Heute haben wir den ...**
7.9.85   (**siebten neunten fünfundachtzig**)
11.12.71   (**elften zwölften einundsiebzig**)

A longer way of saying the date is:
Heute ist der ...
14. April 1985   (vierzehnte April neunzehnhundertvierundachtzig)
3. August 1978   (dritte August neunzehnhundertachtundsiebzig)
but: **heute haben wir den dritten August, den vierzehnten April**, etc.

16 Translate into German: (Answers p.200)

a. Today is the tenth of May. ....

....

b. On April 27th we'll go on holiday/vacation. ....

....

c. Yesterday was Friday the 13th. ....

....

d. I was born on July 2nd, 1944. ....

....

e. We're having a party on Saturday, October 1st. ....

....

....

Übungen: Lesen

17 Rosarote Wochen! The 'pink weeks' are a special time of the year for cheap travel on the **Deutsche Bundesbahn** (German Federal Railways). Posters showing pink elephants promote bargain fares for families and individuals on posters and in brochures. Read the advertisement below, then answer the questions. (Answers p.200)

Vom 17. September bis 19. Dezember können Sie Sonderrückfahrkarten kaufen. Sie gelten von jedem Bahnhof nach jedem Bahnhof für eine einmalige Hin- und Rückfahrt und für neun Tage. Fahrpreis für eine Person DM 111.– in der 2. Klasse, DM 144.– in der 1. Klasse. Zwei Personen zahlen DM 155.– in der 2. Klasse, DM 199.– in der 1. Klasse. Zwei Erwachsene mit Kindern bis 18 Jahren bezahlen DM 177.– in der 2. Klasse und DM 222.– in der 1. Klasse.

Vocabulary:
die Sonderrückfahrkarte cheap special return/reduced round-trip
gelten to be valid
der Fahrpreis fare

a. During which time of the year can you take advantage of the 'pink weeks' rate?

....

b. Are the cheap specials single (one-way) or return (round trip) tickets?

....

c. For how many days is a ticket valid?

....

d. How much would a family with two young children have to pay for a 2nd class ticket?

....

e. How much would one adult have to pay for a first class ticket?

....

18 Children's express! Have a look at the special attractions the **Königssee** express train offers children. Then translate them into English. (Answers p.200)

Vocabulary:
der Fern-Express long-distance train
der Reisewagen coach, carriage, car
die Kletterleiter climbing frame, jungle gym
die Rutschbahn slide
werden ... betreut are looked after

Kinderland

Eine besondere Attraktion im Fern-Express „Königssee" zwischen Hamburg und Berchtesgaden ist ein spezieller Reisewagen – nur für Kinder von 4 bis 11 Jahren. Hier gibt es viel Spaß: beim Spielen und Lesen, an der Kletterleiter und auf der Rutschbahn. Selbstverständlich werden die Kinder betreut.

Übungen: Radio

19 Listen to the first radio extract – traffic news on **Südwestfunk (SWF 3)**.
Where are the trouble spots in the Stuttgart region? Mark them on the map
below. (Answers p.200)

Vocabulary:
mit Meldungen with news

die Verkehrslage traffic conditions
die Baustelle road works

20 **Ein Reiseruf.** Listen to this radio message for Mr. Friedrich Trappe and
answer the questions. (Answers p.200)

Vocabulary:
der Reiseruf radio message
unterwegs travelling
amtliches Kennzeichen official registration number
wird gebeten is asked
anrufen (sep.) to telephone

a. What's Mr. Trappe's hometown?

....

b. Where is he travelling?

....

c. What type of car does he drive?

....

d. What's the registration number?

....

e. What's Mr. Trappe asked to do?

....

21 What are visitors of the **Schweizer Mustermesse** (Swiss Trade Fair) supposed to do? **Südwestfunk** Radio gives them some advice. Write a brief summary (in English) down below. (Answers p.200)

Vocabulary:
die Fachmesse Trade Fair
der Anschluß exit, junction
das Fahrzeug vehicle
abstellen (sep.) to leave
der Dienst service

Visitors are advised to ....

....

....

....

22 Listen to extract no. 4 and complete the transcript below. (Answers p.209 in transcript)

In ....

Uhr ....

SWF 3 .... aus ....

Keine .... über ....

behinderungen.

 Übungen: Sprechen Sie selbst

23 Your turn to speak. Imagine you're at the railway station, asking for a ticket of your choice to . . . Also ask how many trains a day are leaving for your destination, if you have to pay a surcharge, when the last train would leave, when you'd be arriving, etc. On the cassette Corinna wants to go to Munich and gives you some sample questions.

24 You want to rent a car and are making some enquiries. Make up at least five questions, e.g. is the particular type of car you want available, what's the daily/weekly rate (remember the word **Pauschale**!), how can you pay..... etc. Then listen to Klaus' questions on tape.

4 Woher kommen Sie?

You will learn

- how to start a conversation with a stranger
- how to make yourself comfortable in a guest house
- what to say at dinner parties

... and you will hear a sad but true story about an accident-prone bridegroom

Study guide

		Seite
	Dialog 1 + Übungen	56
	Dialog 2 + Übungen	58
	Dialog 3 + Übungen	60
	Dialog 4 + Übungen	62
	Wörter und Wendungen	64
	Grammatik	65
	Lesen	67
	Radio	68
	Sprechen Sie selbst	70

Dialog 1: In Heidelberg

Ruth	Sind Sie hier im Urlaub?
Student	Ja.
Ruth	Seit wann?
Student	Schon seit drei Tagen.
Ruth	Und wie gefällt es Ihnen?
Student	Mir gefällt es gut hier, weil das Wetter schön ist und die Leute dann freundlich sind.
Ruth	Reisen Sie alleine?
Student	Ja, ich bin mit dem Rucksack unterwegs.
Ruth	Und woher kommen Sie eigentlich?
Student	Ich komm' aus Nürnberg.
Ruth	Aus Nürnberg. Ist das 'ne interessante Stadt?
Student	Für die Touristen ist es interessant, ja, aber wenn man sein ganzes Leben schon in Nürnberg gewohnt hat, möchte man auch mal was anderes sehen.

♦ **wie gefällt es Ihnen?** how do you like it? Answer: **mir gefällt es gut hier**
♦ I like it very much here; similar: **wie gefällt Ihnen der Film?** how did you like the movie? **er gefällt mir/er gefällt mir nicht** I like it/I don't like it.

weil das Wetter schön ist und die Leute dann freundlich sind because the weather is nice and the people are friendly. Note the position of **ist** and **sind**: both verbs go to the end of the sentence after **weil** (because).

ich bin mit dem Rucksack unterwegs I'm travelling with my rucksack/
♦ backpack (lit. *the* rucksack); **unterwegs** on the road, on the move.

wenn man sein ganzes Leben schon in Nürnberg gewohnt hat...
if one has spent all one's life in Nürnberg ...

Übungen

1 Two things to fill in. First, write an appropriate word under each picture, then fill in the second missing word from the list below. (Answers p.201)

freundlich   interessant   schön   allein

a. Das .... ist ....

b. Die .... sind ....

c. Für die .... ist Nürnberg ....

d. Ich bin mit dem .... unterwegs. Ich reise ....

2 Try to complete this dialogue by supplying the appropriate questions to the answers. (Answers p.201)

a. ....
Ich komme aus Hamburg.

b. ....
Ja, ich bin hier auf Urlaub.

c. ....
Seit zwei Wochen.

d. ....
Mir gefällt es gut.

e. ....
Nein, ich reise mit meinem Freund.

 3 And now it's your turn to meet a tourist and ask him the same questions as in Exercise 2. Andrew will prompt you on the cassette.

Dialog 2: In der Pension

Birtha Das hier ist also Ihr Zimmer. Brauchen Sie noch irgend etwas?
Ruth Ja, ein Glas Wasser bitte.
Birtha Das bring' ich Ihnen sofort. Und hier drüben steht Ihr Bett. Möchten Sie vielleicht eine extra Decke? Glauben Sie, daß es warm genug ist?
Ruth Wissen Sie, was ich gerne hätte: das ist eine Wärmflasche.
Birtha Ja, die hab' ich auch, die kann ich Ihnen dann füllen.
Ruth Und wo ist denn bitte das Badezimmer?
Birtha Das ist gleich, wenn Sie zur Tür rauskommen, links.
Ruth Haben Sie einen Adapter für mich?
Birtha Den werden Sie nicht brauchen.
Ruth Gut.
Birtha Hm – was haben Sie denn morgen vor?
Ruth Ach, das weiß ich noch nicht genau. Ich möchte ganz gerne vielleicht 'n Ausflug machen.
Birtha Ja – wir könnten meinen Wagen nehmen und ein paar kleine Dörfer in der Nähe ansehen.
Ruth Das klingt gut.
Birtha Es gibt dort auch ein paar schöne Museen und Kirchen, und anschließend könnten wir noch ein Glas Wein trinken gehen.
Ruth Prima.

hier drüben over here
♦ **die Decke** blanket
glauben to think, to believe
♦ **die Wärmflasche** hot-water bottle

♦ **das Museum, die Museen**
    museum, museums
anschließend after that
prima excellent, great

wissen Sie, was ich gerne hätte ... do you know what I'd like (to have) ...

die kann ich Ihnen dann füllen I can fill it for you later; **die = die Wärmflasche**. You can omit **Wärmflasche** because it's obvious what they are talking about. Things are often just referred to by **der, die, das,** or **den: den (Adapter) werden Sie nicht brauchen** you won't need it.

♦ **was haben Sie denn morgen vor?** what are your plans for tomorrow? **vorhaben** (sep.) to plan s.th.: **ich habe eine Reise vor** I'm planning a trip.

♦ **'n** (= **einen**) **Ausflug machen** to go on an outing

wir könnten meinen Wagen nehmen we could take my car; **der Wagen** or **das Auto** car

♦ **(wir könnten) ein paar kleine Dörfer in der Nähe ansehen** we could have a look at a few small villages nearby; **das Dorf** village; **ansehen** (sep.) to look at; **in der Nähe** (lit. in the near) nearby.

das klingt gut that sounds good.

Übungen

4 Try this word puzzle. Write the missing words in the squares. You'll find all the sentences in Dialogue 2, but try not to look at them. The letters marked 1–7 will describe something which is very useful to the traveller. (Answers p.201)

a. Haben Sie einen .... für mich? A ☐ ☐₁ ☐ ☐ ☐

b. Wissen Sie, was ich gerne hätte?

Eine .... Ä ☐ ☐ ☐ ☐ ☐ ☐ ☐₂

c. Und hier .... steht Ihr Bett. ☐ R ☐ ☐₃

d. Es gibt dort auch ein paar schöne .... ☐ ☐₄ ☐ N

e. Das hier ist also Ihr .... ☐ ☐₅ M ☐ ☐

f. Was haben Sie denn .... vor? M ☐₆ ☐ ☐ ☐

g. Glauben Sie, daß es warm .... ist? ☐ ☐ ☐₇ G

☐₁ ☐₂ ☐₃ ☐₄ ☐₅ ☐₆ ☐₇

5 Complete the questions by filling in the appropriate verb form in German. (Answers p.201)

a. (need) .... Sie noch etwas?

b. (would like) .... Sie eine extra Decke?

c. (think) .... Sie, daß es warm genug ist?

d. (have) .... Sie einen Adapter für mich?

e. Was (plan) .... Sie denn morgen

.........................?

6 Turn to the tape now for the speaking exercise. You'll be asked to play the guest. Corinna is your hostess, trying to make you feel at home.

Dialog 3: Noch einen Apéritif?

H. Scheuermann	Möchten Sie nicht noch einen Apéritif trinken, bis die letzten Gäste kommen?
Herr Schmitt	Gern.
Frau Schmitt	Wir könnten den Wein probieren, den wir mitgebracht haben.
Herr Schmitt	Wir waren nämlich im letzten Urlaub in Portugal.
Biba	Ach ja?
Herr Schmitt	Danke schön.
Biba	Ach, das werden jetzt die Frauenfelds sein, unsere letzten Gäste. Einen kleinen Moment, ich mach' mal schnell auf. – Ach, guten Tag, Herr Frauenfeld. Aber Sie sind ja ganz alleine!
H. Frauenfeld	Guten Abend, Frau Scheuermann. Ich muß leider meine Frau entschuldigen. Sie mußte zu Hause bleiben, weil unser Babysitter, den wir bestellt haben, nicht gekommen ist.
Biba	Ach, das tut mir aber leid. Das ist aber wirklich schade.
H. Frauenfeld	Darf ich Ihnen ein kleines Geschenk geben?
Biba	Ach, das wär' aber nicht nötig gewesen. Vielen Dank, Herr Frauenfeld. Darf ich Sie vorstellen: Das ist Frau Schmitt, Herr Frauenfeld, Herr Schmitt ...
Alle	Guten Abend. – Guten Abend. – Guten Abend.

einladen (sep.) to invite
der Gast, die Gäste guest(s)
das Geschenk present

Wir könnten den Wein probieren we could try the wine.
Wir könnten (we could) is the subjunctive form of **können** (can). The subjunctive is often used in polite speech; see also above:
♦ **möchten Sie ... einen Apéritif trinken?** would you like (to drink) an apéritif? and below: **das wäre aber nicht nötig gewesen** that would not have been necessary, i.e. you shouldn't have ... More about the subjunctive in Unit 12, p.193.

das werden die Frauenfelds sein that will be the Frauenfelds.

♦ **ich muß leider meine Frau entschuldigen** I'm afraid I have to apologize on behalf of my wife (lit. I have to excuse my wife); **leider** is often translated as 'I'm sorry to say that': **er kann leider nicht kommen** I'm afraid he cannot come.

den wir bestellt haben whom we've hired; **bestellen** lit. to order.

♦ **das tut mir aber leid** I'm sorry to hear that.

♦ **das ist aber wirklich schade** that's really a pity.

♦ **darf ich Sie vorstellen ...** may I introduce you ... **vorstellen** (sep.) to introduce: **er stellt seine Frau vor** he introduces his wife. But if there is another verb (here: **darf**), a separable verb does *not* split.

Übungen

7 Wer macht was? Make sure you understand Dialogue 3, then answer the questions below in German. (Answers p.201)

a. Wer war im letzten Urlaub in Portugal?

....

b. Wer ist der letzte Gast?

....

c. Wer hat Wein mitgebracht?

....

d. Wer bekommt ein Geschenk?

....

e. Wer ist nicht zu den Frauenfelds gekommen?

....

f. Wer konnte nicht zum Essen zu Scheuermanns kommen?

....

8 Translate the phrases below into German. (Answers p.201)

a. Would you like an apéritif?

....

b. We could try the wine from Portugal.

....

c. I have to apologize on behalf of my wife.

....

d. May I give you a small present?

....

e. May I introduce you, Herr Frauenfeld?

....

9 Your turn to say a few polite phrases which might be useful if you are invited to somebody's home. This time you won't be asked to take part in a conversation, but Andrew will ask you to recall some phrases you've met in the dialogue.

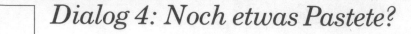

Dialog 4: Noch etwas Pastete?

Biba	Darf ich Ihnen noch etwas von dieser Pastete anbieten?
Frau Schmitt	Oh nein, danke, es tut mir leid, ich bin Vegetarierin.
Biba	Ach, aber dann nehmen Sie noch etwas von diesem Salat vielleicht?
Frau Schmitt	Ja, gern. Danke.
Biba	Und Sie, Herr Frauenfeld, nehmen Sie noch von dieser Pastete?
H. Frauenfeld	Oh ja, gerne.
Biba	Bitte sehr.
H. Frauenfeld	Danke.
Herr Schmitt	Ist diese Pastete selbstgemacht?
Biba	Ja, das ist ein Rezept meiner Mutter.
Herr Schmitt	Hm, schmeckt sehr fein.
Frau Schmitt	Da haben Sie aber ein wundervolles Gemälde an der Wand. Das gefällt mir ja sehr gut.
Biba	Ja, das hat mein Mann zum Geburtstag von seiner Firma bekommen.
Frau Schmitt	Ah, ja. Ach, Sie hatten Geburtstag vor kurzem . . .
H. Scheuermann	Ja . . .
Alle	Herzlichen Glückwunsch . . . Herzlichen Glückwunsch . . . Alles Gute.

♦ **der Vegetarier/die Vegetarierin** vegetarian   **das Gemälde** painting
das Rezept recipe   **die Firma** firm, company
♦ **selbstgemacht** homemade (lit. self made)

♦ **darf ich Ihnen noch etwas von dieser Pastete anbieten?** may I offer you
a bit more of this pâté? **anbieten** (sep.) to offer: **sie bietet ihm Zigaretten
an** she offers him cigarettes. Again **anbieten** is not split here because of the
second verb **darf**.

(das) schmeckt sehr fein (that) tastes very nice; you'll more often hear:
♦ **das schmeckt sehr gut** that tastes very good.

zum Geburtstag for (his) birthday

vor kurzem a short while ago, recently

♦ **herzlichen Glückwunsch** congratulations. Apart from **alles Gute** (all the
best) you'll also hear **gratuliere** I congratulate (you).

Übungen

10 Die richtige Antwort. Do you remember the conversation in Dialogue 4? Match up the questions and answers below, e.g. **a/C**. The words are slightly different from the dialogue. (Answers p.201)

a. Möchten Sie noch etwas von dieser Pastete?
b. Darf ich Ihnen noch etwas Salat anbieten?
c. Ist diese Pastete selbstgemacht?
d. Woher haben Sie das Gemälde an der Wand?
e. Hatten Sie vor kurzem Geburtstag?

A. Ja, nach einem Rezept meiner Mutter.
B. Von der Firma meines Mannes.
C. Nein, danke, ich bin Vegetarierin.
D. Ja, vor ein paar Tagen.
E. Danke, gerne.

11 Another word puzzle. The clues are in English, but fill in the answers in German. The column in the middle, read from top to bottom, gives you the name of a famous wine growing area in Germany. (Answers p.201)

a. Frau Schmitt refuses to eat it

b. They gave Mr Scheuermann a birthday present

c. Someone who doesn't eat meat

d. Frau Schmitt likes to eat it

e. Biba used one of her mother's for the pâté

 12 Your turn to take part in a dinner conversation now. Andrew will prompt you on the cassette.

Wörter und Wendungen

Starting a conversation

Wie gefällt es Ihnen?	How do you like it (here)?
Mir gefällt es gut/nicht gut	I like it/don't like it
Sind Sie hier im Urlaub?	Are you on holiday/vacation here?
Reisen Sie alleine?	Are you travelling on your own?
Woher kommen Sie?	Where are you from?
Seit wann sind Sie schon unterwegs?	Since when have you been travelling?

Staying somewhere

Brauchen Sie noch irgend etwas?	Do you need anything else?
Hier ist . . .	Here is . . .
das Bett	the bed
eine Decke	a blanket
eine Wärmflasche	a hot water bottle
das Badezimmer	the bathroom
Was haben Sie morgen vor?	What are your plans for tomorrow?
Wir könnten . . .	We could . . .
einen Ausflug machen	go on a trip
ein paar Dörfer/Museen/ Kirchen ansehen	have a look at a few villages/ museums/churches

Dinner party talk

Möchten Sie . . .	Would you like . . .
einen Apéritif?	an apéritif?
ein Glas Wein?	a glass of wine?
etwas Pastete?	some pâté?
noch etwas?	some more?
Darf ich Ihnen . . . anbieten?	May I offer you . . .?
Darf ich vorstellen?	May I introduce?
Das schmeckt gut	That tastes good
Das ist selbstgemacht	That's homemade
Ich bin Vegetarier(in)	I'm a vegetarian
Einen kleinen Moment	Just a moment
Ich muß leider meine Frau/ meinen Mann entschuldigen	I must apologize on behalf of my wife/husband
Das tut mir aber leid	I'm sorry to hear that
Das ist aber schade	That's a pity
Nein, danke	No, thank you
Ja, bitte	Yes, please
Bitte sehr	Here you are
Herzlichen Glückwunsch	Congratulations

Grammatik

The use of 'nicht' (not)

It is relatively easy in German to make a sentence negative, e.g. to say that you *don't* do something. In most cases you just need the word **nicht** (not):

Ich rauche I smoke
Ich rauche <u>nicht</u> I don't smoke (lit. I smoke not)
Wir gehen nach Hause We go home
Wir gehen <u>nicht</u> nach Hause We don't go home
Er geht zur Schule He goes to school
Er geht <u>nicht</u> zur Schule He doesn't go to school

As you can see from the above examples, in simple sentences **nicht** follows the verb. If there are two verbs in a sentence, **nicht** comes after the first verb:

Ich kann <u>nicht</u> schwimmen I can't swim
Sie ist <u>nicht</u> nach Wien gefahren She didn't go to Vienna
Es wird <u>nicht</u> regnen It isn't going to rain

In questions subject and verb are switched, so that **nicht** follows the subject:

Können Sie <u>nicht</u> schwimmen? Can't you swim?
Rauchen Sie <u>nicht</u>? Don't you smoke?
Hat es <u>nicht</u> geregnet? Didn't it rain?

In longer and more complex sentences the position of **nicht** can easily change, but for the time being just keep in mind that **nicht** stays close to the verb, and – in questions – to the subject.

13 Put these phrases into the negative by putting **nicht** in the right place. (Answers p.201)

a. Ich tanze ....

b. Ich kann singen ....

c. Wer kann schwimmen? ....

d. Bist du nach Bonn geflogen? ....

e. Das war nett ....

f. Es ist kalt geworden ....

In subordinate clauses, i.e. in sentences which start with **daß**, **weil**, **ob**, etc. the verb goes to the *end* of the sentence, and **nicht** goes with it:

Es tut mir leid, daß er <u>nicht</u> kommt I'm sorry he's not coming
Ich bin traurig, weil wir <u>nicht</u> wegfahren I'm sorry because we're not going away

The use of 'nichts' (nothing)

The difference does not just lie in the 's' – **nicht** and **nichts** have quite a different meaning:

Ich weiß nicht I don't know
Ich weiß nichts I don't know anything (lit. I know nothing)
Ich will nicht I don't want to
Ich will nichts I don't want anything
Er versteht nicht He doesn't understand
Er versteht nichts He doesn't understand anything

The use of 'kein'

Kein basically means 'no' as in 'no money' – **kein Geld**. But it can also be translated by 'not . . . a' as in 'I haven't got a car' – **Ich habe kein Auto**, or 'not . . . any' as in 'They haven't (got) any children' – **Sie haben keine Kinder**. Here are some more examples:

Ich habe ein Haus.
I have a house.

Ich habe <u>kein</u> Haus.
I don't have a house.

Ich besitze eine Wohnung.
I own an apartment.

Ich besitze <u>keine</u> Wohnung.
I don't own an apartment.

Er hat einen Sohn.
He has a son.

Er hat <u>keinen</u> Sohn.
He hasn't got a son.

Sie mag Tiere.
She likes animals.

Sie mag <u>keine</u> Tiere.
She doesn't like animals.

Haben Sie Brot?
Have you got any bread?

Nein, wir haben <u>kein</u> Brot.
No, we haven't got any bread.

The endings of **kein** are exactly as the endings for **ein** (see Unit 2, p.34).

14 Translate into German: (Answers p.201)

a. I don't speak any English.

....

b. I don't want any wine.

....

c. I have no telephone.

....

d. Mountains? I don't see any mountains.

....

Übungen: Lesen

15 Wir geben eine Party. Have a look at this section from the magazine
FREUNDIN which gives you some useful hints on how to organise your party.
Then answer the questions below in detail on a separate sheet.
(Answers p.201)

Man soll die Feste feiern, wie sie fallen . . .
. . . aber trotzdem nicht alles improvisieren

Ein Fest in den eigenen vier Wänden
zu feiern, eine tolle Idee. Man freut
sich, doch gleichzeitig hat man
Angst: was passiert, wenn die Gäste
sich langweilen? Jeder, der eine
größere Party geben will, kennt diese
gemischten Gefühle. Man kann nicht
vorhersagen, ob eine Party ein Erfolg
wird – man weiß nicht, wie die 20
oder 30 Leute aufeinander reagieren.
Man sollte sich aber vorher
überlegen:

- wen möchte ich einladen?
- wo möchte ich feiern?
- wie will ich die Gäste unterhalten?

Das beste Prinzip ist nach wie vor,
nur die Leute einzuladen, mit denen
man wirklich feiern möchte:

- also keine 'Muß-Einladungen' – sie
  könnten die Stimmung verderben.
- auch nicht die Freunde einladen,

die große Partys nicht mögen.
Lieber warten, bis man im
kleineren Kreise feiert.

- für eine lustige Party braucht man
  aktive Gäste – Leute, die keine
  Angst davor haben, auch mal den
  ersten Schritt zu tun . . .

Aber die beste Party kann ein Flop
werden, wenn die passenden Räume
fehlen. Fragen Sie sich:

- ist zum Beispiel genug Platz zum
  Tanzen da?
- ist zuviel Platz da?
- gibt es auch Möglichkeiten, sich zu
  zweit oder dritt in eine Ecke zu
  setzen?

. . . und vergessen Sie nicht: die
Nachbarn vorher informieren. Denn
die schönste Stimmung ist kaputt,
wenn ein ärgerlicher Nachbar vor der
Tür steht und über den Krach
schimpft.

Vocabulary:
man soll die Feste feiern, wie sie fallen never miss out on a party
passende Räume suitable rooms
trotzdem in spite of
was passiert what happens
gemischte Gefühle mixed feelings
vorhersagen (sep.) to predict
aufeinander reagieren relate to each other
in den eigenen vier Wänden in one's own four walls
die Einladung invitation
verderben to spoil
der Platz here: space
der Nachbar neighbour
ärgerlich annoyed

schimpfen to complain
der Krach noise
zu zweit in groups of two
zu dritt in groups of three

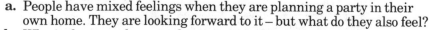

a. People have mixed feelings when they are planning a party in their
    own home. They are looking forward to it – but what do they also feel?
b. Why is there an element of uncertainty about any big party?
c. To start with, you should think about three points. Which are they?
d. What kind of people should you *not* invite?
e. What kind of guests are ideal for a successful party?
f. What should the rooms be like?
g. Who could spoil a party instantly? How could you avoid this?

16 **Herzlichen Glückwunsch!** On a **Südwestfunk** radio show Frank Metzler delivers birthday greetings. Listen, then try to take notes of the main points in the box below. (Answers p.201)

Vocabulary:
lächerlich ridiculous
die Oma (coll.) granny, grandma
der Enkel, das Enkelkind grandchild
der Grillbraten grilled meat
ich hab ... den Tisch gedeckt gekriegt the table was set for me
von vorne bis hinten richtig verwöhnt thoroughly spoilt, pampered

---

Whose birthday: ....

Living at: ....

Age today: ....

Number of grandchildren: ....

Celebrations:

morning ....

afternoon ....

evening ....

Südwestfunk

● ● **Vorwiegend Stereoprogramme**

4.30 Radiowecker. Dazw. 5.00 Nachr. — **5.30** Nachr. — **5.35 Guten Morgen aus Mainz.** Dazw. 5.55 Wort in den Tag / 6.55 Aktuelle Botschaft. — **8.00** Nachr. — **8.05 Gute Laune aus Südwest.** Dazw. 9.00 und 10.00 Nachrichten / 10.05 Wunschkonzert. Dazw. 11.00 Nachrichten — **11.50** Landfunk. — **12.00** Nachrichten — **12.05 Rheinland-Pfalz-Echo.** — **13.00** Heute mittag. — **14.00** Nachr., Börse. — **14.05** Für junge Hörer: Mit dem Mikro unterwegs. — **14.30 Radiotreff.** Dazw. stündlich Nachrichten

18.00 Tribüne der Zeit
18.20 Tagesspiegel
18.30 Zur Unterhaltung
19.00 Nachrichten
19.05 RO des SWF
19.30 Politik / Aktuelles
20.00 Nachrichten
20.05 FRÖHLICHER ALLTAG

22.00 Nachr., Politik
22.15 Boulevard
23.00 Nachrichten
23.05 Mitternachts-spitzen
24.00 Nachrichten
0.06–4.30 Nachtprogr.

SWF 2

4.30–5.35 wie 1. Progr. — **5.35 Morgenmelodie.** — **5.55** Wort in den Tag. — **6.00** Nachr. — **6.03 Kon-zert.** — **6.55** Aktuelle Botschaft. — **7.00** Nachr., Presse. — **7.17 Musikal. Kaleidoskop.** — **8.00** Nachr. — **8.05** RSO Saar-brücken. — **9.00 Schul-funk.** Niels Bohr. Physik und Erkenntnis. — **9.30** Nachr. — **9.35** Religionen und ihre Musik (2). — **10.30** Der grüne Punkt. — **11.00 Hörer wünschen Klas-sik.** — **12.00** Rundfunkor-chester des SWF. — **12.30** Blickpunkt

13.10 Konzert Werke von Gluck, Che-rubini, Mozart
14.30 Französ. Lieder und Kammermusik
15.00 Nachrichten
15.05 Fortsetzung folgt Heine: „Reisebilder"
15.30 Konzert Johs. Brahms, Beetho-ven, Bartok, Schönberg, Mahler, Berio
17.00 Schulfunk La Gendarmerie Nationale
17.30 Nachrichten
17.35 Kultur regional
18.00 SO des SWF
19.00 Blickpunkt
19.30 Jazzplatte
20.00 Kultur aktuell
20.20 Kreisler-Trio Werke von Beethoven, Kirchner, Schubert
22.00 Hochschulreport
22.15 Aus Wissen-schaft und Technik
23.00 Nachrichten
23.05 Musik nach 1900
24.00 Nachrichten
0.05–2.00 siehe WDR 3
2.00–4.30 Nachtprogr.

17 Hochzeit mit Hindernissen. No celebration at all so far for bridegroom Ken, who wants to get married but was stopped twice by the same event. Which one? Listen to our second radio extract, which is also printed – slightly simplified – below, but the sentences are not in the right order. Re-arrange them after listening. (Answers p.201)

Vocabulary:
Hochzeit mit Hindernissen wedding hitches
eigentlich actually
heiraten to get married
der Polterabend eve of the wedding day
er nahm einen großen Anlauf zum Standesamt he made a dash for the registry office
verschoben postponed
der Bräutigam bridegroom
im Streckverband in plaster
die Braut nimmt's gelassen auf the bride takes it in her stride

Hals- und Beinbruch best of luck; break a leg

a. Aber er brach sich wieder ein Bein.
b. Ken wollte im Frühjahr heiraten.
c. Die Hochzeit wird verschoben.
d. Aber er brach sich am Polterabend ein Bein.
e. Der Bräutigam liegt noch drei Monate im Krankenhaus.
f. Jetzt versuchte er es zum zweiten Mal.
g. Die Braut nimmt's gelassen auf.
h. Und aus der Hochzeit wurde nichts.

a. ....

b. ....

c. ....

d. ....

e. ....

f. ....

g. ....

h. ....

18 You meet someone on a trip and start chatting. Ask at least five questions –
e.g. where is he from, is he travelling alone, does he like the area, etc. On
the cassette Corinna will have some questions for you to compare.

19 You're having a guest for the weekend and are showing her her room. Ask
her if she's comfortable, if she needs anything, tell her where the bathroom
is, breakfast times, etc. There'll be a sample version to listen to afterwards.

5 Wie ist die Arbeitslage?

You will learn

- something about the job market in West Germany
- to talk about your own job
- to write a curriculum vitae

... and you'll get a chance to hear a listener's problems on the radio

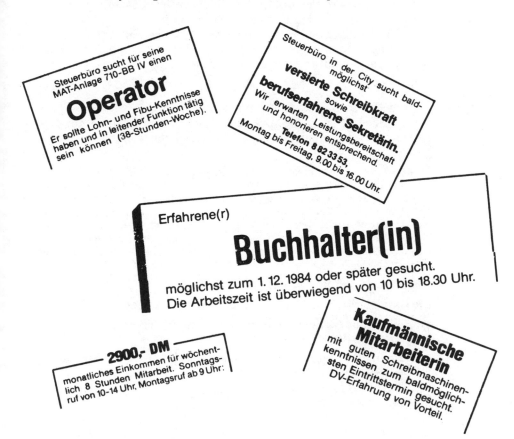

Steuerbüro sucht für seine
MAT-Anlage 710-BB IV einen
Operator
Er sollte Lohn- und Fibu-Kenntnisse
haben und in leitender Funktion tätig
sein können (38-Stunden-Woche).

Steuerbüro in der City sucht bald-
möglichst
versierte Schreibkraft
sowie
berufserfahrene Sekretärin.
Wir erwarten Leistungsbereitschaft
und honorieren entsprechend.
Telefon 8 82 33 53,
Montag bis Freitag, 9.00 bis 16.00 Uhr.

Erfahrene(r)
Buchhalter(in)
möglichst zum 1. 12. 1984 oder später gesucht.
Die Arbeitszeit ist überwiegend von 10 bis 18.30 Uhr.

2900,- DM
monatliches Einkommen für wöchentlich 8 Stunden Mitarbeit. Sonntags-
ruf von 10-14 Uhr, Montagsruf ab 9 Uhr:

Kaufmännische Mitarbeiterin
mit guten Schreibmaschinen-
kenntnissen zum baldmöglich-
sten Eintrittstermin gesucht.
DV-Erfahrung von Vorteil.

Study guide

Dialog 1: Auf dem Arbeitsamt

Ruth	Frau Blumental, wie ist im Moment die Arbeitslage?
F. Blumental	Leider gar nicht rosig. Hier in Heidelberg haben wir 7,5 Prozent Arbeitslose, und in der Bundesrepublik sogar 8,9.
Ruth	Wer ist besonders betroffen?
F. Blumental	Unter den Männern sind das insbesondere die Lager- und Transportarbeiter. Bei den Frauen die Verkäuferinnen, und bei Männern und Frauen außerdem die Lehrer und Sozialarbeiter.
Ruth	Was passiert, wenn jemand seine Arbeit verliert?
F. Blumental	Er kommt zum Arbeitsamt – je früher, desto besser – und wir suchen nach einer Stelle für ihn. Wenn wir keine haben, dann kann er Arbeitslosenunterstützung bekommen.
Ruth	Für wie lange?
F. Blumental	Maximal für ein Jahr.
Ruth	Welche Berufe haben im Moment gute Chancen?
F. Blumental	Das sind vor allem der Maurer, der Tischler, der Kellner, der Zahnarzt auch, ebenso wie die Krankenschwester.

Many words in this dialogue are built around **die Arbeit** (work) or
♦ **arbeiten** (to work): **das Arbeitsamt** labour exchange/employment office;
♦ **der Arbeitsmarkt** job market, **die Arbeitslage** job situation, **arbeitslos**
♦ out of a job, unemployed; **die Arbeitslosen** (pl.) the jobless, **der Arbeiter/
die Arbeiterin** male/female worker, **der Lagerarbeiter** storeman, **der
Transportarbeiter** transport worker, **der Sozialarbeiter** social worker,
♦ **die Arbeitslosenunterstützung** unemployment benefit (**unterstützen** to
support).

rosig rosy; **die Rose** rose

die Bundesrepublik (Deutschland) the Federal Republic of Germany

wer ist besonders betroffen who is particularly affected (from
betreffen to affect).

unter den Männern among the men; similarly: **unter den Frauen**
among the women

♦ **der Beruf** job, profession; Frau Blumental mentions a number of
professions: **der Lehrer** teacher, **der Maurer** bricklayer, **der Tischler**
carpenter (from **Tisch** table), **der Kellner** waiter; by changing the article
to **die** and by adding **-in** to the noun you will get the female form: **die
Lehrerin** etc; similarly: **der Verkäufer/die Verkäuferin** sales assistant,
der Zahnarzt/die Zahnärztin dentist; but: **die Krankenschwester**
(female) nurse (**krank** sick; **Schwester** sister).

was passiert, wenn ... what happens if ...

je früher, desto besser the sooner the better.

♦ **die Stelle** job, situation; also: vacancy; **es sind Stellen frei** there are
vacancies.

wenn wir keine haben if we haven't got any.

Übungen

1 Fill in the gaps! Listen to the dialogue as often as you feel you have to, but try not to look at the text opposite. Note that the sentences here are slightly different. (Answers p.201)

a. In Heidelberg sind im Moment .... Prozent

arbeitslos, in der Bundesrepublik sogar ....

b. Unter den Männern haben besonders ....- und

.... arbeiter keine Stelle.

c. Unter den Frauen sind auch .... ohne Arbeit.

d. Unter Männern und Frauen gibt es viele arbeitslose ....

.... und ....

e. Wenn das .... keine Stelle findet, bekommt

man ...., maximal für ....

....

2 A job quiz. Fill in the squares. All the jobs required here have occurred in Dialogue 1. The numbered squares 1–11 will give you the word for what used to be a 'dream job'. (Answers p.201)

a. Er baut Häuser ⬛M⬛⬛⬛⬛⬛₁

b. Er serviert Essen und Getränke ⬛⬛₂⬛⬛L⬛⬛⬛

c. Er arbeitet viel mit Holz ⬛⬛₃⬛⬛H⬛⬛R⬛

d. Sie hat mit kranken Menschen zu tun
⬛K⬛⬛⬛⬛⬛⬛₄⬛⬛⬛⬛⬛⬛E⬛⬛

e. Er arbeitet in der Schule ⬛⬛₅⬛R⬛⬛

f. Er braucht starke Muskeln ⬛₆A⬛⬛R⬛⬛₇₈⬛⬛R⬛

g. Zu ihm geht niemand gern Z⬛⬛⬛⬛⬛₉

h. Er arbeitet im Geschäft ⬛₁₀⬛⬛Ä⬛⬛₁₁

⬛₁⬛₂⬛₃⬛₄⬛₅⬛₆⬛₇⬛₈⬛₉⬛₁₀⬛₁₁⬛

3 In order to practise some of the quite difficult words connected with **Arbeit**, repeat Klaus's statements after him on the cassette.

Dialog 2: Keine feste Stelle

Ruth Was sind Sie von Beruf?
Biba Ich bin freie Journalistin.
Ruth Haben Sie sich auch andere Berufe überlegt?
Biba Ja, früher wollte ich mal Lehrerin werden, aber das ist heute nicht mehr so einfach. Es gibt sehr viele arbeitslose Lehrer. Und natürlich habe ich auch an eine feste Anstellung gedacht, beim Rundfunk oder bei einer Zeitung.
Ruth Warum sind Sie dann freie Journalistin geworden?
Biba Zunächst einfach deswegen, weil ich keine feste Stelle gefunden habe.
Ruth Und sind Sie denn mit Ihrem Beruf zufrieden?
Biba Ja und nein. Insgesamt glaube ich schon, daß ich die richtige Entscheidung getroffen habe, denn mein Beruf ist sehr abwechslungsreich. Ich komme ständig mit neuen Leuten zusammen und muß viele neue Ideen entwickeln. Aber er hat auch viele Nachteile. Zum Beispiel habe ich manchmal Geldsorgen, oder ich verdiene während des Urlaubs kein Geld. Oder wenn ich krank bin, verdiene ich kein Geld, und das sind große Unsicherheiten.

einfach simple, easy
zufrieden happy, content
♦ **abwechslungsreich** varied

die Geldsorgen (pl.) money worries
entwickeln to develop
♦ **die Unsicherheit** insecurity

♦ **was sind Sie von Beruf?** what's your job? (lit. what are you of profession?)

♦ **ich bin freie Journalistin** I'm a freelance journalist; similar: **ich bin Lehrer/Tischler/Krankenschwester (von Beruf)** I'm a teacher/carpenter/nurse.

Haben Sie sich auch andere Berufe überlegt? Did you consider other jobs as well?

♦ **früher wollte ich mal Lehrerin werden** at one time I wanted to be a teacher.

♦ **natürlich habe ich auch an eine feste Anstellung gedacht** of course I thought of a steady job as well; **die Anstellung** or **die Stelle** position, job; **ich habe ... gedacht** lit. I have thought. This is the *perfect tense*, see **Grammatik** for more details.

... daß ich die richtige Entscheidung getroffen habe that I made the right decision; **eine Entscheidung treffen** to make a decision.

ich komme ständig mit neuen Leuten zusammen I constantly meet new people; **zusammenkommen** to meet (lit. come together) is a separable word: **ich komme nicht oft mit ihm zusammen** I don't often meet him.

♦ **... viele Nachteile** many disadvantages; **der Nachteil** disadvantage, **der Vorteil** advantage.

Ich verdiene während des Urlaubs kein Geld I don't earn any money during my holiday/vacation; note that **während** takes the genitive case: **während des Krieges/der Party/des Festivals** during the war/the party/the festival.

Übungen

4 Which sentences in the dialogue are similar to the ones printed below?
Underline them in the dialogue. (Answers p.201)

a. Haben Sie sich auch überlegt, ob Sie etwas anderes werden wollen?
b. Es gibt viele Lehrer, die keine Stelle haben.
c. Gefällt Ihnen Ihr Beruf?
d. Ich treffe immer neue Leute.
e. Mein Beruf ist nicht langweilig.
f. Ich habe manchmal finanzielle Schwierigkeiten.

5 Vorteil oder <u>N</u>achteil? Advantage or disadvantage? Read these six
statements about Biba's job and write either **N** or **V** in the boxes.
(Answers p.201)

a. Bibas Beruf ist manchmal unsicher. ☐
b. Sie kommt viel mit Leuten zusammen. ☐
c. Sie muß immer neue Ideen entwickeln. ☐
d. Sie verdient im Urlaub kein Geld. ☐
e. In ihrem Beruf gibt es viel Abwechslung. ☐
f. Wenn sie krank ist, bekommt sie kein Geld. ☐

*Die Journalistin Biba
(links) bei einem Interview*

6 On tape you'll be asked to conduct an interview and ask someone questions
about his career. Andrew will prompt you.

Dialog 3: Ein sicherer Beruf

Ruth   Was sind Sie von Beruf?

Herr Beck   Ich bin Buchhalter in einer großen Exportfirma, und das ist für mich ein ganz sicherer Beruf mit großen Aufstiegsmöglichkeiten. Und vor allen Dingen bekomme ich eine gute Rente, wenn ich pensioniert werde.

Ruth   Und wann gehen Sie in den Ruhestand?

Herr Beck   Ich gehe mit 65 in den Ruhestand.

Ruth   Wie sieht Ihr typischer Arbeitstag aus?

Herr Beck   Mein typischer Arbeitstag beginnt um sieben Uhr und endet um 15 Uhr.

Ruth   Wann haben Sie Mittagspause?

Herr Beck   Ich habe Mittagspause von zwölf bis ein Uhr.

Ruth   Und was machen Sie da?

Herr Beck   Ich gehe in die Kantine, esse da mit Kollegen zusammen.

Ruth   Gibt's bei Ihnen gleitende Arbeitszeit?

Herr Beck   Ja, bei uns gibt's gleitende Arbeitszeit, aber ich selber habe bisher davon noch keinen Gebrauch gemacht.

Ruth   Und wieviel Urlaub haben Sie im Jahr?

Herr Beck   Ich habe vier Wochen Urlaub im Jahr, wobei ich aber dazu sagen muß, daß die Pfingsttage, Ostern oder Weihnachtstage nicht dazu gerechnet werden.

Ruth   Das ist extra?

Herr Beck   Das ist extra, ja.

- **der Buchhalter** accountant
- **die Exportfirma** export firm
- **die Rente** pension

- **die Kantine** canteen, lunch room
- **die Mittagspause** lunch hour, lunch break

- **ein (ganz) sicherer Beruf mit guten Aufstiegsmöglichkeiten** a safe job with good prospects; **die Aufstiegsmöglichkeiten** career prospects; from **Aufstieg** (rise) and **Möglichkeiten** (possibilities)

- **wenn ich pensioniert werde** when I retire (lit. become retired).

- **wann gehen Sie in (den) Ruhestand?** when do you enter retirement?

- **ein typischer Arbeitstag** a typical working day; similar: **ein typischer Ferientag** a typical holiday, **ein typischer Sonntag** a typical Sunday.

- **die gleitende Arbeitszeit** flexitime. Flexitime is becoming more and more popular in Germany as it enables office workers to leave work as early as three or four o'clock in the afternoon – provided you start at about seven in the morning.

  ich habe bisher davon noch keinen Gebrauch gemacht I haven't made use of it yet.

  die Pfingsttage or **Pfingsten** Whitsun, Pentecost

  . . . nicht dazu gerechnet werden are not included (in the holidays).

Übungen

7 Fill in this form with details about Manfred Beck's job. Try it by just listening to the dialogue and refer to the book only when you're stuck. (Answers p.201)

Name: _____

Beruf: _____

Arbeitet wo? _____

Rente – ab wann? _____

Arbeitstag: von _____ bis _____

Mittagspause: von _____ bis _____

macht von gleitender Arbeitszeit Gebrauch:

ja ☐   nein ☐

Urlaub: _____

Extra Urlaub: _____

8 Translate the following words and phrases into German. (Answers p.201)

a. career prospects ....

b. to take one's retirement..

c. lunch break ....

d. canteen, lunch room..

e. flexitime..

f. a good pension...

9 Look at this job profile of a computer expert and put yourself in her shoes. Then turn on the cassette and answer Klaus's questions accordingly.

Einzelheiten details **das Gehalt** salary **brutto** gross, before tax

Name: Cornelia Martens
Beruf: Computer-Expertin
Arbeitgeber: Siemens
Alter: 35 Jahre
Einzelheiten: gleitende Arbeitszeit
40-Stunden-Woche
5 Wochen Jahresurlaub
Firmenrente
Gehalt: DM 6 000 brutto pro Monat

Dialog 4: Ein neues Leben

Silke Also, ich hab' die Schule so früh wie möglich verlassen; ich wollte nämlich ziemlich schnell Geld verdienen. Und da hab' ich 'ne Zeitlang in der Fabrik gearbeitet – am Fließband. Und da ich noch mehr Geld verdienen wollte, machte ich dann Akkordarbeit. Aber das war ziemlich anstrengend. Wenn ich abends nach Hause kam, kam ich mir vor wie eine Maschine. Ich konnte nichts Richtiges mit mir anfangen, ich war völlig kaputt. Und dann entschloß ich mich nach einer Weile, was anderes zu machen. Es war mir egal, ob ich mehr Geld in der Tasche hatte oder nicht. Ich ging daher zum Arbeitsamt und ließ mich beraten. Und jetzt bin ich Arzthelferin. Ich komme mit Menschen zusammen – das ist zwar auch anstrengend, aber ich hab' das Gefühl, daß ich was wirklich Wichtiges mache.

▶ **die Fabrik** factory
die Akkordarbeit piece work
das Fließband production line

▶ **anstrengend** exhausting
die Tasche pocket, bag

▶ **ich habe ... verlassen** I (have) left ...

▶ **Ich wollte nämlich ziemlich schnell Geld verdienen** I wanted to earn money rather quickly, you know.

'ne Zeitlang short for **eine Zeitlang** for a while

ich kam mir vor wie eine Maschine I felt like a machine; **sich vorkommen** (sep.) to feel like ...: **er kommt sich wie ein Held vor** he feels like a hero.

ich konnte nichts Richtiges mit mir anfangen I didn't know what to do with myself (lit. I couldn't start anything right with myself).

ich war völlig kaputt I was completely worn out; **kaputt** (lit. broken, smashed), coll. for **müde, erschöpft** tired, exhausted

und dann entschloß ich mich nach einer Weile ... and then I decided after a while ... **sich entschließen** to decide, to make up one's mind: **er kann sich nicht entschließen** he can't make up his mind.

es war mir egal I did not care; **es ist mir egal** I don't care.

ich ließ mich beraten I asked for advice (lit. I let myself be advised).

was wirklich Wichtiges something really important.

die Arzthelferin doctor's assistant. An **Arzthelfer/in** is more than just a doctor's receptionist; he/she would have some medical training and assist the doctor with the patients as well as having clerical duties.

Übungen

10 Re-translate the following phrases into German by using Silke's words from the dialogue. (Answers p.201)

a. I wanted to earn money fast.

....

b. I worked in a factory on the production line.

....

c. I was completely worn out.

....

d. I went to the labour exchange/employment office.

....

e. I'm a doctor's assistant now.

....

f. I have the feeling I'm doing something important.

....

11 Below are some words from the previous dialogues in a different context: Cordula has written a letter to her aunt, asking her for some advice on her future career. Fill the words in the appropriate blanks. (Answers p.201)

Idee Menschen Geld Arbeitsamt Maschine Interesse Schule Beruf

Liebe Tante Emma,
Vielen Dank für Deinen Brief und für Dein
.... an meinen Berufsplänen. Ich ging
gestern zum .... und ließ mich
beraten. Du weißt ja, im Juli verlasse ich
die .... Ich möchte einen ....,
der interessant ist, und wo ich viel mit
.... zu tun habe. Natürlich möchte
ich auch genügend .... verdienen.
In einer Fabrik möchte ich nicht arbeiten –
da komme ich mir vor wie eine ....
Hast Du eine gute ....?
Viele liebe Grüße,
Deine
Cordula

12 On the cassette Corinna will ask you some questions about what you did after leaving school. Answer according to Andrew's prompts. Here are some imperfect forms you'll be using:

ich ging   ich wollte   ich war   ich hatte   ich machte

Wörter und Wendungen

About your job

Was sind Sie von Beruf?	What's your job?
Ich bin ...	I am a ...
Lehrer/in	teacher
Transportarbeiter/in	transport worker
Krankenschwester	nurse
Ich bin freie Journalistin	I'm a freelance journalist
Ich habe eine feste Stelle	I've got a permanent job
Ich arbeite ...	I'm working ...
in der Fabrik	in a factory
bei einer Exportfirma	at an export firm
am Fließband	on the production line
Ich mache Akkordarbeit	I do piece work
Mein Beruf ist sehr ...	My job is very ...
abwechslungsreich	varied
anstrengend	exhausting
sicher/unsicher	secure/insecure
Mein Beruf hat viele Vorteile/ Nachteile	My job has many advantages/ disadvantages
Es gibt ...	There is/are ...
gute Aufstiegsmöglichkeiten	good promotion prospects
gleitende Arbeitszeit	flexitime/flextime
eine Kantine	a canteen
eine Stunde Mittagspause	one hour lunch break
vier Wochen Urlaub	four weeks holiday/vacation
ein gutes Gehalt	a good salary
nette Kollegen	nice colleagues
eine Rente	a pension
Ich gehe (mit 65) in den Ruhestand	I'll take my retirement (at 65)
Ich habe die Schule früh verlassen	I left school early
Ich will/wollte ...	I want/wanted ...
Lehrer werden	to be a teacher
viel Geld verdienen	to earn a lot of money

At the labour exchange

das Arbeitsamt	labour exchange/employment office
die Arbeitslage	job situation
arbeitslos	unemployed
die Arbeitslosen	the unemployed
die Arbeitslosenunterstützung	unemployment benefit

Grammatik

The perfect tense

Sentences such as **Ich habe gearbeitet** (I have worked) or **Ich habe gelacht** (I have laughed) use the perfect tense in order to talk about something that happened in the past. The perfect tense is the past tense form most often used in everyday speech. It is often applied when you would have to use the imperfect (see **Grammatik** Unit 8) in English, e.g. **Ich habe gestern gearbeitet** – I worked yesterday.

Here is a reminder of how the perfect is formed: In most cases you use the present tense of **haben** plus the past participle of a verb. To get the past participle you put **ge-** in front and (**e**)t after the verb stem. For example:

verb: **machen** (to do, to make)
verb stem: **mach**
past participle: **gemacht**
perfect tense: **ich habe gemacht, du hast gemacht, er/sie/es hat gemacht, wir haben gemacht, ihr habt gemacht, Sie/sie haben gemacht**

13 Follow the above example (**machen**) with the verbs **lernen, kochen, antworten** (to learn, to cook, to answer). Remember that you add **-et** if the stem of a verb ends in **t**. (Answers p.202)

Note the word order: **haben** usually goes in second place in statements and in first place in questions, with the past participle right at the end of the sentence:

Ich habe von der gleitenden Arbeitszeit keinen Gebrauch gemacht.
Ich habe ein Zeitlang in der Fabrik gearbeitet.
Haben Sie schon Mittagspause gemacht?
Hat er bei der Exportfirma gearbeitet?

14 Put the following sentences into the perfect tense. (Answers p.202)

a. Was machen Sie am Sonntag?

....

b. Ich lerne Deutsch.

....

c. Was kochst du heute abend?

....

d. Ich antworte dir nicht.

....

Note: There are quite a few verbs which do not add **ge-** in front, e.g. **garantieren** (to guarantee), **studieren** (to study): **ich habe garantiert, ich habe studiert**. Words which already have a prefix do not add **ge-** either, e.g. **besichtigen** (to have a look at s.th.), **erleben** (to experience): **ich habe besichtigt, ich habe erlebt**.

A few verbs form their perfect tense with **sein** instead of **haben**. They are usually verbs expressing change or movement, e.g. **reisen** (to travel):

ich bin gereist	**wir sind gereist**
du bist gereist	**ihr seid gereist**
er/sie/es ist gereist	**sie/Sie sind gereist**

Dictionaries and grammar books state which verbs use **haben** and which use **sein** for their perfect tenses.

Strong verbs

The same rules for position and the use of **sein** and **haben** apply to the so-called strong verbs (see p.215), but those verbs form their past participle in a different and less predictable way. They add **-en** and not **-t** to the stem, and the stem itself frequently changes, for example:

treffen (to meet): **Ich habe ihn getroffen**
werden (to become): **Ich bin Lehrerin geworden**
finden (to find): **Ich habe mein Buch gefunden**

There is sometimes a resemblance between English and German strong verbs, e.g. **singen – gesungen** (to sing – sung), **fallen – gefallen** (to fall – fallen) which may help you to recognize the verb forms. There is little point in trying to learn them all by heart at once. Try to remember those you've come across, and when in doubt consult a dictionary or a grammar book that has a list of strong verbs.

15 Translate the following sentences which use the perfect tense of strong verbs. Here are the participles mixed up: **geschlafen, gegessen, gefunden, gesungen, getrunken**. (Answers p.202)

a. I have drunk wine. ....

....

b. Have you slept well? ....

....

c. What have you eaten? ....

....

d. He has sung a song. ....

....

e. I have found your book. ....

....

Übungen: Lesen

16 Here is an extract from an information sheet about unemployment among young immigrants. Study it, then read the statements below and decide whether they are true or false – **Richtig oder Falsch**. (Answers p.202)

Viele ausländische Jugendliche sind arbeitslos

Unter den ausländischen Jugendlichen gibt es besonders viele Arbeitslose. Warum? Sie sind oft schlechter auf das Berufsleben vorbereitet als die deutschen Jugendlichen. Ihr Deutsch ist nicht gut genug und ihre Allgemeinbildung ist voller Lücken, besonders, wenn sie erst spät in die Bundesrepublik Deutschland kamen und keinen Schulabschluß haben.

Aus diesem Grund können sie nur Hilfsarbeiter werden – aber Hilfsarbeiter gibt es jetzt schon zuviele. Wie kann man helfen? Das Arbeitsamt kann Sprach- und Ausbildungskurse finanzieren, um den ausländischen Jugendlichen bessere Chancen auf dem Arbeitsmarkt zu geben.

Vocabulary:
ausländisch foreign
der/die Jugendliche youth
das Berufsleben professional life
vorbereitet prepared
die Allgemeinbildung general education

die Lücke gap
der Hilfsarbeiter unskilled labourer
der Ausbildungskurs training course

a. Youth unemployment is not quite so severe among immigrants.
R   F

b. Young immigrants are not as well prepared for their future careers as their German counterparts. R   F

c. Their job opportunities are better when they have come to Germany relatively late. R   F

d. Very often their German is not good enough and they have no diploma. R   F

e. They can only be unskilled labourers. R   F

f. The labour exchange can provide money for special language and training courses. R   F

g. There is no demand for unskilled labourers. R   F

17 When applying for a new job you will nearly always be asked to provide a curriculum vitae – **einen Lebenslauf** – sometimes handwritten. Here's one from the author of 'Breakthrough Further German' – read it, then answer the questions below. (Answers p.202)

Lebenslauf

Ich wurde am 1.5.48 als Tochter von Josef Rach und seiner Frau Hilde in Biberach geboren.
Nach 4 Jahren Grundschule (von 1955-59) besuchte ich das Mädchengymnasium Ulm. 1966-67 verbrachte ich als Stipendiatin des American Field Service (AFS) in Cincinnati (Ohio) und bekam zum Abschluß das 'American High School Diploma.'
1968 machte ich in Ulm das Abitur ('Hauptfächer: Deutsch, Mathematik, Französisch, Englisch. Danach studierte ich in West Berlin, München und Aberystwyth (Wales) die Fächer Philosophie, Anglistik und Germanistik.
1975 machte ich das Staatsexamen und ging dann nach England. Ich unterrichtete 5 Jahre Deutsch an den Universitäten Sussex und Bath, anschließend arbeitete ich als Journalistin beim Deutschsprachigen Dienst der BBC London. Ich lebe in Sussex und habe eine kleine Tochter, Dewi Jessica. Meine Hobbies sind Schreiben, Malen und Reisen.

Vocabulary:

ich wurde geboren I was born
die Grundschule primary school, elementary school
das Gymnasium grammar school, high school
studieren to study
das Staatsexamen state exam qualifying you to teach – equivalent to an M.A.
unterrichten to teach
Deutschsprachiger Dienst German Service
die Stipendiatin (female) holder of a scholarship

a. For how many years did Ruth go to elementary school? ....

b. What were her main subjects before she left school? ....

c. Who sponsored her stay in the United States? ....

d. At which universities did she study? ....

e. What was she doing at Sussex University? ....

f. What are her hobbies? ....

Übungen: Radio

18 Below you'll find a printed version of our first radio excerpt advertising the American movie 'Flashdance'. But eight words are wrong. Can you cross them out and fill in the right ones after listening? (Answers p.210 in transcript)

Er träumt den Traum von der kleinen Karriere. Doch selbst wenn ein Traum niemals wahr wird, verändert er das Leben für immer. Flashdance. Er tanzt sich ganz nach unten in Flashdance – die Diskosensation aus den USA. Ein Film ohne Träume und voll kalter Musik. Flashdance. Ein Film, der in die Beine geht. Jetzt im Theater. Und die Flashdance-Hits gibt's jetzt auch auf LP und Kassette.

19a Listen to the first part of the next extract, where Alexander Borrell, who hosts a 'problem programme' on **Südwestfunk** Radio, reads out a listener's letter. What are her problems? Complete the summary of her letter. (Answers p.202)

Vocabulary:

die Hörerin (female) listener
der Hörer (male) listener
die Hotelkauffrau (female) hotel manager
die Serviermeisterin head waitress
sich bewerben to apply (for a job)
auf die Dauer in the long run
die Lust am Leben love of life

das Inserat classified advertisement
allerdings but
das Fältchen small wrinkle
der Schönheitschirurg plastic surgeon
der Bekanntenkreis circle of friends

Ich bin seit einem Jahr .... Mein

Problem ist mein .... Alle Arbeitgeber

wollen eine .... Das ist so deprimierend,

daß ich die .... verloren habe. Auch die

Männer im Inserat wollen jüngere Frauen. Und ich frage mich, ob

ich zu einem .... gehen soll.

19b Now go back to the cassette and listen to Alexander Borrell's advice. What does he suggest? Mark the correct boxes in the questions below.
(Answers p.202)

auf gar keinen Fall on no account
ob Sie nun geliftet sind oder nicht whether you had a face lift or not
Flausen im Kopf haben to have fancy ideas in one's head
einstellen (sep.) to employ
imponieren to impress
das braucht Sie gar nicht zu kümmern you needn't worry about that
umgekehrt the other way around
der Lebensgefährte companion, partner
eine Frau in reifen Jahren a mature lady
die Zuneigung affection

a. Should the lady have cosmetic surgery?

☐ yes
☐ no

b. Should she admit her age when applying for a job?

☐ yes
☐ no

c. Would some employers value her experience if she were honest about her age?

☐ yes
☐ no

d. Would it be a good idea if she placed an ad herself in order to find a partner?

☐ yes
☐ no

e. Should she lie about her age in the ad?

☐ yes
☐ no

Übungen: Sprechen Sie selbst

20 Make up your own answers to the questions below. First read out the question, then give your answer. On the cassette you can then listen to a few examples of what other people said.

Was sind Sie von Beruf?
Wo arbeiten Sie?
Sind Sie mit Ihrem Beruf zufrieden?
Wieviel Urlaub haben Sie im Jahr?

21 Have another look at the **Lebenslauf** on p.84, then talk about your own life in a similar way. Use the perfect or imperfect tense as often as possible. On the cassette you'll then hear a sample **Lebenslauf**.

6 Schönes Wochenende

You will learn

- to say what you do during the weekend
- to talk about sports and hobbies
- to deal with time

... and you'll hear something about a very special service to liven up your weekend

Study guide

Dialog 1: Ostern nach Zell

Ruth Wir wollen gerne Ostern nach Zell am See – so 'ne Art verlängertes Wochenende. Was kann man da denn alles machen?

Frau Jonas Also als erstes würde ich Ihnen empfehlen, daß sie rechtzeitig buchen. Das ist nämlich sehr stark gebucht. Und Sie können dort also – wenn's Wetter schön ist – am See irgendwas unternehmen: Bootfahren, Surfen . . . Sie können auch wandern. Sehr viele Spazierwege gibt's dort . . . könnte natürlich auch sein, daß es noch Schnee gibt, und dann können Sie skifahren. Das heißt also Langlauf, oder auch unter Umständen Abfahrtsski.

Ruth Und was machen wir, wenn's regnet?

Frau Jonas Wenn's regnet, gibt's also sehr viele Möglichkeiten. Sie können ins Schwimmbad, Sie können in die Sauna, es gibt Kegelbahnen, es gibt Tanzveranstaltungen . . . das ist überhaupt kein Problem.

Zell am See resort in Austria
- **das Bootfahren** boating
- **das Surfen** here: windsurfing
- **der Langlauf** cross-country skiing

- **Abfahrtsski** downhill skiing
- **die Kegelbahn** bowling alley
- **die Tanzveranstaltung** dance

- **so 'ne Art (=eine Art) verlängertes Wochenende** a kind of long weekend.

- **. . . daß Sie rechtzeitig buchen** that you book well ahead.

- **das ist nämlich sehr stark gebucht** it gets very heavily booked, you know. If something is fully booked you'd say **es ist ausgebucht**.

  . . . könnte natürlich sein, daß es noch Schnee gibt Ostern; it would have been correct to say: **es könnte natürlich sein, daß es Ostern noch Schnee gibt** it could be, of course, that you'll have snow at Easter.

  wenn's regnet, gibt's also sehr viele Möglichkeiten if it rains there are many possibilities (i.e. things to do); note that **also** doesn't mean 'also' but is just a 'filler' with no special meaning, often used in colloquial speech: **also, ich gehe jetzt** well, I'll be going.

- **Sie können ins Schwimmbad** you can go to the swimming pool; it is quite acceptable to drop the **gehen** (go) in colloquial speech:
- **Sie können in die Sauna** you can go to the Sauna; similar: **du kannst da jetzt nicht rein** you can't go in there now.

  unter Umständen possibly (lit. under cirumstances).

88

Übungen

1 Ostern in Zell am See – what would you do? Many different things, depending on the weather. Listen to the dialogue and complete the list. (Answers p.202)

bei Sonnenschein	bei Schnee	bei Regen
Bootfahren		

2 Complete the sentences without looking at the text opposite. (Answers p.202)

a. Ruth plant ein .... Wochenende.

b. Sie will .... nach Zell am See fahren.

c. Sie sollte .... buchen, weil Zell immer

.... gebucht ist.

d. Man kann am See viel ....

e. Auch wenn es regnet, gibt es viele ....

f. Das ist .... kein ....

3 Your turn to speak. You're planning to spend a weekend at the **Chiemsee**, a popular lake in Bavaria. Klaus will ask you what there is to do. Answer him according to Andrew's prompts.

Dialog 2: Zu Hause

Horst Am Samstagnachmittag, da mach' ich erst mal das Übliche: Auto waschen, im Garten arbeiten – also je nach Jahreszeit zum Beispiel umgraben, Hecken schneiden, Unkraut jäten, Rosen schneiden, düngen, undsoweiter. Dann hab' ich noch einen kleinen Gemüsegarten. Das ist ziemlich viel Arbeit, aber ich mach's trotzdem recht gerne.
Und dann mach' ich meine ganzen Hobbys – 'Do-it-yourself', wissen Sie. Ich hab' schon einen Tisch gebaut, und eine Bank, und jetzt mach' ich gerade ein Bücherregal. Gegen Abend leg' ich mich dann in die Badewanne.

Heide Ich geh' meine Eltern besuchen, die wohnen nicht weit weg, gleich um die Ecke. Meistens nehm' ich die zwei Kinder mit. Wir trinken Kaffee, essen Kuchen und reden miteinander. Oder ich leg' mich einfach faul in die Sonne, in den Garten, lese ein Buch ... Und einmal im Monat gehe ich zum Kaffeekränzchen. Da gibt's immer was zu plaudern und zu lachen.

Horst Am Sonntag machen wir uns meistens einen ruhigen Tag. Wir stehen spät auf, außer Claudia, die steht um acht schon auf und geht um neun in die Kirche. Oft fahren wir ins Grüne, gehen im Wald spazieren, kehren dann in einem Gasthof ein. Am Abend gibt's dann meistens Fernsehen.

▶ **das Übliche** the usual (things)
umgraben (sep.) to dig
düngen to fertilize

das Bücherregal bookshelf
die Badewanne bathtub

je nach Jahreszeit depending on the time of the year; similar: **je nach Tageszeit** depending on the time of the day.

Hecken schneiden to cut hedges, **die Hecke** hedge.

Unkraut jäten to weed, **das Unkraut** weed, **das Kraut, die Kräuter** herb (**Unkraut**: the prefix **un** denotes that this **Kraut** isn't edible!).

wir reden miteinander we talk (to each other).

▶ **das Kaffeekränzchen** lit. coffee circle, meeting friends in the afternoon for coffee and cakes and a chat.

wir machen uns einen ruhigen Tag we take it easy (lit. we make ourselves a quiet day).

▶ **wir stehen spät auf** we get up late.

▶ **wir fahren ins Grüne** we go to the country (lit. to the green).

▶ **wir kehren in einem Gasthof ein** we stop off at an inn; **einkehren** (sep.) to go to a pub, inn or restaurant: **wir sind im 'Weißen Bock' eingekehrt** we stopped off at the 'Weißer Bock'.

Übungen

4 Here are some weekend activities. Match the right words from each column and connect them with arrows. We've done one for you. (Answers p.202)

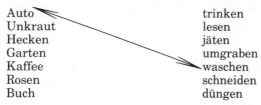

Auto	trinken
Unkraut	lesen
Hecken	jäten
Garten	umgraben
Kaffee	waschen
Rosen	schneiden
Buch	düngen

5 Have a look at this account of Heide's Saturday. It's not quite right. Can you spot the mistakes and underline them? (Answers p.202)

Heide always sees her parents, but they live quite far away. She always takes her two children with her. They all have coffee and cakes together and talk to each other. Or Heide sunbathes in her own garden, swims in the pool and reads a book. Twice a month she meets her friends for coffee and cakes.

6 What do Horst and his family do on Sundays? Have another look at the last part of Dialogue 2 and underline the phrases corresponding to the ones below. (Answers p.202)

a. Wir bleiben lange im Bett
b. Wir fahren aufs Land
c. Wir besuchen ein Gasthaus

7 What do *you* do at the weekend? Switch on your cassette and do the speaking exercise according to Andrew's prompts.

Dialog 3: Große Pläne

Ingrid	Mir ist so langweilig. Was machen wir denn heute abend?
Günter	Also ich hab' – wie immer – einen ganz tollen Plan. Ich hab' mir das alles schon genau überlegt.
Ingrid	So?
Günter	Um sechs gehen wir zuerst ins 'Zagreb' zum Essen. Da gibt es sehr gute jugoslawische Spezialitäten.
Ingrid	Das ist schon mal 'ne gute Idee. Und dann?
Günter	Um halb acht gibt's ein Promenadenkonzert im Freien. Im Rosengarten, mit der Heidelberger Mozartgruppe. Die spielen da die 'Kleine Nachtmusik'.
Ingrid	Und dann?
Günter	Und dann geht's ins Kino. Ein ganz heißer Film, ein Klassiker: 'M – eine Stadt sucht den Mörder' von Fritz Lang.
Ingrid	Aha. Und dann?
Günter	Danach wird getanzt. Im 'Club 87'.
Ingrid	Ist ja ein tolles Programm! Und so gut geplant . . . Weißt du, daß es schon zehn nach sieben ist? Und dann – schau mal aus dem Fenster. Es regnet! Und übrigens: dein 'heißer Film' wird erst nächste Woche gespielt . . .

das Promenadenkonzert
promenade concert
▸ **im Freien** open-air
die Heidelberger Mozartgruppe
the Heidelberg Mozart players
die 'Kleine Nachtmusik' 'A Little
Night Music'

der Klassiker classic
der Mörder murderer
übrigens by the way

▸ **mir ist langweilig** I'm bored; **ist dir langweilig?** are you bored?
▸ **langweilig** boring; **ein langweiliger Abend** a boring evening; **die Langeweile** boredom.

▸ **ich habe einen ganz tollen Plan** I have a really exciting plan; **toll** (lit. mad) often used colloquially for 'super', 'great'.

▸ **ich hab' mir das genau überlegt** I've thought it all out; **sich etwas überlegen** to think about s.th. in detail, to ponder: **ich muß mir das noch einmal überlegen** I have to give it another thought; **ich habe es mir anders überlegt** I've changed my mind.

danach wird getanzt after that it's dancing time (lit. it is danced, a passive construction, see Unit 11 p.178).

dann geht's ins Kino then (we're) off to the cinema/to the movies.

▸ **ein ganz heißer Film** a really great movie; **heiß** (lit. hot) coll. for 'great', 'fantastic', **ein heißer Tip** a hot tip.

zehn nach sieben = zehn Minuten nach sieben ten (minutes) past seven.

Übungen

8 The great night out. What are Günter's plans? Write them down in order in the chart below. (Answers p.202)

1.	Restaurant 'Zagreb'	essen	jugoslawische Spezialitäten
2.			
3.			
4.			

9 Wie war das Konzert? To find out, try to solve this word puzzle. All the clues are in German. The letters in the middle column read will tell you what the concert was like. (Answers p.202)

a. Ingrid findet Günters Plan . . .
b. Eine Farbe (so ist der Himmel oft)
c. Dort spielt man Filme
d. Die Woche hat sieben . . .
e. Der 'König der Tiere'
f. Ein alkoholisches Getränk
g. Noch ein alkoholisches Getränk
h. 'M' ist ein . . . von Fritz Lang
i. Gegenteil von 'kalt'
j. Wie **d.**

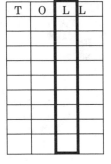

T	O	L	L

10 Was machen Sie am Sonntag?
We've got hold of a page from your diary for Sunday. Use this as a base for telling Corinna about your Sunday. After her question, start with **'Um elf Uhr gehe ich ins Orgelkonzert'**, etc. There'll be no prompts, but Klaus will tell you what you should have said.

SONNTAG 15.2.

11 Uhr : Orgelkonzert

1 Uhr : Essen im Restaurant "Krone"

3 Uhr : Spaziergang

halb sechs : Kino

8 Uhr : Abendessen mit Carola

Dialog 4: Der Sportler

Horst	Also, ich finde, du treibst entschieden zu viel Sport.
Mark	Wie kommst du denn darauf?
Horst	Ja, schau doch mal hin: Am Sonntagmorgen bist du auf dem Fußballplatz, am Sonntagnachmittag bereits wieder auf dem Handballplatz. Und während der Woche machst du alles: Schwimmen, Reiten, Tennisspielen, Leichtathletik, alles.
Mark	Das siehst du falsch. Zum Beispiel Fußball spiele ich schon seit meiner frühesten Jugend. Und die anderen Sportarten, die du aufgezählt hast, mach ich zwar nicht jede Woche, aber ich treib' sie als Ausgleichssport.
Horst	Ich finde, du könntest als Ausgleich einmal an einem Sonntagmorgen ein gutes Buch lesen. Das würde dir und deiner Familie bestimmt gut tun.
Mark	Ich weiß nicht, ob das meiner Familie gut tut, wenn ich ein Buch lese und irgendwo in der Ecke sitze.
Horst	Vielleicht wirst du dadurch etwas gescheiter.
Mark	Also ich bin ganz zufrieden mit meiner Intelligenz.

- ◆ **(das) Tennisspielen** tennis
- ◆ **(die) Leichtathletik** athletics
-   **aufzählen** to number
-   **gescheit** clever
-   **der Sportler** sports enthusiast
- ◆ **der Fußball** football (soccer)
- ◆ **(das) Reiten** (horse) riding; **reiten** to ride
- ◆ **(das) Schwimmen** swimming, **schwimmen** to swim

- ◆ **du treibst entschieden zuviel Sport** you definitely do too many sports.

- ◆ **Sport treiben** to go in for sports.

   wie kommst du denn darauf? what (on earth) makes you think that?

   schau doch mal hin just think (lit. just look at it), **hinschauen** (sep.) to look at.

- ◆ **am Sonntagmorgen** Sunday morning, **am Montagmorgen** Monday morning, etc. Do not confuse **der Morgen** (the morning) with **morgen** tomorrow.

- ◆ **am Sonntagnachmittag** Sunday afternoon.

   das siehst du falsch you're getting it all wrong (lit. you see it wrong).

   seit meiner frühesten Jugend since my earliest days (lit. youth); **die Jugend** youth, adolescence.

- ◆ **die anderen Sportarten** the other sports; **die Sportart** (kind of) sport.

   ich treib' sie als Ausgleichssport I do them to have a balance (e.g. to my sedentary work); **der Ausgleich** balance.

   wenn ich . . . irgendwo in der Ecke sitze if I'm sitting somewhere (tucked away) in a corner.

   ich bin zufrieden I'm satisfied.

Übungen

11 Der Sportfanatiker. Answer the questions below in German.
(Answers p.202)

a. Wann ist Mark auf dem Fußballplatz?

....

b. Wann ist Mark auf dem Handballplatz?

....

c. Wann geht Mark zum Schwimmen?

....

d. Seit wann spielt Mark Fußball?

....

e. Wann sollte Mark ein gutes Buch lesen?

....

12 Have a look at these drawings of various sports and mark the sports Mark
doesn't go in for. (Answers p.202)

a. Fußball   **b. Leichtathletik**

c. Skifahren   **d. Tennis**

e. Gewichtheben   **f. Schwimmen**

 13 A busy schedule. Imagine you are a sports enthusiast and talk about your
life. You're doing a different sport every night – they are listed below. Start
with **Am Sonntag gehe ich zum Reiten**, etc. Then listen to Corinna who
will tell you the correct version.

Sunday	Monday	Tuesday	Wednesday	Thursday	Friday	Saturday
riding	dancing	swimming	tennis	karate	basketball	squash

Wörter und Wendungen

When to do things

am Wochenende	during the weekend
am Samstag/Sonntag	on Saturday/Sunday
am Samstagabend	on Saturday evening
am Sonntagmorgen/nachmittag	on Sunday morning/afternoon
heute/morgen	today/tomorrow
je nach Jahreszeit	depending on the time of the year
ein verlängertes Wochenende	a long weekend

What to do

Ich...

mache meine Hobbys	pursue my hobbies
arbeite im Garten	work in the garden
gehe zum Kaffeekränzchen	go for coffee and cakes and chat
lege mich faul in die Sonne	laze about in the sun
besuche meine Eltern	see my parents

Wir...

I...

We...

stehen spät auf	get up late
fahren ins Grüne	go to the country
gehen in die Sauna/ins Schwimmbad	go to the sauna/the swimming pool
kehren in einem Gasthof ein	stop off at an inn

Planning a weekend

Ich habe...

I have...

einen tollen Plan	a great plan
eine tolle Idee	a good idea
ein tolles Programm	a great programme/schedule
es mir genau überlegt	thought it all out
Sie müssen rechtzeitig buchen	You must book well ahead
Es ist alles ausgebucht	Everything is fully booked

Sports

Ich treibe Sport	I go in for sports
Die Sportarten:	Various kinds of sports:
Fußball	football (soccer)
Handball	handball
Schwimmen	swimming
Reiten	(horse) riding
Tennis	tennis
Leichtathletik	athletics
Surfen	surfing
Skifahren	skiing
Langlauf	cross-country skiing
Abfahrtslauf	downhill skiing

Grammatik

Telling the Time

Wie spät ist es? What is the time?
Es ist genau 6 Uhr. It's 6 o'clock precisely.
Es ist viertel nach 7. It's a quarter past 7.
Es ist viertel vor 7. It's a quarter to 7.
Es ist 20 (Minuten) nach 6. It's 20 (minutes) past 6.
Es ist 20 (Minuten) vor 6. It's 20 (minutes) to 6.

In everyday speech you say **es ist zehn Uhr, es ist fünf vor/nach zehn, es ist viertel vor/nach elf** (it's ten o'clock, it's five to/past ten, it's a quarter to/past eleven) etc. **Zehn Uhr** (ten o'clock) for example can mean both ten in the morning or ten in the evening. There is no equivalent of a.m. and p.m., but you might hear **zehn Uhr morgens** (ten in the morning) or **elf Uhr abends** (eleven o'clock in the evening).
Officially though the 24-hour-system is used, and on the radio or at stations, airports etc. 10.00 pm is always **zweiundzwanzig Uhr**, 6.00 pm **achtzehn Uhr**, etc. You write:
11.46 Uhr *but* you say **11 Uhr 46 = elf Uhr sechsundvierzig.**

14 Express the following times in figures for both a.m. and p.m.
(Answers p.202)

Example: **Viertel nach drei = 3.15 or 15.15**

a. Viertel nach zwei = ...

b. Viertel vor fünf = ...

c. Zwanzig vor neun = ...

d. Fünf nach drei = ...

e. Halb eins = ...

f. Halb zwei = ...

g. Viertel nach vier = ...

h. Fünf vor zehn = ...

15 Now write out in full the times shown below. Use informal speech, e.g. 15.20 = **zwanzig nach drei.** (Answers p.202)

a. 17.12 = ...

b. 8.15 = ...

c. 21.30 = ...

d. 12.45 = ...

Don't forget that e.g. **halb sechs** in German means half past *five*. It's *not* the equivalent of the British 'half six'.

Times of the day

gestern yesterday	**der Morgen** morning
vorgestern the day before yesterday	**der Vormittag** late morning
heute today	**der Mittag** noon, midday
morgen tomorrow	**der Nachmittag** afternoon
übermorgen the day after tomorrow	**der Abend** evening
	die Nacht night

gestern abend last night, yesterday evening
heute morgen this morning, *but* **morgen früh** tomorrow morning
gestern mittag at noon yesterday
morgen nachmittag tomorrow afternoon
heute nacht tonight

am Morgen/Mittag/Vormittag	in the morning/at noon/in the afternoon
am Samstag/Dienstag/Freitag	on Saturday/Tuesday/Friday
am Sonntagmorgen/Dienstagabend	on Sunday morning/Tuesday evening
but **in der Nacht**	during the night
um halb sieben/zwölf Uhr	at half past six/twelve o'clock
im Sommer/Winter/Frühjahr/ Herbst	in the summer/winter/spring/ autumn
im Juli/September/Dezember	in July/September/December

16 Translate into German: (Answers p.202)

a. In the evening ....

b. On Sunday morning ....

c. In May ....

d. In June ....

e. At 10 o'clock ....

f. At half past five ....

Some more useful expressions:

gegen Abend towards the evening	**bald** soon	**immer** always
früh am Morgen early in the morning	**oft** often	**schon** already
spät am Abend late at night	**wieder** again	**sofort** at once
jeden Sonntag/Montag every Sunday/Monday		

17 Translate into English: (Answers p.202)

a. Sie kommt immer um sieben Uhr. ....

b. Der Film fängt sofort an. ....

c. Der Sommer ist schon da. ....

d. Ich will wieder nach Berlin fahren. ....

e. Ich denke oft an Jessica. ....

Übungen: Lesen

18 I hate weekends! That's a statement by 13-year-old Klaus. Read this essay he has written, and you'll know why. – Below you'll then see a pictorial account of Klaus's weekend. Have a look at the drawings and pick a phrase from the text which would be suitable as a caption, as we have done for drawing **a**. You can alter them slightly. (Suggested answers p.203)

> Ich hasse das Wochende! Überall sieht man dasselbe Bild: die Väter waschen Autos, arbeiten im Garten oder machen ihre langweiligen Hobbys. Mein Vater zum Beispiel hat schon vier Tische gebaut – einer wackliger als der andere. Der Sonntag gefällt mir noch weniger als der Samstag. Morgens geht's in die Kirche, dann wird im Garten gegrillt – immer Würstchen! Am Nachmittag gibt's dann einen Spaziergang. Man trifft immer dieselben Leute, man muß immer höflich grüßen: 'Guten Tag, Herr Hinz, guten Tag, Frau Kunz...' Einfach scheußlich! Und dann kommt der Höhepunkt: Kaffeekränzchen bei Tante Elsbeth! So etwas Langweiliges. Abends sitzt unsere ganze Familie dann beim Fernsehen. Meistens gibt's einen uralten schlechten Film oder eine Talk-Show mit 90-jährigen. Ich bin froh, wenn ich ins Bett kann. Da freut man sich ja fast wieder auf die Schule...

Vocabulary:
hassen to hate **höflich** polite
wacklig wobbly **grüßen** to greet
dasselbe }
dieselben } the same

a. Mein Vater hat schon vier wacklige Tische gebaut.

b. ....

c. ....

d. ....

e. ....
....

f. ....
....

Übungen: Radio

19 Viel Spaß mit 'Knallbonbon'. Listen to a radio report about a very special party service a firm called **Knallbonbon** (cracker) has to offer. As the report is rather long, you'll hear it in three parts. Listen to part one first, then mark the correct boxes below. (Answers p.203)

Vocabulary:

gerettet saved
... zur Partyverschönerung to ensure the success of your party
der Schornsteinfeger chimney sweep
die Putzfrau cleaner
mieten to rent
die Fete (coll.) party
heimisch at home
die Nummer act, party sketch
der Renner the favourite

platzen to burst
desjenigen of the (particular) person
für den sie bestimmt ist on whose behalf she's there
sich entblättern here: to shed one's disguise, to strip
todschick terribly chic
ansprechend appealing
aufziehen (sep.) (coll.) to start
feiern to celebrate

a. What's the home town of **Knallbonbon**?

☐ Ulm
☐ Köln
☐ Bonn

b. How many different attractions are in **Knallbonbon's** programme?

☐ over 30
☐ over 50
☐ over 200

c. How much is one 'performance'?

☐ around 20 marks
☐ around 200 marks
☐ around 2000 marks

d. The service is run by Jutta Lüssen. What was her job before she started **Knallbonbon?**

☐ journalist
☐ waitress
☐ teacher

20 Putzfrau Schmitz und Tarzan – Cleaning lady Schmitz and Tarzan are two of **Knallbonbon's** most popular acts. Write a few sentences about what Putzfrau Schmitz and Tarzan do when they visit a party. (Suggested answers p.203)

Putzfrau Schmitz: ....

....

....

Tarzan: ....

....

....

21 What were Jutta's reasons for starting a party service in spite of the recession? Listen and write them down – in German. (Answers p.203)

a. Ich hab' ....

....

b. Ich kann...

....

c. Ich kenne ....

....

d. Ich habe mir gesagt: ....

....

Übungen: Sprechen Sie selbst

22 What do you do during the weekend? Say a few sentences and try to use phrases like **am Samstagmorgen**, **am Nachmittag**, **am Samstagabend**, **am Sonntagmorgen**, etc. Corinna will tell you something about her weekend on the cassette.

23 Make up at least six sentences using the time, specific months, days, or times of the day, for example:
Um halb sieben gehe ich ins Kino
Im Dezember fahre ich nach Amerika, etc.
You'll hear four more examples on the cassette for comparison.

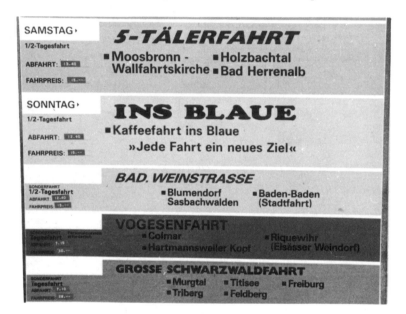

7 *Presse, Rundfunk, Fernsehen*

You will learn

- to select a paper or a magazine
- to say what you think of radio or television
- to choose your radio or TV programme

... and you'll get some general information on the media in West Germany

Study guide

		Seite
Dialog 1 + Übungen		104
Dialog 2 + Übungen		106
Dialog 3 + Übungen		108
Dialog 4 + Übungen		110
Wörter und Wendungen		112
Grammatik		113
Lesen		115
Radio		117
Sprechen Sie selbst		118

Dialog 1: Beim Zeitschriftenhändler

Ruth	Ich möchte eine Frauenzeitung.
Frau Huber	Ja, das haben wir.
Ruth	Was haben Sie denn alles?
Frau Huber	Frau im Spiegel, Neue Post, Tina ...
Ruth	Haben Sie eine mit Mode, bitte?
Frau Huber	Ja, haben wir da – Neue Mode oder Burda ...
Ruth	Was kostet die Burda?
Frau Huber	Vier Mark fünfzig.
Ruth	Dann nehme ich die Burda ... Und haben Sie auch ausländische Zeitungen?
Frau Huber	Nein, leider nicht – nur das Reader's Digest, in Englisch.
Ruth	Und wo kann ich 'ne ausländische Zeitung bekommen?
Frau Huber	In der Stadt: in der Buchhandlung oder am Hauptbahnhof.
Ruth	Vielen Dank.
Frau Huber	Bitte.

▸ **der Zeitschriftenhändler** newsagent, newspaper store
die Mode fashion
die Buchhandlung book shop

▸ **die Zeitung** newspaper
▸ **die Zeitschrift** magazine

Frau im Spiegel, Tina, Neue Post titles of German women's magazines.

▸ **die Frauenzeitung, die Frauenzeitschrift** women's magazine. Similar:
▸ **die Modezeitschrift** fashion magazine, **die Wochenzeitschrift** weekly magazine. A **Zeitschrift** can also be called **Magazin: das Sportmagazin** sports magazine, **das Hobbymagazin** hobby magazine, **das politische Magazin** political magazine.

Neue Mode, Burda names of fashion magazines.

'ne ausländische Zeitung short for **eine ausländische Zeitung** a foreign newspaper. In colloquial speech bits of **ein, eine, einen** are often swallowed: **wo kann ich 'n (=ein) Buch/'ne (=eine) Zeitung/'nen (=einen) Fernseher kaufen?** where can I buy a book/newspaper/TV set?

Übungen

1 Try this puzzle by filling in the squares according to **a**, **b**, **c** etc. The numbered squares, read from 1 to 8, will give you a popular girls' (and women's magazine's) name in Germany. (Answers p.203)

a. Dort kann man ausländische Zeitungen kaufen

H				⁶	¹					

b. Name einer Modezeitschrift

		²		

c. Frauenname und Frauenzeitschrift

⁷	³		

d. Dort gibt es Bücher

B										⁴

e. 'Frau im ....' ist eine Zeitschrift

S	⁵		⁸	

¹	²	³	⁴	⁵	⁶	⁷	⁸

2 **Richtig oder falsch?** True or false? Mark the right box. (Answers p.203)

a. **Neue Post** ist eine Modezeitschrift R F

b. Bei Frau Huber gibt es keine Modezeitschrift R F

c. Die **Burda** kostet vier Mark zwanzig R F

d. Ruth kauft eine Modezeitschrift R F

e. Ruth möchte das 'Reader's Digest' kaufen R F

f. Ausländische Zeitungen gibt es in der Stadt R F

 3 You are at a newsstand and want to buy a sports magazine. Andrew will prompt you as usual.

Vocabulary:
das Tauchen scuba diving
das Segelfliegen gliding

Dialog 2: Die Presse

Herr Frauenfeld Tageszeitungen – wir haben da zwei Arten von Tageszeitungen, die regionalen und die überregionalen. Die wichtigsten der überregionalen sind etwa die Süddeutsche Zeitung, die eher liberal ist, die Frankfurter Allgemeine Zeitung, die sehr konservativ ist, und vielleicht noch die Frankfurter Rundschau, die linksliberal ist.

Von den regionalen Zeitungen gibt es sehr viele. Sie bringen auch Lokalnachrichten und sind sehr wichtig für die Bevölkerung. Dann gibt es natürlich noch die Boulevardpresse, diese Sensationsblätter, die eigentlich nur aus Schlagzeilen und Bildern bestehen und sehr wenig Information bringen.

Sonntagszeitungen gibt es beinahe keine. Dafür aber gibt es Wochenblätter und politische Magazine, die wöchentlich erscheinen. Von den Wochenblättern zum Beispiel Die Zeit, die liberal ist, und als politisches Magazin Der Spiegel.

♦ **die Presse** the press
wichtig important
♦ **liberal** liberal
♦ **konservativ** conservative

linksliberal liberal to left-wing
die Bevölkerung population, people
♦ **die Sonntagszeitung** Sunday paper

♦ **die regionalen und die überregionalen** the regional and the national papers. On the whole there are more regional and fewer national papers in Germany; even the nationals are regional in origin, as their names show: **Frankfurter Rundschau, Süddeutsche Zeitung**, etc.

♦ **diese Sensationsblätter** those tabloids. **Das Blatt** is another word for newspaper: **das Wochenblatt, das Sonntagsblatt** weekly paper, Sunday paper. Remember that **Blatt** can also mean sheet (of paper): **das Blatt Papier** and leaf (of a plant): **das Palmenblatt** palm leaf.

♦ **... die eigentlich nur aus Schlagzeilen und Bildern bestehen** which actually just consist of headlines and pictures. Herr Frauenfeld is mainly referring to **Bild**, the most popular tabloid in the Federal Republic.

... die wöchentlich erscheinen which appear weekly. Similar: **sie erscheinen täglich/monatlich/jährlich** they appear daily/monthly/yearly.

Übungen

4 What did Herr Frauenfeld have to say about three major German dailies? Listen to the first part of Dialogue 2 again and mark the details in the grid below, as we have done for **Süddeutsche Zeitung**. (Answers p.203)

Zeitungen	regional	überregional	liberal	konservativ	linksliberal
Süddeutsche		✔	✔		
Frankfurter Allgemeine					
Frankfurter Rundschau					

5 Complete the sentences by inserting the following words:

Sensationsblätter   Sonntagszeitungen   Wochenblättern Regionale Zeitungen (Answers p.203)

a. Es gibt nicht viele .... in der

Bundesrepublik.

b. .... sind wichtig für die Bevölkerung,

weil sie auch Lokalnachrichten bringen.

c. .... haben viele Bilder und

Schlagzeilen und zu wenig Information.

d. Die Zeit gehört zu den ....

 6 Now read sentences **a–d** of Exercise 5 out loud, then switch on the cassette and listen to Klaus to check a. if you've inserted the right words and b. your pronunciation. Speak and listen to each sentence one by one.

Dialog 3: Radio oder Fernsehen?

Henning and Silke prefer radio to television. Why?

Henning   Weil mir die Reporter besser gefallen, und weil ich die Sendungen interessanter finde.
Biba   Welche Sendungen hörst du am liebsten?
Henning   Die Single-Hit-Parade am Sonntag.
Biba   Und was noch?
Henning   Die Sportreportagen.
Biba   Und wieviel Stunden hörst du Radio?
Henning   Ich höre eigentlich nur am Wochenende Radio – samstags vier Stunden, und sonntags drei Stunden.

Biba   Und welche Sendungen hören Sie im Radio am liebsten?
Silke   Ich höre am liebsten Regionalsendungen, und zwar für unseren Bereich Südfunk Stuttgart, weil da die Musik sehr gut ist. Die gefällt mir. Es wird auch Politik gesendet und aktuelle Beiträge.
Biba   Und wieviel Stunden hören Sie Radio?
Silke   Das kommt darauf an, ganz verschieden.

- **das Radio** radio
- **das Fernsehen** television
- **fernsehen** (sep.) to watch television

- **der Bereich** here: region
- **am Wochenende** during weekends

weil mir die Reporter besser gefallen because I prefer the reporters (on radio). Remember **gefallen** to like, e.g. **die Musik gefällt mir** I like the music (lit. the music pleases to me).

- **die Sportreportage** sports report; **die Reportage** report. Similarly: **die aktuelle Reportage** report on current events.

- **die Regionalsendung** regional programme; **die Sendung** radio programme, broadcast; **senden** to broadcast: **es wird auch Politik gesendet** there are also programmes on political issues (lit. politics are being broadcast). Remember that **senden** also means 'to send': **einen Brief senden** to send a letter.

- **aktuelle Beiträge** current features; **der Beitrag** contribution, here: radio feature.

das kommt darauf an that depends.

ganz verschieden (that's) quite different, it varies.

Übungen

7 Who listens to what? And at what times? Put your mark in the correct box. (Answers p.203)

	Henning	Silke
Regionalsendungen		
Politik		
Single-Hit-Parade am Sonntag		
aktuelle Beiträge		
Sportreportage		
... und wann?		
nur am Wochenende		
ganz verschieden		

8 What's what? Match the German expressions with the appropriate English definition below. (Answers p.203)

**Sportreportagen   Regionalsendungen   Reporter
aktuelle Beiträge   Single-Hit-Parade   Wochenende**

a. Someone investigating and covering news...

b. Radio features on current events ....

c. The last two days of the week   ....

d. Radio programmes on local news ....

e. 'Top twenty' programme...

9 On the cassette you'll talk to Klaus, who prefers radio to television. Ask him questions according to Andrew's prompts.

Vocabulary:
die klassische Musik classical music
die Literatur literature

Dialog 4: Fernsehen

Günter and Amin prefer television.

Günter Hm – ich finde, daß das Fernsehen oft umfassender und anschaulicher informiert als der Rundfunk.

Biba Und was halten Sie vom Werbefernsehen?

Günter Eigentlich nichts. Ich glaube, es verführt nur zum Konsum.

Biba Wieviel Stunden sehen Sie fern?

Günter Es mögen vielleicht drei bis vier Stunden in der Woche sein – ich suche mir die Sendungen meist aus.

Amin Ja, ich sehe eben gerne Filme, und im Fernsehen kann ich mir öfters Filme anschauen, die hier in der Stadt im Kino nicht laufen.

Biba Und was halten Sie vom Werbefernsehen?

Amin Gar nichts. Ich finde, jeder soll selbst entscheiden, welche Produkte er kauft.

Biba Und was sehen Sie am liebsten?

Amin Am liebsten sehe ich diese leichten, amüsanten amerikanischen Komödien aus den dreißiger Jahren von Frank Capra, von William van Dyke . . . und die Sportschau.

▶ **der Rundfunk** radio
eigentlich actually
anschauen (sep.) to watch
entscheiden to decide

das Produkt product
leicht light
amüsant amusing
▶ **die Komödie** comedy

. . . daß das Fernsehen oft umfassender und anschaulicher informiert
. . . that television often gives you more comprehensive and clearer information; **umfassend** comprehensive, **anschaulich** clear (lit. graphic).

▶ **was halten Sie vom Werbefernsehen?** what do you think of ads on television? Similarly: **was halten Sie von den Nachrichten?** what do you think of the news? **das Werbefernsehen** time given to commercials. Advertising spots can be seen on nearly all channels in Germany but only in short blocks, never after eight o'clock and not on Sundays.

es verführt nur zum Konsum it only tempts you to spend money; **der Konsum** lit. consumerism; **verführen** to tempt, to seduce.

Filme, die hier nicht laufen films which aren't shown here; **laufen** lit. to run.

jeder soll selber entscheiden everyone should decide for himself.

aus den dreißiger Jahren from the thirties; also **die vierziger Jahre** the forties **die sechziger Jahre** the sixties, etc.

▶ **die Sportschau** most popular sports programme on West German television. There are three TV channels: **1. Programm** (first programme), **2. Programm** (second programme) and **3. Programm** (third programme). All networks are government controlled, there are no commercial TV stations.

Übungen

10 After having listened to the dialogue several times, fill in the right forms of the missing verbs in the sentences below. (Answers p.203)

aussuchen informieren laufen verführen entscheiden

a. Das Fernsehen .... umfassender als der

Rundfunk.

b. Das Werbefernsehen .... zum Konsum.

c. Ich .... mir die Sendungen meistens

....

d. Im Fernsehen gibt's Filme, die in der Stadt nicht ....

e. Jeder soll selber ...., welche Produkte er kauft.

11 Partytime! Everyone is talking about the media, but about what in particular? About **Kino**, **Rundfunk**, **Sport**, **Komödien**, or **Werbefernsehen**? Fill in the captions as we have done for **a.** below. (Answers p.203)

Also, ich gehe mindestens einmal pro Woche...

Ich nicht! Im Fernsehen laufen viel bessere Filme als dort!

Ich interessire mich sehr für Sport und sehe sie jeden Samstag.

Ach ja?

a. *Kino* ....

b. ....

Er informiert längst nicht so umfassend wie das Fernsehen!

Aber die Reporter sind viel besser!

Ich halte überhaupt nichts davon!

Ich auch nicht! Ich will selbst entscheiden, was ich kaufe!

c. ....

d. ....

Also, am liebsten mag ich die aus 30 er Jahren!

Ja, die von Frank Capra!

Oder die von William van Dyke!

e. ....

12 Time to speak! Switch on the tape, then answer Corinna's questions according to Andrew's prompts.

Wörter und Wendungen

Die Presse

die Zeitung	paper
die Zeitschrift ⎫	
das Magazin ⎭	magazine
Ich möchte gern eine ...	I'd like a ...
Mode/Frauen/Sportzeitschrift	fashion/women's/sports magazine
Tages/Sonntags/Wochenzeitung	daily/Sunday/weekly paper
die Boulevardpresse	popular press
das Sensationsblatt	tabloid
die Schlagzeile	headline
die Lokalnachrichten	local news
Diese Zeitung/Zeitschrift ist ...	This paper/magazine is ...
regional	regional
überregional	national
konservativ	conservative
liberal	liberal

Rundfunk und Fernsehen — Radio and television

der Rundfunk/das Radio	radio
das Fernsehen	television
die Sendung	broadcast
fernsehen	to watch television
Radio hören	to listen to the radio
Ich sehe gern ...	I like watching ...
Filme	films
Komödien	comedies
die Sportschau	the sports programme
aktuelle Beiträge	news features
Ich höre gern ...	I like listening to ...
Reportagen	reports
Nachrichten	news
Musik	music
Regionalsendungen	regional programmes
Was halten Sie vom ...	What do you think of ...
Rundfunk?	the radio?
Fernsehen?	television?
Werbefernsehen?	TV commercials?

Grammatik

Questions

You may have found some of the dialogues quite difficult, but the grammar section is easy in this unit. It is not at all difficult to form questions (**Fragen**) in German if you observe a few basic rules, e.g.

- Questions which can be answered with 'yes' or 'no' are formed by inversion, i.e. switching subject and verb, so that the verb is then in the first place:

Sie ist krank. She is ill.
▶ *Ist* **sie krank?** Is she ill?
Ich wohne in London. I live in London.
▶ *Wohnen* **Sie in London?** Do you live in London?
Es schneit. It is snowing.
▶ *Schneit* **es?** Is it snowing?

13 Turn the statements below into questions. (Answers p.203)

a. Es regnet ....

b. Er fährt nach Berlin ....

c. Du trinkst Wein ....

d. Sie (=*they*) haben Urlaub ....

e. Sie ist verheiratet ....

- 'W'-questions are questions beginning with the following words:

wo (where)   **wer/wem/wen** (who/m)
wie (how)   **wohin** (where to)
was (what)   **woher** (where from)
wann (when)   **warum** (why)
wieviel (how much)   **welche/r/s** (which)
wie viele (how many)

The 'w'-words are followed by the verb and then usually by the subject and the rest of the sentence:

Wo	ist	der Bahnhof?	Where is the station?
Warum	hat	er kein Geld bekommen?	Why didn't he get any money?
Was	sehen	Sie am liebsten?	What do you most like watching?
Wann	gehen	wir nach Hause?	When do we go home?
Wie	geht	das?	How does it work?

Watch the word order after **wieviel** and **welche/r/s** which require an object before the verb:

| **Wieviel** | Geld | hast du? | How much money have you got? |
| **Welches** | Haus | verkauft er? | Which house is he selling? |

Do not confuse **wer** (=who) with **wo** (=where). **Wer**, by the way, changes slightly depending on which case it is:

Wer ist das? Who is that? (*Nominative* – **wer** is the subject.)
Wen kennst du? Whom do you know? (*Accusative* object – **wer** becomes we**n**.)
Wem gehört das? To whom does it belong? (*Dative* object – **wer** becomes we**m**)
Wessen Buch ist das? Whose book is this? (*Genitive* object – **wer** becomes **wessen**, which is, however, not often used.)

Welche/r/s changes its ending according to the gender and the case of the noun it precedes, so that it behaves like an adjective, e.g.

der **Welcher Mann ist das?** Which man is that? (*Nom.*)

Mann ◆ **Welchen Mann hast du gesehen?** Which man did you see? (*Acc.*)
Welchem Mann gehört das? To which man does this belong? (*Dat.*)

die **Welche Frau ist das?** Which woman is that? (*Nom.*)

Frau ◆ **Welche Frau siehst du?** Which woman do you see? (*Acc.*)
Welcher Frau gehört das? To which woman does this belong? (*Dat.*)

das **Welches Kind ist das?** Which child is that? (*Nom.*)

Kind ◆ **Welches Kind siehst du?** Which child do you see? (*Acc.*)
Welchem Kind gehört das? To which child does this belong? (*Dat.*).

14 Translate into German: (Answers p.203)

a. When is he coming?

....

b. Where are you going?

....

c. Where do you (=**Sie**) come from?

....

d. Why are you laughing?

....

e. Who is the woman over there?

....

f. To whom shall we give the money?

....

g. How many hours do you listen to the radio?

....

h. Which size are you (=**Sie**)?

....

i. Which house is for sale?

....

Übungen: Lesen

1. Programm

10.00 **HEUTE**
10.03 **Die Sportschau**
10.30 **Schiff ohne Heimat**
12.10 **Die Könige aus dem Jemen**
12.55 **Presseschau**
13.00 **HEUTE**
13.15 **Videotext für alle**
   Eine Auswahl aus dem Angebot
13.40 **Vorschau**
14.10 **Tagesschau**
14.15 **Für Kinder**
   Sesamstraße
14.45 **ARD-Ratgeber: Essen und Trinken**
   Was Großmutter noch wußte über Milch und Käse
15.30 **Nonstop Nonsens**
   Von und mit Dieter Hallervorden
   Didi – ein Glückspilz?
   Regie: Heinz Liesendahl
   (Erstsendung 20. 6. 1978)
16.15 **Neues vom Kleidermarkt**
   Antonia Hilke berichtet über die Mode im Herbst/Winter 1983
17.00 **Blickfeld**
   Kirche und Gesellschaft
18.00 **Tagesschau**
18.05 **Die Sportschau**
   u. a. Fußball-Bundesliga

2. Programm

11.50 **ZDF – Ihr Programm**
   mit Vorschau auf die kommende Woche
   Nachbarn in Europa
   Information und Unterhaltung für Ausländer und Deutsche
   Mit Beiträgen aus:
12.15 **Griechenland**
13.00 **Spanien**
13.45 **Jugoslawien**
   Im Studio: Ekkehard Kuhn
14.30 **HEUTE**
14.32 **Pinocchio**
   Zeichentrickserie
   Schreck in der Morgenstunde
14.55 **1, 2 oder 3**
   Ratespiel für Kinder
   Durch die Sendung führt Michael Schanze
15.35 **Schau zu – mach mit**
   Tips und Anregungen
16.00 **Black Beauty**
   Das Leben eines edlen Pferdes
16.45 **Enorm in Form**
   Tele-Aerobic für die Familie
   Folge 21
17.02 **Der große Preis**
   10 000 Mark für Sie?
   Und Bekanntgabe der Wochengewinner
17.05 **HEUTE**
17.10 **Länderspiegel**
   Informationen und Meinungen aus der Bundesrepublik

Vocabulary:
das Ratespiel guessing game
die Anregung suggestion
das Pferd horse
in Form fit, in shape
der Preis prize

die Bekanntgabe announcement
der Gewinner winner
Länderspiegel programme on events in the Federal Republic
die Meinung opinion

15 Above you see an extract from the day's TV programme. Where and when would you tune in if you wanted to: (Answers p.203)

	time	title of programme	1st or 2nd channel
a. watch football			
b. see if you'd won a prize			
c. get fit			
d. find out about fashion			
e. watch a religious programme			
f. be informed about domestic affairs			
g. get the children out of your way for 40 minutes			

16 Magazine, Magazine ... Below you see the titles of four different magazines and four articles from those magazines. Match them up by writing the correct magazine title under each article. (Answers p.203)

**Zum Vorlesen:
Olli kommt auf
eine andere
Schule**

**Billigmarken
im Supermarkt:
Qualität und
Preise im
DM-Vergleich**

a. ....

b. ....

**extra:
Die tollen
neuen Video-
Maschinen**

**Ein perfekter
Haarschnitt für drei
Frisuren**

c. ....

d. ....

Übungen: Radio

17 On the cassette you'll hear three radio commercials about three different magazines – **Sieben Tage**, **Aero** and **Karina**. Listen carefully, then answer the multiple choice questions below. (Answers p.203)

Vocabulary:

Sieben Tage:
die Unterhaltung entertainment
erleben to experience
das Schicksal fate
erleiden to suffer

Karina:
edel here: classy
lässig casual
zum Selberstricken for knitting at home
zärtlich tender
im Handel on sale

Aero:
das Sammelwerk partwork
der Senkrechtstarter vertical take-off plane
die Grundlage basics
das Luftkampfmanöver air manoeuvre
zivil civilian

a. **Sieben Tage** is a magazine for
☐ people interested in royalty
☐ followers of fashion
☐ music lovers

b. **Sieben Tage** is published
☐ daily
☐ weekly
☐ on Sundays

c. **Aero** magazine appeals to someone
☐ interested in games
☐ interested in history
☐ who loves all kinds of planes

d. Where can you buy **Aero**?
☐ at the newspaper store
☐ you subscribe to it
☐ you order it from the publisher

e. **Karina** would find readers among
☐ young women
☐ mothers with babies
☐ fitness fanatics

f. In **Karina** you'll find articles on
☐ sewing
☐ travelling
☐ better homemaking

18 What's on the radio? Listen to the preview on **Südwestfunk** and write down the times, names of programmes and special topics in the chart below. (Answers p.203)

das Magazin here: (radio)
   programme
aktuell topical, current
folgende Themen the following
   topics
die Großmacht super power
die Mittelstreckenrakete medium
   range missile
die Massenflucht mass exodus

der Kinderbuchautor author of
   children's books
das Schmökerlexikon (coll.)
   encyclopedia of light fiction
der Hörer listener
ausgefallen unique
die Kosmetikerin beautician
der Lippenstift lipstick

time	which programme?	topics for the day
13.00	**Heute Mittag** (Magazin)	1. Verhandlungen über Mittelstreckenraketen 2. 3.

Übungen: Sprechen Sie selbst

19 Your turn to speak again: try to come up with a few words on your favourite paper or magazine. Say what it's about and why you like it. On tape Corinna and Klaus will tell you about their favourite magazines and papers.

8 Immer gute Stimmung?

You will learn

- to invite someone out
- to ask what's on at the theatre
- to talk about good and bad nights out you've known

... and you'll read and hear something about films and film festivals

6., 7., 8. Dezember, 20 Uhr, Urania

Münchner Lach- und Schießgesellschaft

Neues Programm: „Auf Nummer Sicher"/Regie: S. Drechsel

1. und 27. Dezember, 20 Uhr, ICC

Gala-Ballettabend in 3 Bildern
Tschaikowskys Meisterwerk

Der Nußknacker

mit dem
Rumänischen Staats-
Ballett Fantasio

60 Tänzerinnen und Tänzer
Prunkvolle Ausstattung
Das entzückende Ballett-Märchen
in glanzvoller Aufführung.

Dienstag, 27. November, 20 Uhr, ICC
Alexander ROY London Ballet Theatre

„Ein Sommernachtstraum" Ballett nach der
Shakespeare-Komödie

Musik: Gioachino Rossini – Choreographie: Alexander Roy

Study guide

Dialog 1: Eine Einladung

Amin Gnädige Frau, nach diesen ganzen Interviews mache ich Ihnen jetzt einen Vorschlag: Wir gehen zusammen aufs Weinfest an die Mosel.

Biba Ja, wann wäre das denn? Und was gibt es denn da so alles?

Amin Sie waren noch nie auf einem Weinfest?

Biba Nein, ich glaube nicht – nein.

Amin Da haben Sie was versäumt. Ein Weinfest an der Mosel – ist immer gute Stimmung, da trinkt man ein paar Viertel Wein, und manchmal fangen auch Leute noch an zu singen, eine Kapelle spielt, und wir könnten auch ein bißchen tanzen...

Biba Das hört sich nicht schlecht an. Aber eigentlich bin ich eine Biertrinkerin.

Amin Zigarette?

Biba Nein, vielen Dank.

Amin Ja, wissen Sie, auf diesen Weinfesten kann man natürlich auch Bier trinken, aber ich würde Sie schon gerne von dem neuen Moseler Wein überzeugen. Ich glaube, der würde Ihnen auch schmecken.

Biba Also gut, ich überleg's mir mal. Telefonieren wir noch mal?

Amin Ich glaube, es ist besser, wenn wir jetzt gleich zusammen aufs Weinfest fahren. Da gibt es auch noch ein Feuerwerk am Ende, und ich bin mir ganz sicher, daß Sie sich sehr gut mit mir amüsieren werden.

Gnädige Frau madam
♦ **der Vorschlag** suggestion

♦ **das Feuerwerk** fireworks

nach diesen ganzen Interviews after all these interviews.

♦ **das Weinfest** wine festival – one of the big attractions in all wine-producing areas in Germany; they are usually in the autumn when you can try new wines as well as older brands, and they can last for a few days.

da haben Sie was (short for **etwas**) **versäumt** there you have missed something; **etwas versäumen** to miss something.

♦ **(da) ist immer gute Stimmung** Amin swallowed the **da**: there is always a good atmosphere.

♦ **da trinkt man ein paar Viertel Wein** you can have a few glasses (lit. quarter litres) of wine.

manchmal fangen auch Leute noch an zu singen sometimes people also start to sing; **anfangen** to start (a separable verb), e.g.
♦ **ich fange an zu tanzen** I start dancing.

eine Kapelle spielt a band plays/is playing; remember: there is no continuous form (i.e. play*ing*) in German.

wir könnten tanzen we could dance.

♦ **das hört sich nicht schlecht an** that does not sound bad; she could also have said **das hört sich gut an** that sounds good.

Zigarette? cigarette? The shortest – and not at all an impolite – way of offering someone a cigarette.

ich würde Sie schon gerne von dem neuen Moseler Wein überzeugen I'd like to convince you of (the quality of) the new Moselle wine; **der Moseler Wein** or **der Moselwein** = Moselle wine.

der würde Ihnen auch schmecken you would like it too; **der** = **der Wein**; **schmecken** lit. to taste.

Übungen

1 There are lots of activities going on at a wine festival – but could you do *all* these things? Answer **Richtig oder Falsch** – True or False. (Answers p.204)

a. Man kann Wein trinken R F

b. Man kann kochen R F

c. Man kann Bier trinken R F

d. Man kann Musik hören R F

e. Man kann ein Theaterstück sehen R F

f. Man kann einen Film sehen R F

g. Man kann tanzen R F

h. Man kann ein Feuerwerk sehen R F

i. Man kann singen R F

k. Man kann sich gut amüsieren R F

2 Find the phrases in the dialogue which most closely correspond to the expressions printed below and underline them. (Answers p.204)

a. Haben Sie noch nie ein Weinfest besucht?

b. Da ist immer eine gute Atmosphäre!

c. Man trinkt ein paar Gläser Wein.

d. Das klingt gut.

e. Eigentlich trinke ich Bier.

f. Ich glaube, den Wein würden Sie auch gut finden.

g. Ich bin ganz sicher, daß es Ihnen mit mir gut gefallen wird.

 3 Your turn to speak, i.e. it's your turn to persuade Corinna to come to the wine festival with you. Andrew will help you on the cassette as usual.

♦ **ich überleg's mir mal** I'll think about it.

♦ **daß Sie sich sehr gut mit mir amüsieren werden** that you'll have a good time with me; **sich amüsieren** to have fun, to have a good time; **ich habe mich gestern gut amüsiert** I had fun yesterday.

Dialog 2: *Haben Sie noch Karten?*

Kundin	Guten Tag.
Kassiererin	Guten Tag. Was kann ich für Sie tun?
Kundin	Was spielen Sie am Donnerstag?
Kassiererin	Da haben wir eine Premiere der Oper *Eugen Onegin*.
Kundin	Oh gut – haben Sie noch Karten?
Kassiererin	Ja, in den ersten zwei Preisgruppen nicht mehr, aber in der dritten zu neunzehn Mark und siebzig und im zwoten Rang zu zwölf Mark und vierzig.
Kundin	Zwei Karten.
Kassiererin	Das käme dann neununddreißig Mark und vierzig.
Kundin	Gut. Bitte schön.
Kassiererin	Danke sehr. – Bitte schön.
Kundin	Danke. Wann beginnt denn die Aufführung?
Kassiererin	Um zwanzig Uhr.
Kundin	Was spielen Sie denn sonst noch in der Woche?
Kassiererin	Da haben wir einen Liederabend mit Werken von Hugo Wolf, Richard Wagner, Johannes Brahms, Otto Rino-Respighi, Richard Strauß und Gustav Mahler.
Kundin	Haben Sie noch Karten?
Kassiererin	Ja, dafür haben wir noch Karten in allen Preisgruppen.
Kundin	Gut. Vielen Dank. Das überlege ich mir dann noch. Danke.
Kassiererin	Bitte sehr.
Kundin	Auf Wiedersehn.
Kassiererin	Auf Wiedersehn.

die Kundin customer (fem.)
der Kunde customer (m.)
‣ **die Premiere** premiere, first night
‣ **die Theaterkasse** box office
die Kassiererin ⎱ cashier
der Kassierer ⎰

die Preisgruppe price range
die Aufführung performance
‣ **der Liederabend** song recital

was kann ich für Sie tun? what can I do for you? Note that the equivalent of 'do' (**tun**) goes right to the end of the sentence – see **Grammatik** for more details.

‣ **im zwoten Rang** in the second tier; you'll often hear **zwo** instead of **zwei** (=two) in spoken German in order not to confuse **zwei** with **drei** (=three).

das käme dann ... that would come to ... she could also have said **das kommt dann ...** that comes to ... or **das macht dann ...** that makes ...

‣ **was spielen Sie denn sonst noch in der Woche?** what else is playing this week? lit. what else do you play this week?

‣ **mit Werken von ...** with works by ... **das Werk** the (artistic) work; e.g. **eine Ausstellung mit Werken von Rembrandt** an exhibition with works by Rembrandt.

Übungen

4 Buying opera tickets. Can you complete the dialogue below by making out the questions? Listen to Dialogue 2 on the cassette carefully – it's very similar. (Answers p.204)

a. ....

Am Sonntag spielen wir die Oper 'Aida' von Verdi.

b. ....

Ja, wir haben noch Karten.

c. ....

Sie kosten zwischen 15 und 45 Mark.

d. ....

Die Aufführung beginnt um 19.30 Uhr.

e. ....

Wir haben noch einen Liederabend mit Werken von Schubert.

5 Lots of music! Fill in the squares. The letters in the squares marked 1–6 will give you the name of a famous German composer. The other letters are there to help you. (Answers p.204)

a. In dieser Woche gibt es einen

		D		A 1			

mit Werken von Hugo Wolf und Richard Wagner.

b. Am Donnerstag spielen wir die

		2

Eugen Onegin.

c. Wir haben noch Karten im ersten

	3	

d. Wann beginnt denn die

U			4		N	

?

e. Wir bringen diese Woche auch Lieder von Gustav

5		H		R

f. Für den Liederabend haben wir Karten in allen

P			6					N

1	2	3	4	5	6

6 Here is an extract from a letter Ruth has written to her friend Agnes. As you see Ruth is an opera fan. Read the letter first, then turn on the cassette for your speaking exercise. The letter will help you when you are asked to speak according to Andrew's prompts.

```
Liebe Agnes,

Am Montag gehe ich ins Theater. Man spielt eine Oper von

Richard Wagner: Tristan und Isolde. Ich habe eine sehr

gute Karte und freue mich schon auf die Aufführung. Du

weißt ja, ich bin ein Wagner-Fan. Die Aufführung beginnt

schon um sechs Uhr und dauert bis um elf....
```

Dialog 3: *Nur ein kleiner Kater*

Ruth Amin, du siehst etwas müde aus. Ist dir nicht gut?

Amin Ach doch. Ich habe nur einen kleinen Kater.

Ruth Hm – zuviel gefeiert, was?

Amin Ja, eigentlich wollten wir ja ganz früh nach Hause gehen, aber schließlich sind wir doch noch im 'Hades' gelandet.

Ruth Was, in diesem Lokal?

Amin Ja, im 'Hades'. Da sollte nämlich eine gute Band spielen. Wir wollten mal wieder richtig klassisch tanzen, so wie früher in der Tanzschule: Foxtrott, Walzer, Tango ... Wir haben zwanzig Mark gezahlt pro Person, und das Lokal war knallvoll. Ja, und dann hieß es, die Band kann nicht kommen. Na ja, was hätten wir machen sollen?

Ruth Ja, gab's denn keine andere Band?

Amin Ja, doch. Wir blieben erstmal da und warteten auf die Ersatzband. Aber die war fürchterlich: laut und langweilig. Man konnte sein eigenes Wort nicht verstehen. Und ich sag dir, ich schlief im Stehen ein ... Tanzen konnte man sowieso nicht, weil das Parkett zu voll war. Ständig trampelte mir jemand auf den Füßen 'rum, und die Luft war zum Schneiden dick. Mein Jackett war zerknittert, ich sag dir, einfach ein völliger Reinfall. Und das Eintrittsgeld bekamen wir auch nicht mehr zurück.

♦ **der Kater** here: hangover
die Tanzschule dancing school
der Walzer waltz
knallvoll (coll.) very crowded

fürchterlich awful, terrible
das Parkett dance floor
♦ **das Eintrittsgeld** entry fee

♦ **das Lokal** establishment for eating, drinking or dancing, e.g. **das Speiselokal** restaurant, **das Tanzlokal** dance hall.

du siehst etwas müde aus you look a bit tired; **aussehen** (sep.): **er sieht gut aus** he looks well/good.

♦ **zuviel gefeiert?** short for **hast du zuviel gefeiert?** have you been celebrating (too much)? **feiern** to celebrate: **ich habe meinen Geburtstag gefeiert** I have been celebrating my birthday; remember **der Feierabend** time after work.

wir sind im Hades gelandet we ended up at 'Hades'; **landen** lit. to land: **das Flugzeug ist gelandet** the plane has landed.

wir wollten wieder mal richtig klassisch tanzen we wanted to do old-time dancing again.

dann hieß es then they said; **hieß** from **heißen: wie heißt du** what's your name.

was hätten wir machen sollen? what should we have done?

wir warteten auf die Ersatzband we waited for the replacement (band).

tanzen konnte man sowieso nicht you couldn't dance anyway.

ständig trampelte mir jemand auf den Füßen 'rum constantly someone trampled on my feet.

die Luft war zum Schneiden dick the air was very stuffy (lit. the air was so thick you could have cut through it).

mein Jackett war zerknittert my jacket was creased.

Übungen

7 In Dialogue 3 quite a few verbs appeared in the imperfect tense (see **Grammatik**), e.g. **konnte, trampelte, wollte**. Try to translate the sentences below into German, using the following imperfect forms where appropriate. (Answers p.204)

wir blieben   wir warteten   wir bekamen   war   wir wollten man konnte

a. We wanted to dance
b. The band was noisy
c. One could not dance
d. We stayed and waited for a replacement band
e. We didn't get our money back

8 A pictorial account of Amin's big night out at 'Hades', but somehow the captions got all mixed up. Can you sort them out and match them with the right picture? (Answers p.204)

a. Die Luft war zum Schneiden dick.

b. Das Lokal war knallvoll.

c. Jetzt hab' ich einen kleinen Kater.

d. Die Band war fürchterlich.

e. Ständig trampelte mir jemand auf den Füßen 'rum.

9 You've had a big – and bad – night out. So you are a bit short-tempered when Corinna asks you about it, assuming you had a great time. Andrew will prompt you.

Dialog 4: Geister und Gespenster

Amin Ja, und dann kam uns plötzlich die Idee, daß wir ja auf den Fasching gehen könnten. Im 'Adler' gab's einen Tanz unter dem Motto 'die weißen Nächte'. Das heißt, jeder mußte sich weiß anziehen. Wir fuhren schnell nach Hause und verkleideten uns als Geister und Gespenster. Na ja, nicht sehr originell, aber trotzdem. Das Auto ließen wir gleich zu Hause. Man kann ja nie wissen, ob nicht plötzlich die Polizei um die Ecke wartet und wir ins Röhrchen blasen müssen! Na ja. Das Fest war schon in vollem Gang, wir trafen auch ein paar Freunde. Ja, und sogar meine Tante war da, weißt du, die dicke, lustige. Sie war als Ölscheich verkleidet. Es war wirklich toll. Wir tranken viel Bier, tanzten bis zum Umfallen, und morgens um vier Uhr hatten wir einen riesigen Hunger. Und da gingen wir dann zum 'Goldenen Eck' – das hat ja um diese Zeit immer schon offen, und aßen ein paar Bratwürste, die fränkischen. Das Lokal war voll von den komischsten Faschingsfiguren: Clowns und Hawaiimädchen, Eskimos und Neger, Fußballspieler und Eishockeyspieler ...

der Geist ghost
das Gespenst spectre, phantom
▶ **der Fasching** carnival
der Ölscheich oil sheik
der 'Adler' ⎱ names of pubs/
das 'Goldene Eck' ⎰ taverns

dann kam uns die Idee then we had the idea (lit. the idea came to us).

unter dem Motto with (lit. under) the theme ...

▶ **wir verkleideten uns als ...** we dressed up as ... **sich verkleiden** to dress up; **ich verkleide mich als Cowboy** I dress up as a cowboy.

aber trotzdem but never mind.

ins Röhrchen blasen to blow into the little nozzle (i.e. the mouth piece for the bag when you're breathalized).

▶ **das Fest war schon in vollem Gang** the party was already in full swing.

wir tanzten bis zum Umfallen we danced until we were absolutely exhausted (lit. until falling over).

wir hatten einen riesigen Hunger we were ravenous (lit. we had a gigantic hunger); **riesig** gigantic, **der Riese** giant.

wir aßen ein paar Bratwürste we ate a couple of sausages.

voll von den komischsten Faschingsfiguren full of the most amazing carnival figures; **komisch** funny, strange.

Übungen

10 Here is an account of Amin's fancy-dress party, but it's not quite right. Underline the words or phrases which are wrong. (Answers p.204)

Wir gingen in den Adler zum Tanzen. Das Motto war an dem Abend: 'die schwarzen Nächte', das heißt, jeder mußte sich schwarz anziehen. Und so gingen wir nach Hause und verkleideten uns als Eskimos. Wir fuhren mit dem Auto, aber leider wartete die Polizei um die Ecke und wir mußten ins Röhrchen blasen.

Das Fest war in vollem Gange, aber wir kannten niemand. Wir tranken viel Wein und tanzten. Morgens um 5 hatten wir ein wenig Hunger, und so gingen wir zum 'Silbernen Eck' und aßen ein paar Wiener Würstchen.

11 Answer the questions by picking the right German expression from the box below. (Answers p.204)

a. What would you say if you felt ravenous?

....

b. What would you say if you had danced all night?

....

c. What would you say if the police had breathalized you?

....

d. What would you say if you had been dressing up as an Indian?

....

> Ich habe mich als Indianer verkleidet
> Ich mußte ins Röhrchen blasen
> Ich habe bis zum Umfallen getanzt
> Ich hatte einen Riesenhunger

12 In the speaking exercise you will be asked to talk about your weekend, practising the past tense at the same time. Use the following expressions:

wir gingen, wir fuhren, wir gingen tanzen, wir trafen, wir verkleideten uns, ich trank, ich mußte Auto fahren.

Wörter und Wendungen

A night out

Ich mache Ihnen einen Vorschlag	I have a suggestion
Wir gehen . . .	We'll go (to) . . .
aufs Weinfest	the wine festival
zum Fasching	the carnival
zum Feuerwerk	the fireworks
tanzen	dancing
Wir werden uns gut amüsieren	We'll have a good time
Da ist immer gute Stimmung	There's always a good atmosphere
Eine Kapelle spielt	There's a band playing
Das Fest war/ist in vollem Gang	The party was/is in full swing
Wir treffen/trafen Freunde	We meet/met friends
Das hört sich nicht schlecht an	That doesn't sound bad
Ich überleg's mir mal	I'll think about it
der Kater	hangover
das Lokal	pub/restaurant/dance hall/bar
ein Fest/einen Geburtstag feiern	to have a party/celebrate a birthday

Buying tickets

Was spielen Sie . . .	What's playing . . .
heute?	tonight?
diese Woche?	this week?
am Montag?	on Monday?
Haben Sie noch Karten?	Have you still got tickets?
Welche Preisgruppe?	What price range?
Im ersten/zweiten Rang	In the first/second tier
Wann beginnt die Aufführung?	When does the performance start?
das Theater	theatre
die Theaterkasse	box office
die Oper	opera
das Werk	the (artistic) work
der Liederabend	song recital

Grammatik

The imperfect tense

Sentences such as **'Die Band <u>war</u> laut'** or **'Ich <u>hatte</u> Hunger'** use the imperfect tense for telling you something that happened in the past. In spoken German it is used less than the perfect tense (**Ich <u>habe</u> ein Buch gelesen, ich <u>bin</u> gestern <u>gekommen</u>**) but it is still an important tense to learn. The most important forms to remember are the imperfect forms of **sein** and **haben** because they are used a lot.

sein – to be	*haben* – to have
ich war	**ich hatte**
du warst	**du hattest**
er/sie/es war	**er/sie/es hatte**
wir waren	**wir hatten**
ihr wart	**ihr hattet**
Sie/sie waren	**Sie/sie hatten**

Most other verbs (the so-called 'weak verbs') form their imperfect by adding **-te, -test, -tet** or **-ten** after the stem. This is not unlike English where you add -(e)d: play – played, dance – danced. For example, here are the imperfect forms of the verb **tanzen** (to dance). The stem of **tanzen** is **tanz**.

ich tanz<u>te</u>
du tanz<u>test</u>
er/sie/es tanz<u>te</u>
wir tanz<u>ten</u>
ihr tanz<u>tet</u>
Sie/sie tanz<u>ten</u>

13 Translate the following forms into German (Answers p.204):

a. I learned ....

b. You (**du**) believed ....

c. He heard ....

d. We wanted ....

e. You (**Sie**) wanted ....

f. They heard ....

The other group of verbs, the so-called strong verbs, are not so easy to handle. They like to change their stems in the imperfect, and also have different endings from the weak verbs. For example:

gehen – to go	
ich ging (no extra ending)	**wir gingen**
du gingst	**ihr gingt**
er/sie/es ging (no extra ending)	**Sie/sie gingen**

Quite often you can see a resemblance between the English and the German imperfect forms which can help you to recognize the verbs, for example:

kommen	**kam**	to come	came
trinken	**trank**	to drink	drank
singen	**sang**	to sing	sang

14 Fill in the correct imperfect form of the infinitives given in brackets.
(Answers p.204)

a. Er .... ins 'Goldene Eck'   (gehen)
b. Wir .... nach Hause   (fahren)
c. Wir .... das Auto zu Hause   (lassen)
d. Ich .... Freunde   (treffen)
e. Im 'Adler' .... es einen Tanz   (geben)

Word order in sentences with two verbs

In sentences where you have two verbs the second verb goes right to the end of the sentence, for example:

Man <u>konnte</u> sein eigenes Wort nicht verstehen

Wir <u>könnten</u> auch ein bißchen tanzen

Wir <u>wollten</u> mal wieder richtig klassisch tanzen

Der Wein <u>würde</u> Ihnen bestimmt schmecken

Da <u>sollte</u> eine gute Band spielen

Jeder <u>mußte</u> sich weiß anziehen

The same rule applies for questions: the second verb goes to the end, for example:

<u>Kannst</u> du gut schwimmen?

Wann <u>wirst</u> du morgen kommen?

Warum <u>konntest</u> du nicht aufs Weinfest gehen?

Wann <u>müssen</u> wir nach Hause fahren?

<u>Mußt</u> du heute viel arbeiten?

15 Here are 5 sentences that have fallen to pieces – can you put them together again? Mind the word order! (Answers p.204)

a. ich kann
skifahren
gut

b. gestern abend
er konnte
nicht kommen

c. im Sommer
nach Afrika
will ich
fahren

d. wir wollten
einen langen Spaziergang
am Sonntag
machen

e. zuerst
ins Theater
gehen
wollten sie

Übungen: Lesen

16 Here is an extract from a brochure with day trips organized by the German Federal Railway (**Deutsche Bundesbahn**). What's on the programme? Read carefully, then answer the questions below. (Answers p.204)

Stimmung – Tanz – Wein
"La Mosella"

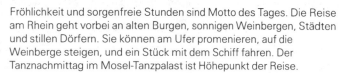

Sonntag 10. Juli, Reise Nr. 63 306

Fahrtstrecke:

Neckargemünd – Heidelberg – Weinheim – Mannheim – Ludwigshafen – Frankenthal

Fröhlichkeit und sorgenfreie Stunden sind Motto des Tages. Die Reise am Rhein geht vorbei an alten Burgen, sonnigen Weinbergen, Städten und stillen Dörfern. Sie können am Ufer promenieren, auf die Weinberge steigen, und ein Stück mit dem Schiff fahren. Der Tanznachmittag im Mosel-Tanzpalast ist Höhepunkt der Reise.

Reisepreise: von Heidelberg: 55 DM
von Mannheim: 53 DM
inklusive: Bahnfahrt 2. Klasse, Mittagessen, Tanz

Vocabulary:
die Fahrtstrecke route
die Fröhlichkeit fun, gaiety
sorgenfrei carefree
die Burg castle

der Weinberg vineyard
der Tanzpalast dance hall
der Höhepunkt highlight

a. When does the excursion take place?

....

b. Along which river?

....

c. How much is the fare from Heidelberg?

....

d. Is lunch included?

....

e. When is the dance, afternoon or evening?

....

f. What is the motto of the day?

....

g. What else can you do, apart from dance?

....

Here is a review of a film that became popular overnight – and which you might have seen or heard about yourself. The text is taken from a film review – and it is, by the way, a good illustration of how much English has become part of the German language. Read the extract, then do the exercises below.

DIVA . . .

. . . ein Thriller, ein Synthetikfilm, ein Medienspektakel. Ein Film für die Generation von Disney und Popkultur. Ironisch, laut, brutal, utopisch . . .

Die Story des Films ist kompliziert. Es geht um den jungen Postboten Jules und sein Idol Cynthia, die Diva, eine Opernsängerin . . . Die ewige Geschichte von Liebe und Kunst, aber hier erzählt als Action Thriller.

1980 machte Beneix, ein New-comer Regisseur, den Film Diva. Es war ein langer Film; in Paris sahen ihn nur ein paar Cineasten, das war alles. Diva war ein Reinfall, ein 'Flop'. Aber Irene Silbermann, die Produzentin, glaubte an den Film, zeigte ihn in den USA und dort wurde er ein riesiger Erfolg. Er kam zurück nach Paris, aber diesmal im Triumph. Auf einmal sah man die tollen Farben, Schnitte, die Schocks und Gags – Diva wurde Mode, wurde zum Kultfilm.

Vocabulary:

kompliziert complicated
der Postbote postman
der Sänger/die Sängerin singer
erzählt told
der Regisseur director (film or theatre)
der Cineast movie buff
der Produzent/die Produzentin producer
der Schnitt cut
die Mode fashion

ewig eternal
die Kunst art
wurde became

17 Are the statements below true or false – **Richtig oder Falsch?**
(Answers p.204)

a. The story line is simple |R |F |

b. It is about a young postman and his idol, a popstar |R |F |

c. It is the old story of love and art |R |F |

d. When first shown, 'Diva' was no success at all |R |F |

e. In the United States, too, people thought it was a flop |R |F |

f. Back in Paris though, 'Diva' became a triumphant success |R |F |

g. But it never became a cult film |R |F |

18 Can you find the 'German' equivalents of the following words?
(Answers p.204)

a. a media spectacle: ....

b. his idol: ....

c. shock: ....

d. cultfilm: ....

Übungen: Radio

19 Popshop is a pop programme for young people broadcast by **SWF 3**
(**Südwestfunk 3**). **Popshop** will be going on the road, broadcasting live – but
where and when? Listen to the radio extract on the cassette, then fill in the
missing words in the transcript below. (Answers p.212 in complete transcript)

Popshop unterwegs. Die .... pause ist vorbei,
es geht wieder los. SWF 3, Popshop unterwegs. Am ....
.... in Griesheim in der Hegelsberghalle, von
...., und mit dabei, live aus ....
...., die 'Münchner Freiheit'. Also, nicht
vergessen, kommenden Samstag, 10. September, Griesheim,
Hegelsberghalle, von 18 bis 22 Uhr. SWF 3, Popshop unterwegs. So,
und wer noch wissen will, wo Griesheim liegt – da gibt's nämlich
mehrere Griesheim in der ganzen .... das liegt
bei Erbarmstadt – Darmstadt.

20 Listen to the extract from **Funkboutique**, a cultural programme, then mark
the right boxes below. (Answers p.204)

Vocabulary:

kommunal communal
Obervolta Upper Volta
skandinavisch Scandinavian
die Ostblockländer the East
European countries

die Konservenbüchse can, tin
witzig amusing
überrascht surprised
der Maler/die Malerin painter
abliefern (sep.) to deliver

a. Die Filme sind für
- [ ] alte Leute
- [ ] Teenager
- [ ] Kinder

b. Das Festival zeigt Filme
- [ ] nur aus Europa
- [ ] aus der ganzen Welt
- [ ] nur aus Deutschland

c. 'Konrad aus der Konservenbüchse' ist ein Film aus
- [ ] der DDR
- [ ] der Schweiz
- [ ] der Bundesrepublik Deutschland

d. Der Film 'Konrad aus
der Konservenbüchse' ist
- [ ] lustig
- [ ] traurig
- [ ] langweilig

e. Ein 'Instant-Kind' ist
- [ ] ein kluges Kind
- [ ] ein Kind aus der Konserve
- [ ] ein besonders kleines Kind

21 Name (in English) all the countries mentioned in the Film Festival report.
(Answers p.204)

....

....

Übungen: Sprechen Sie selbst

22 Imagine you're at the box office, wanting to buy tickets. What kind of questions would you ask the cashier? Try to make up at least 4 questions, then listen to Klaus's questions on the cassette. Remember that yours could be quite different.

23 What did you do when you last had a night out? Try to speak for at least half a minute, then listen to Klaus's version.

24 Try to make up a story. The details are up to you, but you must use the following words (the sequence does not matter): **am Sonntag**, **Maria**, **Oper**, **Diva**, **Eintrittsgeld**, **essen**. There are two versions on the tape – but do try to come up with your own first, before listening.

9 Ab morgen Diät!

You will learn

- to talk about your health
- to shop at your local pharmacy
- to describe an accident

... and you'll find out how to stay (or get) slim and fit

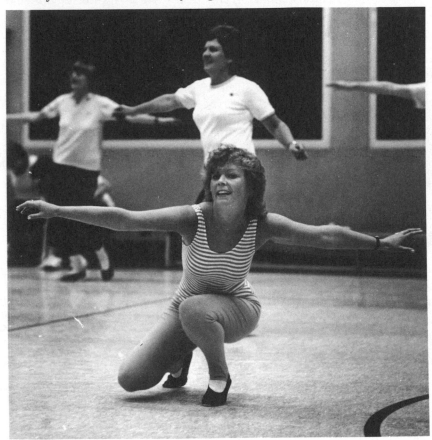

Study guide

Dialog 1: Ab morgen Diät!

Silke Also, morgen beginne ich mit meiner Diät.
Biba Warum denn das?
Silke Ach, ich fühle mich so schlaff und ungesund und unbeweglich.
Biba Was für eine Diät machst du denn?
Silke Also erst mal eine Saftkur, zur Entschlackung, und dann mach' ich
eine Kaloriendiät, streng nach Plan: 800 Kalorien am Tag.
Biba Was ißt du denn dann?
Silke Ja, so fettarmes Essen, Salate, mageres Fleisch, Fisch, wenig
Kohlehydrate – ist halt sehr teuer.
Biba Hm – und natürlich keinen Alkohol?
Silke Ja . . . nee . . .
Biba Und keine Süßigkeiten?
Silke Ja . . . nee . . .
Biba Das könnte ich nicht!
Silke Ja, wieso siehst du denn so gesund aus?
Biba Also, ich – ich mach' jeden Tag ein bißchen Gymnastik, und dann
geh' ich noch zum Schwimmen, einmal in der Woche; ja – und dann
achte ich darauf, daß ich genug schlafe.

▸ **die Diät** diet
▸ **abnehmen** (sep.) to lose weight
  zunehmen (sep.) to gain weight

  warum denn das? why that, for heaven's sake?

  ich fühle mich so schlaff, ungesund und unbeweglich I feel so listless
  (lit. limp), unhealthy and unfit; **gesund** healthy,
▸ **die Gesundheit** health; **beweglich** supple, fit.

  was für eine Diät machst du? what kind of diet will you go on?
▸ **eine Diät machen** to go on a diet.

  erst mal = erst einmal first of all.

  die Saftkur fruit juice diet, **die Kur** lit. cure, course of treatments; **die
  Hungerkur** fast (lit. hunger cure).

  zur Entschlackung for purification.

▸ **die Kalorie** calorie; **streng nach Plan** following a strict plan.

▸ **fettarmes Essen** food with very little fat.

  wenig Kohlehydrate few carbohydrates.

  ist halt sehr teuer that is (unfortunately) very expensive; **halt** is a 'filler'
  word here – don't confuse it with **halt** = stop.

▸ **keinen Alkohol** no alcohol.

▸ **keine Süßigkeiten** no sweets.

▸ **das könnte ich nicht** (**tun**) I could not do that.

  wieso siehst du denn so gesund aus? why do you look so healthy?

▸ **ich mach' Gymnastik** I do my exercises.
  und dann achte ich darauf . . . and then I make sure (lit. take care that).

Übungen

1 In spite of her diet plans, Silke loves eating. Here are just a few of her favourite foods and drinks. Which ones would *not* fit into her low-calorie diet? (Answers p.204)

Eierlikör	Limonade	Karottensalat	Grüne Bohnen
Hühnchen	Tee mit Rum	Käsekuchen	Kartoffeln mit
Champignons	Eisbein	Forelle	Butter

2 **Diät-Details.** Make sure you've understood Dialogue 1 really well, then complete the details about Silke's diet in the grid below. (Answers p.204)

a.	Wann?	Ab:
b.	Warum?	Sie fühlt sich:
c.	Was für eine Diät?	1. 2.
d.	Wieviel Kalorien pro Tag?	
e.	Was darf sie essen?	
f.	Was nicht?	

3 Silke has written a letter to her friend Katrin telling her about her diet, suggesting that Katrin went on a diet too. Here is Katrin's reply. Read it, then pretend you're Katrin on the tape and answer Klaus's questions.

> Liebe Silke,
> Vielen Dank für Deinen Vorschlag. Aber ich werde keine Diät machen. Ich habe Spaß am Kochen und am Essen. Außerdem ist mir eine Diät zu teuer. Warum müssen denn alle Leute schlank sein? Ich bin lieber ein bißchen dick. Fit bin ich trotzdem, denn ich mache viel Gymnastik. Also, laß mich so, wie ich bin! Alles Gute und viel Erfolg,
>
> Deine Katrin

Vocabulary:
ich habe Spaß am ... I enjoy ...
schlank slim
dick fat

Dialog 2: Eine Familienepidemie

Heide   Also letzte Woche war die ganze Familie krank. Zuerst hatte Claudia die Grippe. Kein Wunder bei dem Wetter! Halsweh, Schnupfen, Fieber, eben so alles, was dazu gehört ... Kopfweh ... Dann wurde mein Mann auch noch krank. Ihm war ständig schlecht, hatte Magenschmerzen, Durchfall, keinen Appetit, und er konnte nicht schlafen. Der Arzt sagte, er hätte 'ne Darmgrippe. Und dann wurde ich schließlich auch noch krank. Ich weiß gar nicht, was es ist. Ich habe Muskelschmerzen, meine Augen sind ganz rot, mir wird ständig heiß, und dann wieder kalt ... Wir können bald sowas wie 'ne Privatklinik aufmachen.

> **die Familienepidemie** family epidemic
> ▶ **die Grippe** flu
> ▶ **der Schnupfen** running nose
> ▶ **das Fieber** fever, temperature
>
> ▶ **der Durchfall** diarrhoea
>   **die Darmgrippe** intestinal flu
> ▶ **der Arzt** doctor
> ▶ **die Ärztin** female doctor

▶ **letzte Woche war die ganze Familie krank** last week the entire family was sick; **krank sein** to be ill, sick; **krank werden** to fall ill/get sick: **dann wurde mein Mann auch noch krank** then my husband fell ill/got sick as well.

  kein Wunder bei dem Wetter no wonder with this weather.

▶ **(das) Halsweh** sore throat. You'll also hear **die Halsschmerzen** (lit.
▶ throat pains); similar: **das Kopfweh** or **die Kopfschmerzen** headache, **die Magenschmerzen** stomach pains, **die Muskelschmerzen** sore muscles; **der Schmerz** ache, pain; **wo tut es weh?** where does it hurt?

▶ **ihm war ständig schlecht** he felt sick all the time; **mir ist schlecht** I feel sick.

  mir wird ständig heiß, dann wieder kalt I keep getting hot and cold flushes.

  wir können bald sowas wie 'ne Privatklinik aufmachen soon we can open (something like) a private clinic.

Übungen

4 Was fehlt ihnen? What's wrong with them?
Have a look at the drawings, then write your diagnosis. (Answers p.204)

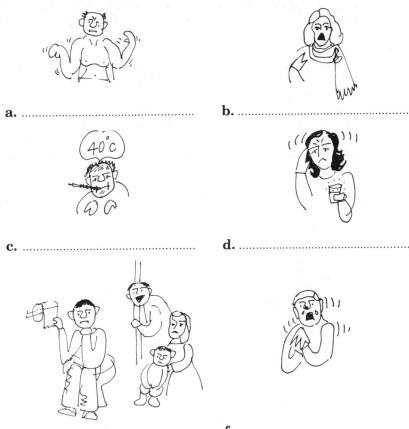

a. ....

b. ....

c. ....

d. ....

e. ....

f. ....

 5 Now you are ill. You feel sick, you have a headache, you have no appetite, but what exactly is wrong with you? Answers Corinna's questions after Andrew's prompts.

Dialog 3: In der Apotheke

Ruth　　　Guten Tag.

Herr Keidel　Guten Tag.

Ruth　　　Also, ich fahre in die Berge, und da möchte ich mir 'ne ganz kleine Reiseapotheke mitnehmen. Können Sie mich da beraten, können Sie mir da helfen?

Herr Keidel　Ja, gerne. Wo fahren Sie denn hin?

Ruth　　　Ich fahre in die Berge, nach Österreich.

Herr Keidel　Nach Österreich, ja. Da brauchen Sie ein starkes Sonnenschutzmittel, wenn Sie in die Berge fahren, weil die Sonne da sehr intensiv scheint. Dann würde ich Ihnen noch ein Verbandszeug empfehlen, für die erste Hilfe: Binden, Pflaster, vielleicht noch Desinfektionsmittel oder ein Antiseptikum für kleine Wunden. Auch den Insektenschutz sollten Sie nicht vergessen.

Ruth　　　Ja, und da gibt's doch auch 'n Spray, nicht?

Her Keidel　Ja, man kann ein Spray nehmen, würd' ich Ihnen aber nicht empfehlen in den Bergen. Wenn die Sonne scheint, wird die Spraydose sehr heiß und kann explodieren. Ich würde Ihnen ein Gelee empfehlen. Das kühlt und erfrischt.

> ◆ **die Apotheke** pharmacy
> **der Apotheker** pharmacist
> ◆ **die Reiseapotheke** medical kit
> for travelling
> **scheinen** to shine

> **das Antiseptikum** antiseptic
> **der Insektenschutz** insect repellent
> ◆ **das Pflaster** sticking plaster
> **explodieren** to explode

können Sie mich da beraten? can you advise me? can you give me some advice?

◆ **das Sonnenschutzmittel** sun cream or lotion; **das Mittel** (lit. means, e.g. **das Transportmittel** means of transport) can also be used for 'medication, medicine': **haben Sie ein Mittel gegen Kopfschmerzen?** have you something for a headache? See also **Desinfektionsmittel** (disinfectant) below.

◆ **das Verbandszeug** bandage, dressing (for wounds): **eine Wunde verbinden** to dress a wound; **die Binde** bandage.

und da gibt's doch auch 'n Spray, nicht? and there is also a spray, isn't there?

ich würde Ihnen ein Gelee empfehlen I would recommend a gel.

das kühlt und erfrischt that is cooling and refreshing (lit. that cools and refreshes).

Übungen

6 Here is a rather more extensive **Reiseapotheke** containing more items than the ones suggested by Herr Keidel. What doesn't fit? (Answers p.204)

Binden	Lippenstift
Augentropfen	Shampoo
Desinfektionsmittel	Insektenschutz
Pflaster	Gesichtscreme
Seidentuch	Haarpomade
Sonnenschutz	Puder

7 Translate into German (use **Sie** for 'you'): (Answers p.204)

a. I'd like to take a small medical kit with me.

....

b. Can you help me? Can you give me some advice?

....

c. You shouldn't forget the insect repellent.

....

d. You can use a spray.

....

8 It's your turn to buy some things at the pharmacy now (and a chance to practise **möchten** and **würden**). Andrew will prompt you as usual.

Dialog 4: Glück im Unglück

Horst   Gestern hab' ich bei einem Unfall einen großen Schreck bekommen.
Frauenfeld   Ich fuhr so auf der Landstraße. Mir kam ein Lastwagen entgegen.
Plötzlich scherte hinter dem Lastwagen ein BMW aus und kam
direkt auf mich zu. Ich konnte vor Schreck nur noch das Steuer nach
rechts reißen und bin in den Graben gefahren. Ich hab' mich
zweimal überschlagen und konnte trotzdem aus dem Auto
herauskriechen. Der BMW-Fahrer war verletzt. Gottseidank hat
dann der Lastwagenfahrer die Ambulanz gerufen. Die kamen auch
sofort und haben den verletzten BMW-Fahrer und mich mit ins
Krankenhaus genommen.

▸ **der Unfall** accident   ▸ **verletzt** injured
plötzlich suddenly   **Gottseidank** thank goodness
der Graben ditch   ▸ **das Krankenhaus** hospital

ich habe ... einen großen Schreck bekommen I got the fright of my life;
der Schreck(en) fright, shock; **vor Schreck** out of fright.

der Lastwagen lorry, truck; **mir kam ein Lastwagen entgegen** a lorry
came towards me.

plötzlich scherte hinter dem Lastwagen ein BMW aus suddenly a
BMW pulled out from behind the lorry; **ausscheren** (sep.) to pull out.

ich konnte nur noch das Steuer nach rechts reißen all I could do was to
pull the steering wheel over to the right.

ich hab' mich zweimal überschlagen I turned over twice.

der Lastwagenfahrer hat die Ambulanz gerufen the lorry driver called
the ambulance; instead of **Ambulanz** you'll also often hear
▸ **der Krankenwagen: Rufen Sie einen Krankenwagen!** Call an
ambulance!

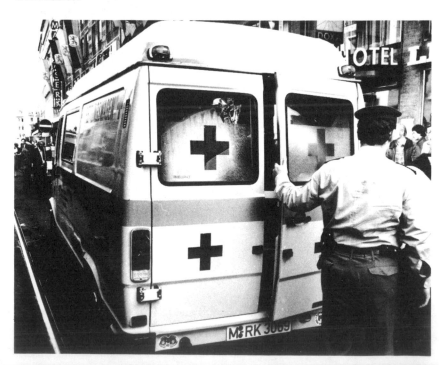

Übungen

9 Here is a picture story of Horst Frauenfeld's accident. Pick the right captions from the box and write them under the appropriate picture. (Answers p.204)

a. ....

b. ....

c. ....

d. ....

....

e. ....

f. ....

....

....

Ich konnte vor Schreck nur noch das Steuer nach rechts reißen.

Plötzlich scherte ein BMW hinter dem Lastwagen aus.

Der Lastwagenfahrer rief die Ambulanz.

Die Ambulanz nahm mich und den Fahrer des BMW mit ins Krankenhaus.

Ein Lastwagen kam mir entgegen.

Ich konnte aus dem Auto herauskriechen.

---

10 Translate the phrases below into German. Remember that 'you must not' is **Sie dürfen nicht**. (Answers p.204)

a. You cannot park here. ....

b. You must not pass now. ....

c. You must brake. ....

d. Please stop. ....

e. You must turn left. ....

11 In the speaking exercise you'll be asked to say aloud the phrases from **Übung 10**. But Andrew will prompt you nevertheless.

Wörter und Wendungen

Going on a diet

Ich will eine ...	I want to go on a ...
Diät/Saftkur/Hungerkur machen	diet/fruit juice diet/fast
Ich will abnehmen/schlank werden	I want to lose weight/get slim
Ich esse ...	I eat ...
nur 800 Kalorien am Tag	only 800 calories per day
fettarmes Essen	food low in fat
keine Süßigkeiten	no sweets
Ich trinke keinen Alkohol	I drink no alcohol
Ich mache Gymnastik	I do exercises

Your health/illness

die Gesundheit	health
die Krankheit	illness
gesund/krank sein	to be healthy/ill
krank werden	to become ill/sick
Mir ist schlecht	I'm feeling sick
Ich habe ...	I've got ...
Grippe	flu
Halschmerzen	a sore throat
Kopfschmerzen	a headache
Fieber	a temperature
eine Erkältung	a cold
Schnupfen	a running nose
Durchfall	diarrhoea
der Arzt/die Ärztin	male/female doctor

At the pharmacy

die Apotheke	chemist, pharmacy
die Reiseapotheke	medical kit
Ich brauche ...	I need ...
ein Sonnenschutzmittel	sun cream
Verbandszeug	bandages
Pflaster	sticking/adhesive plaster
ein Mittel gegen ...	something for ...

Accidents and traffic regulations

der Unfall	accident
das Krankenhaus	hospital
Ich bin verletzt	I'm injured
Rufen Sie einen Krankenwagen!	Call an ambulance!
Sie dürfen hier nicht ...	You must not ...
parken	park
halten	stop
überholen	overtake/pass here
Sie müssen ...	You must ...
bremsen	brake
links/rechts abbiegen	turn left/right

Grammatik

Modal verbs

The modal verbs (**Modalverben**) are those useful linking words like **können** (can), **müssen** (must), **wollen** (want), etc., e.g. **ich will arbeiten** (I want to work) or **sie kann gut skifahren** (she can ski well). Here is a list of all modal verbs in the present tense.

können (can, to be able to)

ich kann	I can	**wir können**	we can
du kannst	you can	**ihr könnt**	you can
er/sie/es kann	he/she/it can	**Sie/sie können**	you/they can

Ich kann Auto fahren. I can drive.
Sie können alle schwimmen. They all know how to swim.

müssen (must, to have to)

ich muß	I must	**wir müssen**	we must
du mußt	you must	**ihr müßt**	you must
er/sie/es muß	he/she/it must	**Sie/sie müssen**	you/they must

Du mußt Peter besuchen. You have to visit Peter.
Wir müssen jetzt arbeiten. We have to work now.
Note the meaning of **müssen** with **nicht** (not): **Du mußt Peter nicht besuchen** (you don't have to see Peter). **Wir müssen jetzt nicht arbeiten** (we don't have to work now).

wollen (to want)

ich will	I want to	**wir wollen**	we want to
du willst	you want to	**ihr wollt**	you want to
er/sie/es will	he/she/it wants to	**Sie/sie wollen**	you/they want to

Ich will schlafen. I want to sleep.
Was wollen Sie? What do you want?
Note that **ich will** does not mean 'I will.' That is **ich werde**: **Ich werde wieder Arbeit finden.** I will find work again.

dürfen (may, to be allowed to)

ich darf	I may	**wir dürfen**	we may
du darfst	you may	**ihr dürft**	you may
er/sie/es darf	he/she/it may	**Sie/sie dürfen**	you/they may

Sie dürfen rauchen. You may smoke, i.e. you're allowed to smoke.
Sie dürfen nicht rauchen. You're not allowed to smoke.

mögen (to like)

ich mag	I like (to)	**wir mögen**	we like
du magst	you like	**ihr mögt**	you like
er/sie/es mag	he/she/it likes	**Sie/sie mögen**	you/they like

Ich mag jetzt nicht essen. I don't like to eat now.
Das mag schon sein. That may be so.

sollen (shall, to be supposed to)

ich soll	I shall	**wir sollen**	we shall
du sollst	you shall	**ihr sollt**	you shall
er/sie/es soll	he/she/it shall	**Sie/sie sollen**	you/they shall

Vater sagt, du sollst nach Hause kommen. Father says you ought to come home.
Sollen wir sie abholen? Shall we pick her up?

In most cases the modal verbs require a second verb (**Du kannst jetzt gehen**), but sometimes they stand on their own:
Ich mag kein Eis (essen). I don't like ice cream.
Ich kann Deutsch (sprechen). I can speak German.
Ich will Geld (haben). I want (to have) money.
Du sollst das nicht (tun). You are not supposed to do that.

12 Translate into German: (Answers p.205)

a. You (**Sie**) must not park here. ....

b. We want to go now. ....

c. Can you (**du**) speak French? ....

d. Do you (**Sie**) want to wait? ....

e. She doesn't like coffee. ....

f. Can I help you (**Sie**)? ....

g. May I smoke? ....

During this course you have also come across the past tense of the modal verbs:

ich konnte	I could
mußte	had to
wollte	wanted to
durfte	was allowed to
mochte	liked
sollte	was supposed to

Wir wollten mal wieder so richtig klassisch tanzen. We wanted to dance in the old-fashioned way.
Man konnte sein eigenes Wort nicht verstehen. One couldn't understand anything.
You sometimes find some of these verb forms with an **Umlaut**, e.g. **ich könnte** (I could) or **ich möchte** (I would like to). In this case the meaning changes:

Das könnte ich nicht! I couldn't do that.
Ich möchte gern ein Rumpsteak. I would like a rumpsteak.
Er könnte wohl, aber er möchte nicht. He could very well do it, but he doesn't want to. **Könnte, möchte**, etc. are the so-called *subjunctive* forms (see **Grammatik** Unit 12).

13 Translate into German: (Answers p.205)

a. I could not hear her. ....

b. I had to drink water. ....

c. I did not want to talk about it. ....

d. The train was supposed to leave at six. ....

Übungen: Lesen

14 According to statistics, women are the safer drivers – at least the accidents they cause are less serious. However, there are many prejudices against women drivers, which are totally unjustified, as our artist below shows ... Study the drawings and the blurbs, then match them with the right captions, e.g. label them **a.**, **b.**, etc. (Answers p.205)

a. It's a prejudice that women pick their cars according to the size of the rearview mirror.

b. It's also not true that they reject cars if they don't like the colour of the seats.

c. Only rumour has it that some women can't tell the front of a car from the rear.

d. There may be some truth in it that some women don't know all the Japanese makes.

e. They do, however, know all the European models.

f. Often women drivers are more popular with the family.

15 Here is a short article from BRIGITTE about a highly successful dieter. Study it, then decide whether the statements below are true or false. (Answers p.205)

Käthy Christen, 19, aus Genf wollte lieber schlank als mollig sein. Sie hatte Erfolg.

16 Kilo weniger

Käthy kommt aus einer großen Familie, die sich gern und oft zu fröhlichen Festen versammelt. Alle haben Spaß am Kochen und natürlich auch am Essen. Und so blieb es nicht aus, daß alle – von der Oma bis zu den Enkeln – gutgelaunt und ziemlich rund waren. Käthy störte es, daß sie bei Größe 44 hauptsächlich damenhafte und altmodische Kleidungsstücke bekam. Sie hatte viel mehr Lust auf die fröhlich bunte Mode, die es nur in kleineren Größen gibt. Sie nahm in gut drei Monaten 16 Kilo ab.

Vocabulary:
mollig plump
sich versammeln to gather
so blieb es nicht aus ... inevitably
gutgelaunt jolly
Käthy störte es Käthy was bothered by ...
damenhaft ladylike
altmodisch old-fashioned
das Kleidungsstück piece of clothing
die Mode fashion

a. Käthy kommt aus Genf. ⬚R ⬚F

b. Käthy hat keine Geschwister. ⬚R ⬚F

c. Die ganze Familie liebt gutes Essen und ist mollig. ⬚R ⬚F

d. Am Kochen hat niemand Spaß. ⬚R ⬚F

e. Käthy nahm in einem Vierteljahr 16 Kilo ab. ⬚R ⬚F

Übungen: Radio

16a More about dieting. Listen to a commercial about the **Blitzdiät**, a crash diet which appeared in BRIGITTE. **Blitzschnell** – in a flash – is the magic word here. Mark everything in the list below which according to the advertisers could happen **blitzschnell**. (Answers p.205)

a. putting on weight ☐
b. tackling the BRIGITTE crash diet ☐
c. eating spaghetti ☐
d. losing the pounds you gained on holiday ☐
e. cooking five delicious low-calorie meals per day ☐
f. buying the new BRIGITTE ☐
g. remaining seated ☐

Vocabulary:
gut erholt well rested
Sie haben ganz schön charmant zugelegt (iron.) you have gained quite
    a lot of weight
schwinden to disappear
der Vorrat provisions, supply
zubereiten to prepare
auf etwas sitzenbleiben to get stuck with s.th. (lit. to remain seated)

16b Below you'll find the **Natreen** commercial partly translated. Fill in the missing words. (Answers p.205)

der Bundesbürger lit. citizen of the Federal Republic

a. Tell me, did you know that every second German ....
    ....?

b. Yes, and because I don't want to be one of them I sweeten my
    .... and all these sweet

    dishes with Natreen only.

    And why?

c. Because Natreen sweetens without ....
    .... and without ....
    .... This is how I avoid many calories ....

    ....

17 Road safety. How can you protect yourself in case of an accident? Listen to the third commercial, then fill in the transcript below. (Answers in complete transcript p.212)

Die meisten Unfälle passieren ....

Ein Aufprallunfall mit Tempo 50 ist wie ein Sturz ....

Diese Wucht können Sie gar nicht ....

abfangen. Das kann nur der Sicherheitsgurt. Darum, Partner,

fahren Sie ....,

gerade auch in der Stadt.

Vocabulary:
passieren to happen
der Aufprall impact
mit Tempo 50 at 50 km per hour
der Sturz fall
die Wucht abfangen to soften the impact
der Sicherheitsgurt safety belt

Übungen: Sprechen Sie selbst

18 Your turn to speak again. Imagine you're sick with the flu. Name at least three symptoms, then listen to Corinna for comparison.

19 Hopefully you've never been in an accident yourself, but you may have witnessed one. Describe such an accident, then listen to what happened to Klaus.

10 Mein Tagesablauf

You will learn

- how people spend their day
- to describe what you do to relax
- to talk about your language studies

... and you'll hear some revealing statistics about the West German male at home.

Study guide

Dialog 1: Ich bin Hausmann

Helmut Ich bin Hausmann. Mein Tagesablauf sieht ungefähr so aus: Wir frühstücken morgens gemeinsam. Meine Frau fährt dann zur Schule. Sie ist Lehrerin. Ich habe zwei Kinder: einen dreijährigen Sohn und eine zweijährige Tochter. Um neun Uhr bringe ich meinen Sohn zum Kindergarten, gehe dann mit meiner Tochter spazieren – bei schlechtem Wetter in den Zoo, oder in Geschäfte, einkaufen, das ist ganz vom Wetter abhängig. (Ich) bereite mittags etwas zum Essen vor. Je nachdem, wann meine Frau zurückkommt, essen wir gemeinsam, oder ich esse mit meinen Kindern allein.

- **frühstücken** to have breakfast
- **gemeinsam** together
- **morgens** in the mornings
- **mittags** at lunchtime
- **je nachdem** depending on

- **Ich bin Hausmann** I'm a house husband – on the analogy of **die Hausfrau** housewife.

- **mein Tagesablauf sieht ungefähr so aus** my daily routine is something like this; **der Tagesablauf** lit. course of the day; **sieht ... aus** from **aussehen** (sep.) lit. to look like.

  meine Frau ist Lehrerin my wife is a teacher; similar: **mein Mann ist Lehrer** my husband is a teacher.

  ich habe ... einen dreijährigen Sohn und eine zweijährige Tochter I have a three-year-old son and a two-year-old daughter.

  (ich) bereite etwas zum Essen vor I prepare something to eat; **vorbereiten** (sep.) to prepare: **ich bereite meine Hochzeit vor** I'm preparing (for) my wedding.

Der Beruf des Hausmannes bedingt einen Rollenwechsel ...

... den viele Männer nicht verkraften ...

Übungen

1 Here is an account of Helmut's day in English, but it is not quite accurate. Spot the mistakes and underline them. (Answers p.205)

> We have breakfast together, and then my wife goes off to school. At nine o'clock I take my four-year-old son to kindergarten. Then I go for a walk with my daughter. She is three years old. If the weather is good we go to the zoo or we go shopping. At lunchtime we eat out, sometimes with my wife if she is back from work in time, sometimes just me and the children.

2 Complete the sentences below. Try not to look at the dialogue again until you've finished the exercise. (Answers p.205)

a. Wir frühstücken (*together*)...

b. Ich esse mit meinen Kindern (*alone*) ....

c. Wir gehen (*shopping*) ....

d. Ich habe einen (*son*) .... und eine (*daughter*) ....

e. Meine Frau ist (*teacher*) ....

f. Meine Frau fährt zur (*school*) ....

 3 Your turn to speak. Put yourself into the shoes of Helmut's wife and describe your day from her point of view. Andrew will prompt you.

... deren Frauen berufstätig sind.

Dialog 2: Abends Termine

Biba Normalerweise steh' ich so um neun auf. Der Wecker klingelt schon eine halbe Stunde vorher. Dann mach' ich ein bißchen Frühgymnastik, nehm' eine Dusche, höre Radio, les' die Zeitung und mache nebenher das Frühstück.
Danach setz' ich mich an die Arbeit und schreibe einen Artikel. Oder ich gehe in die Bibliothek, wenn ich noch Literatur brauche.
Mittags gehe ich dann einkaufen, mach' die Hausarbeit: aufräumen, staubsaugen, waschen – und dann koch' ich mir noch schnell was Kleines.
Nachmittags schreibe ich dann weiter, oder lese etwas, oder denke nach, was ich als nächstes schreiben werde. Und wenn mir nichts mehr einfällt, geh' ich erst mal spazieren.
Abends hab' ich dann meistens Termine. Entweder ich muß ins Theater gehen, oder in eine Ausstellung, über die ich dann am nächsten Tag schreiben muß.

♦ **die Frühgymnastik** morning exercises
♦ **die Dusche** shower
♦ **nebenher** at the same time
♦ **die Bibliothek** library
aufräumen (sep.) to tidy up

♦ **staubsaugen** (sep.) to vacuum, to hoover (lit. dust sucking)
♦ **der Termin** appointment, engagement
♦ **die Ausstellung** exhibition

♦ **normalerweise steh' ich so um neun auf** I usually get up at about nine; **aufstehen** (sep.) to get up. Biba uses quite a few separable words: **weiterschreiben: nachmittags schreibe ich dann weiter** in the afternoon I go on writing; **nachdenken: ich denke nach, was ich als nächstes schreiben werde** I think about what I'm going to write next.

♦ **der Wecker klingelt schon eine halbe Stunde vorher** the alarm rings half an hour before.

danach setz' ich mich an die Arbeit after that I sit down to work.

und wenn mir nichts mehr einfällt ... and if I can't think of anything, if I don't have any ideas; **einfallen** (sep.) to think of something: **mir fällt heute überhaupt nichts ein** I can't think of anything at all today. Note that the separable word does not split in clauses after **daß**, **weil**, **wenn** (see above).

entweder ... oder ... either ... or ...: **entweder kommst du jetzt, oder ich gehe alleine** either you're coming now or I'll go by myself.

Übungen

4 Bibas Tagesablauf. What does Biba do? Write the missing words in the squares. The letters in the first column will give you a new word – ideally, the meat you buy should always be like that! (Answers p.205)

a. Ich lese die . . .

b. Ich schreibe einen . . .

c. Ich höre . . .

d. Ich habe abends meistens . . .

5 The right combination! Form two compound nouns for each of the three words below – here are the 'second halves' you need: (Answers p.205)

-stück   -mittag   -mann   -arbeit   -gymnastik   -teil

Haus

Früh

Nach

6 Translate the sentences below into German. They'll prepare you for the next speaking exercise. (Answers p.205)

a. The alarm clock rings at seven.

....

b. And I get up at seven thirty.

....

c. I make breakfast and read the paper.

....

d. After breakfast I do the housework – washing, hoovering, tidying up.

....

e. In the afternoon I go to the library.

....

f. In the evening I go to the cinema/movies or the theatre.

....

7 Your turn to speak. Have a conversation with Klaus, who will ask you about your daily routine. Your answers will be very similar to the phrases you've translated in Exercise 6.

Dialog 3: Feierabend

Horst Ich komm' so gegen sechs Uhr abends nach Hause. Dann setz' ich mich erst mal in den Sessel, leg' die Beine hoch, trink' ein Bier, les' die Zeitung, will mich entspannen – so gut das eben geht, wenn man Kinder hat.
Dann helf' ich meiner Frau beim Kochen – nicht immer! Manchmal helfen ihr auch schon die Kinder.
Am Wochenende koch' ich auch mal selbst. Das mach' ich recht gerne, zur Abwechslung. Wir reden über alles Mögliche: die Kinder, die Nachbarn, Ärger bei der Arbeit, Ärger in der Schule...

Heide Und nach dem Essen? Erst waschen wir mit den Kindern das Geschirr ab, und dann gibt's Fernsehen. Manchmal spielen wir auch Karten oder Halma, oder 'Mensch ärgere dich nicht' – nicht so oft, weil ich mich dann immer schrecklich aufrege. Das hängt sehr vom Fernsehprogramm ab, was wir machen. Natürlich gibt's auch Streit über das Programm. Ich interessiere mich mehr für Politik, mein Mann dagegen für Sport. Und die Kinder wiederum sehen lieber Unterhaltungsfilme oder eine Musikshow.

▸ **der Feierabend** time after work
der Sessel armchair
▸ **zur Abwechslung** for a change
▸ **der Ärger** trouble

▸ **der Streit** quarrel, argument
wiederum on the other hand
der Unterhaltungsfilm light feature film

(ich) leg' die Beine hoch (I) put my feet up (lit. my legs, or rather *the* legs, you don't have to say 'my' as long as it's clear whose legs you're talking about).

▸ **(ich) will mich entspannen** (I) want to relax; **sich entspannen** to relax, **die Entspannung** relaxation.

so gut das eben geht as much as possible (i.e. Horst tries to relax as much as he can with his children around).

▸ **wir waschen das Geschirr ab** we wash the dishes; **abwaschen** (sep.) to wash the dishes: **du könntest auch mal abwaschen!** you could do the dishes for once!

'Mensch ärgere dich nicht' ludo/parchisi (lit. don't get angry).

weil ich mich dann immer schrecklich aufrege as I always get terribly worked up; **sich aufregen** (sep.) to get excited, worked up: **reg' dich nicht auf!** relax! calm down!

das hängt vom Fernsehprogramm ab that depends on the television programme; similar: **das hängt vom Wetter ab** that depends on the weather.

Übungen

8 Wer sagt was? Have a look at this pictorial account of Horst's and Heide's **Feierabend**, then complete the captions, then write the correct caption under each picture. Also write **Horst** or **Heide** under each picture, depending on who said what in the dialogue. (Answers p.205)

Ich .... ein Bier

Wir .... Karten

Ich .... mich in den Sessel

Wir .... das Geschirr ab

Ich .... meiner Frau beim Kochen

Ich .... mich immer schrecklich ....

Es .... Streit übers Programm

Ich .... die Beine hoch

a. ....

b. ....

c. ....

d. ....

e. ....

f. ....

g. ....

h. ....

9 On the cassette it's your turn to talk about your **Feierabend**. Andrew will prompt you. Klaus will ask the questions.

Dialog 4: .. und abends Schule

Ingrid So abends nach der Arbeit, da geht meine Arbeit eigentlich erst richtig los. Ich besuch nämlich seit einiger Zeit das Abendgymnasium und will in eineinhalb Jahren Abitur machen. Es fing eigentlich damit an, daß ich früher zur Volkshochschule ging und mich schon immer für Sprachen interessiert habe – so Englisch und Französisch. Englisch kann ich ein bißchen von der Schule her, aber nicht viel.

Was mir noch Schwierigkeiten macht, ist selber sprechen, das ist am schwierigsten, und ich versuch' so zu üben, indem ich Radio hör' in meiner Freizeit. Ich hör' da auch ausländische Sender: BBC London, oder Radio France oder Radio Luxemburg – und das macht Spaß, wenn man dann anfängt, was zu verstehen. Und so nebenbei üb' ich dann auch in der Schule, im Sprachlabor, und demnächst will ich mal in Urlaub fahren: zwei Wochen nach Frankreich und zwei Wochen nach England.

losgehen (sep.) to start
die Schwierigkeit difficulty
schwierig difficult

nebenbei on the side, besides
das Sprachlabor language laboratory
demnächst in the near future

♦ **ich besuche nämlich seit einiger Zeit das Abendgymnasium** I've been going to evening college for some time, you know; **nämlich** (lit. actually, namely) is often translated by 'you know': **ich habe kein Geld – ich bin nämlich arbeitslos** I haven't got any money – I'm out of work, you know.

es fing eigentlich damit an ... it actually started with ...
anfangen (sep.) to start

♦ **... daß ich früher zur Volkshochschule ging** that I went to the adult education centre some time ago. **Die Volkshochschule** is an institution found in virtually every German town. **Volkshochschulen** (lit. people's high schools) offer a wide variety of evening classes and courses.

♦ **daß ... ich mich schon immer für Sprachen interessiert habe** that ... I've always been interested in languages.

... und ich versuch' so zu üben and I try to practise;
♦ **üben** to practise, see below: **nebenbei üb' ich dann auch in der Schule** and besides I practise at school.

ausländische Sender foreign broadcasting stations.

Übungen

10 Answer the following questions: (Answers p.205)

a. When does Ingrid's real work begin?

....

b. When does she want to take her university entrance exam?

....

c. Which languages has Ingrid always been interested in?

....

d. What does she find most difficult?

....

e. How does she try to practise?

....

f. When does she start enjoying her studies?

....

g. How will she spend her next vacation?

....

11 True or False? **Richtig oder Falsch?** (Answers p.205)

a. Ingrid will bald das Abendgymnasium besuchen R F

b. Sie hat sich schon immer für Sprachen interessiert R F

c. Sie ging früher zur Volkshochschule R F

d. Sie hat Englisch nicht in der Schule gelernt R F

e. Sie hört auch ausländische Sender R F

 12 Turn to the tape where you will be asked about your own language learning experience. Andrew will prompt you.

Volkshochschule Heidelberg

Poststraße 15 · Telefon 06221/21882

Berufliche Weiterbildung in der Volkshochschule — der solide Weg zur Arbeitsplatzsicherung und zum Berufserfolg

Wörter und Wendungen

Morgens

der Tagesablauf
der Hausmann/die Hausfrau
Der Wecker klingelt
Ich stehe auf
Wir frühstücken (gemeinsam)
Ich lese Zeitung
Ich höre Radio
Ich mache Frühgymnastik

In the morning

daily routine
house husband/housewife
The alarm rings
I get up
We have breakfast (together)
I read the paper
I listen to the radio
I do my morning exercises

Mittags

Ich mache die Hausarbeit:
    staubsaugen, aufräumen,
        waschen, kochen
als nächstes ...
schnell ...
meistens ...
manchmal ...

At noon

I do the housework:
    hoovering, tidying up, washing,
        cooking
next
quickl(ly)
mostly
sometimes

Nachmittags

Ich ...
    gehe spazieren
    gehe in die Bibliothek/eine
        Ausstellung
    habe Termine

In the afternoon

I ...
    go for a walk
    go to the library/to an exhibition

    have appointments

Abends

der Feierabend
gegen Abend
nach dem Abendessen
Ich ...
    lege die Beine hoch
    entspanne mich
Wir waschen das Geschirr ab
Dann gibt's Fernsehen
Wir spielen Karten
Es gibt Streit
Ärger bei der Arbeit/in der
    Schule

In the evening

time after work (in the evening)
towards evening
after dinner, supper
I ...
    put my feet up
    relax
We wash the dishes
Then we watch TV
We play cards
We have an argument
trouble at work/school

Grammatik

Reflexive verbs

We have reflexive verbs in English, e.g. I wash *myself*. These verbs are also reflexive in German, e.g. **ich wasche <u>mich</u>**.
Here are all the forms of **sich waschen** (to wash oneself) as an example:

ich wasche <u>mich</u>	I'm washing myself
du wäschst <u>dich</u>	you're washing yourself
er wäscht <u>sich</u>	he is washing himself
sie wäscht <u>sich</u>	she is washing herself
es wäscht <u>sich</u>	it is washing itself
wir waschen <u>uns</u>	we are washing ourselves
ihr wascht <u>euch</u>	you're washing yourselves
sie waschen <u>sich</u>	they are washing themselves
Sie waschen <u>sich</u>	you're washing yourself

There are, however, quite a lot of reflexive verbs in German whereas in English the verb often stands alone without an extra pronoun, e.g.
ich interessiere <u>mich</u> für Sprachen – I'm interested in languages, **ich setze <u>mich</u>** – I'm sitting down, **abends entspanne ich <u>mich</u>** – in the evening I relax.

13a. Follow the above example and write out all the forms for **sich setzen** (to sit down) and **sich ärgern** (to be annoyed). (Answers p.205)

....

....

....

....

Some other common reflexive verbs are:

sich erinnern	to remember
sich beeilen	to hurry
sich irren	to be mistaken
sich ausruhen	to rest
sich amüsieren	to enjoy oneself

13b. Try this exercise by translating the English phrases using German reflexive verbs. (Answers p.205)

a. He is mistaken.

....

b. Yes, I remember.

....

c. I relax in the evening.

....

d. I'm enjoying myself.

....

In all the examples mentioned so far, the reflexive pronouns were in the accusative case: **mich**, **dich**, etc. There are, however, some reflexive verbs with pronouns in the dative, but most forms stay the same, apart from **mich** and **dich** which become **mir** and **dir** in the dative:

ich kaufe <u>mir</u> ein Buch	I buy myself a book
du kaufst <u>dir</u> ein Buch	you buy yourself a book
er kauft <u>sich</u> ein Buch	he buys himself a book
sie kauft <u>sich</u> ein Buch	she buys herself a book
wir kaufen <u>uns</u> ein Buch	we buy ourselves a book
ihr kauft <u>euch</u> ein Buch	you buy yourselves a book
sie kaufen <u>sich</u> ein Buch	they buy themselves a book.

Some common reflexive verbs with a dative pronoun are:

sich (etwas) überlegen:	to think about something:
Ich überlege es <u>mir</u> mal.	I'll think about it.
sich (etwas) ansehen:	to have a look at something:
Willst du <u>dir</u> die Kirche ansehen?	Do you want to have a look at the church?
sich (etwas) vorstellen:	to imagine something:
Das kann ich <u>mir</u> nicht vorstellen.	I can't imagine that.

14 Fill in the right pronouns. (Answers p.205)

dir   mir   sich

a. Wie stellen Sie .... Ihren Traumurlaub vor?

b. Wann hast du .... den Mantel gekauft?

c. Ich habe es .... genau überlegt.

d. Du siehst .... immer nur schlechte Filme an.

e. Das kann ich .... gut vorstellen!

Übungen: Lesen

15 Ändern Sie Ihren Tagesablauf – change your daily grind! At least that's what BRIGITTE magazine suggests by saying: **Stellen Sie einmal alles auf den Kopf!** – Turn everything upside down for a change! Have a look at their suggestions, then answer the questions below. (Answers p.205)

> Jeder Tag ist wie der andere? Wenn das für Sie zu langweilig wird, ändern Sie doch einfach mal den Alltagstrott – hier sind ein paar Tips . . .
>
> - Frühstück: Butter, Brötchen, Marmelade schon seit Jahren? Probieren Sie doch mal Obst, Quark, Müsli und Schwarzbrot. Vielleicht fühlen Sie sich viel wohler dabei. Und wie wär's mit klassischer Musik zum Frühstück? Mozart macht munter . . .
>
> - Brauchen Sie ein neues Kleid oder eine neue Hose? Machen Sie einmal ein Experiment: probieren Sie genau das an, was Sie nie kaufen würden, weil Sie denken, es steht Ihnen nicht. Sie werden sich wundern . . .
>
> - Viele Wege führen ins Büro. Entdecken Sie einen neuen Weg – auch wenn es ein Umweg ist. Das ist gut gegen den morgendlichen Routine-Trott . . .
>
> - Machen Sie sich frei von freiwilliger Routine. Zum Beispiel Punkt 12 Uhr essen in der Kantine. Gehen Sie um 1.30 Uhr – und Sie sehen andere Gesichter . . .
>
> - Legen Sie den Arbeitsmenschen ab, wenn Sie abends nach Hause kommen: unter die Dusche gehen, mit Eau de Toilette abreiben von Kopf bis Fuß – und in bequeme Kleidung schlüpfen . . .
>
> - Wie lange haben Sie schon die gleiche Frisur? Probieren Sie Locken! Schneiden Sie den Pony ab – tragen Sie Punk! Haare wachsen wieder . . .

Vocabulary:

der Alltagstrott daily grind	**legen Sie . . . ab** take . . . off
wohler better	**abreiben** (sep.) to rub down
munter wide awake	**bequem** comfortable
es steht Ihnen it becomes you	**schlüpfen** to slip (into s.th.)
sich wundern to be amazed	**die Frisur** hairdo
der Umweg diversion, detour	**die Locke** curl
morgendlich every morning	**der Pony** fringe
freiwillig voluntary	**wachsen** to grow

a. What is BRIGITTE's advice on your 'new' breakfast?

b. What 'experiment' do they suggest when buying new clothes?

c. Going to the office – what could you change about that?

d. Lunch in the canteen at 12 – what's the advantage of going later?

e. How could you start your **Feierabend**?

f. And what could you do with your hair?

16 Ärgerlich, nicht? Aggravating – isn't it? Another item from BRIGITTE – they've done a survey on things people find most annoying in everyday life. Below you'll see some of the common pitfalls illustrated. Study the captions, then try to think of a snappy English caption for each 'troublespot'. (Suggested answers p.205)

Viel Verpackung, wenig drin

a. ....

....

Knöpfe an neuen Hemden und Blusen, die sofort abgehen

b. ....

....

Slalomlaufen zwischen Hundehaufen

c. ....

....

Schmutzige Toiletten, die auch noch Eintritt kosten

d. ....

....

Preisschilder, die nie abgehen

e. ....

....

FAHRzeuge, die auf GEHwegen stehen

f. ....

....

Vocabulary:
die Verpackung packaging, wrapping **der Hundehaufen** dog dirt
wenig drin little contents **das Preisschild** price tag
abgehen (sep.) to come off **der Gehweg** pavement, sidewalk

Übungen: Radio

17 Gleichberechtigung? Listen to the first radio extract, then go over it again slowly and use your pause button as often as you wish while filling in the missing words in the printed part below. (Complete transcript on p.213)

Vocabulary:

die Gleichberechtigung equality
Radiotreff am Nachmittag name of a programme on SWF
das Thema des Tages the topic of the day
amtlich official
die Studie study
im Auftrag commissioned
das Sozialministerium ministry of social affairs
an den Tag ... gebracht brought ... to light

mitgezählt included
das Rollenklischee role cliché
drin deeply ingrained
die Frau Gemahlin/der Herr Gemahl (iron.) the dear spouse
legt mal gnädig Hand an ... lowers himself to help with ...
das Gerät appliance
wuseln (dial.) to busy onself
putzen to clean

Radiotreff am Nachmittag: das Thema des Tages.

Und jetzt haben wir's auch noch amtlich. Eine Studie ....

.... im Auftrag des baden-

württembergischen Sozialministeriums hat es an den Tag

gebracht: Nur acht Prozent ....

sind bereit, sich mit ihren Frauen ....

.... Und dabei sind

noch die Familien mitgezählt, in denen die Frau ....

.... Wie ist es, meine

Herren: ....

Sie nicht, oder .... ?

Ist das alte Rollenklischee noch so drin: Frau Gemahlin ....

.... und wuselt, und der Herr

Gemahl legt mal gnädig Hand ....

.... , zum Beispiel. Das ist nämlich des

.... liebstes Gerät. Geschirrspülen

geht auch noch, aber .... , nee!

---

18 To find out what's in the stars, listen to the horoscope next on the cassette, then answer the questions. (Answers p.205)

Vocabulary:
Widder Aries
die Devise motto
auf Liebe eingestellt ready for love
daran halten Sie sich you stick to that
Waage Libra
fremd gehen to stray, to have a fling
die Hausmannskost home made food
verbrennen to burn
Wassermann Aquarius
unerfüllbare Wünsche wishes that cannot be fulfilled

a. Widder

What's the most important word for an Aries to observe the following day? ....

b. Waage

What will happen if the Libra man/woman feels like having a fling? ....

c. Skorpion

And what should a Scorpio be aware of? ....

....

d. Wassermann

What advice is given to Aquarians? ....

....

Übungen: Sprechen Sie selbst

19 What's your own daily routine like? Describe your day and your **Feierabend** as precisely as possible, then listen to Corinna for comparison.

20 Are you interested in any other languages apart from German? Talk freely about all the languages you speak or have tried to learn, where you learned them, for how long, etc. On the cassette Klaus gives a sample version.

11 Pro und Contra

You will learn

- to talk about schools and education
- to compare country and city life
- to discuss controversial issues

... and you'll begin to understand radio news in German

Study guide

		Seite
	Dialog 1 + Übungen	**168**
	Dialog 2 + Übungen	**170**
	Dialog 3 + Übungen	**172**
	Dialog 4 + Übungen	**174**
	Wörter und Wendungen	**176**
	Grammatik	**177**
	Lesen	**179**
	Radio	**181**
	Sprechen Sie selbst	**182**

Dialog 1: Die Nähe zur Natur

Silke Ich wohne jetzt fünf Jahre auf dem Land, und es hat mir eigentlich sehr gut gefallen, so die Nähe zur Natur – so Berge und Wälder ... Und so mehr Kontakt zu den Leuten zu haben, auch zum Kaufmann. Und irgendwie ist alles viel persönlicher da, kleiner und überschaubarer.
Nachteile, die sich auf die Dauer sehr stark ausgewirkt haben, sind die weite Entfernung zur Stadt – ich hab' kein Auto, muß immer trampen, und ich kriege wenig Besuch, weil wenige meiner Freunde ein Auto haben.
Aus dem Grunde zieh' ich jetzt in die Stadt, um mehr Kontakt zu haben zu Freunden, um auch mehr ins Kino gehen zu können, – eh – um mehr unternehmen zu können.

- **die Nähe** proximity
- **die Natur** nature
  der Kaufmann shopkeeper
  trampen to hitchhike

- **ich wohne jetzt fünf Jahre auf dem Land** I've been living in the country for five years now (lit. I live in the country five years now); in German you can use the present tense for something that started in the past and is continuing into the present: **ich bin schon zehn Jahre in England** I've been in England for ten years, see **Grammatik** for more details.

  Berge und Wälder mountains and woods; **der Berg** mountain, **der Wald** forest.

- **und irgendwie ist alles viel persönlicher da** and somehow everything there is much more personal.

- **kleiner und überschaubarer** smaller and more manageable.

  Nachteile, die sich auf die Dauer sehr stark ausgewirkt haben disadvantages which mattered a lot in the long run; **auswirken** (sep.) to matter, to have an effect on s.th.: **das hat sich negativ ausgewirkt** that had a negative effect.

  die weite Entfernung zur Stadt the considerable distance to the city; **entfernt** distant, far: **es ist nicht weit entfernt** it's not very far.

  ich kriege wenig Besuch I don't have many visitors (lit. I get few visits); **der Besucher/die Besucherin** visitor.

- **aus dem Grunde ziehe ich jetzt in die Stadt** for that reason I'm going to move to the city; the present tense can also be used to express future intentions, e.g. **ich fahre morgen in Urlaub** I'll be going on holiday tomorrow.

Übungen

1 Vorteil oder Nachteil? What are – according to Silke – the advantages and disadvantages of living in the country? Complete the list below in German. (Answers p.205)

Vorteil	Nachteil
Nähe zur Natur	

2 Find the opposite of the words in italics. (Answers p.205/206)

Example: der Bahnhof ist *weit entfernt* → Der Bahnhof ist *sehr nahe*

a. Ich möchte *weniger* Kontakt zu den Leuten.

....

b. Das Leben auf dem Land hat mir *nicht gut* gefallen.

....

c. Dieser Nachteil hat sich auf die Dauer *kaum* ausgewirkt.

....

d. Ich bekomme *wenig* Besuch auf dem Lande.

....

e. Das Leben auf dem Lande ist sehr *unpersönlich*.

....

f. Viele meiner Freunde haben *ein* Auto.

....

3 Your turn to speak. Turn to the cassette, where Corinna will ask you a few questions on urban living. Andrew will prompt you as usual.

Dialog 2: Nachmittags frei

Biba	Wieviel Kinder haben Sie?
Heide	Wir haben zwei Kinder – Niels und Claudia. Niels ist sieben Jahre alt. Er ist jetzt in der ersten Klasse der Grundschule. Davor war er drei Jahre im Kindergarten, und als er ganz klein war und ich noch arbeiten mußte, eine Zeitlang in der Kinderkrippe.
Biba	Und Claudia?
Heide	Claudia ist zwölf. Sie ist seit zwei Jahren auf dem Gymnasium. Sie will auf jeden Fall die Mittlere Reife machen. Also noch vier Jahre Gymnasium, und dann vielleicht auch das Abitur, das wären noch weitere drei Jahre.
Biba	Wie lange dauert eigentlich der Unterricht an der Schule?
Heide	Normal sechs Stunden. Von acht Uhr bis 13 Uhr mittags. Nachmittags ist frei, das heißt, die Kinder haben natürlich Hausaufgaben.
Biba	Ach ja – und was ist, wenn die Kinder später mal beide studieren wollen? Wird das nicht sehr teuer?
Heide	Studieren selbst kostet gar nicht so viel – aber das Leben natürlich ist teuer. Essen, Miete, Bücher ... Man kann von der Regierung ein Stipendium bekommen, das muß man aber später zum Teil zurückzahlen.

♦ **die Kinderkrippe** crèche, day-care centre
♦ **die Hausaufgaben** (pl.) homework
♦ **die Regierung** government

♦ **das Stipendium** scholarship
zurückzahlen (sep.) to pay back
zum Teil partly

♦ **er ist in der ersten Klasse** he is in his first year/grade.

♦ **die Grundschule** primary school, elementary school. The West German school system underwent several reforms recently with certain variations in the various federal states. Basically a child enters primary school at the age of six or seven. After four to six years the academically inclined can go to a **Gymnasium** (grammar school, high school) where they can take the **Mittlere Reife** (school diploma, O-levels) at the age of 16, or the **Abitur** (university entrance exam, A-levels) at the age of 19.

♦ **das wären noch weitere drei Jahre** that would be three more years.

♦ **wie lange dauert eigentlich der Unterricht?** how long do classes last? **Unterrichten** (to teach) is *not* separable: **er unterrichtet Deutsch** he teaches German. **Sechs Stunden** (six hours) here mean six (school) periods of approx. 40 minutes each.

♦ **was ist, wenn die Kinder später mal beide studieren wollen?** what's going to happen if both children will want to go to the unversity later on? **studieren** can mean: to study, to go to university, to read/study a subject (at university): **er studiert den Fall** he studies the case, **sie möchte studieren** she would like to go to university, **er studiert Mathematik** he studies maths.

Übungen

4 Take notes on what you've just heard about Heide's two children in Dialogue 2. (Answers p.206)

	a. Alter	b. Schule	c. seit wann?	d. Pläne
Niels				
Claudia				

5 Fill in the blanks! (Answers p.206)

a. Der Unterricht dauert normalerweise .... Stunden.

b. Nachmittags ist ....

c. Aber die Kinder haben natürlich nachmittags ....

d. .... selbst kostet nicht so viel, aber das

.... ist teuer.

e. Man kann von der .... ein ....

.... bekommen.

6 Welche Schule? Find the right 'school' for the children in the drawings. (Answers p.206)

Grundschule   Kindergarten   Kinderkrippe   Gymnasium

a ....   b. ....   c. ....   d. ....

 7 On the cassette Klaus will ask you a few questions about your children's education. Andrew will prompt you.

Dialog 3: Warum 'Bundesrepublik'?

Biba Was sind die wichtigsten Parteien in der Bundesrepublik?
Ingrid Da sind einmal die Christdemokraten – die CDU/CSU –, eher
rechtskonservative Parteien; die Liberalen – die FDP –, klein, aber
wichtig als Koalitionspartner. Die Sozialdemokraten – die SPD –,
eine eher Mitte-Links-Partei; die Grünen neuerdings, eine auf
Umweltschutz orientierte Partei.
Biba Und wie oft wird in der Bundesrepublik gewählt?
Ingrid Normalerweise alle vier Jahre, manchmal auch früher.
Biba Welche Rolle hat eigentlich der Bundeskanzler?
Ingrid Er steht an der Spitze der Regierung und bildet das Kabinett.
Biba Und wie wichtig ist der Präsident?
Ingrid Er ist relativ unwichtig und hat vor allem repräsentative
Funktionen.
Biba Warum heißt es eigentlich 'Bundesrepublik'?
Ingrid Die Bundesrepublik hat ja eine föderative Struktur. Sie besteht aus
zehn Bundesländern, zum Beispiel Bayern, Hessen ... Diese Länder
haben ihre eigene Hauptstadt und bilden ihre eigene Regierung.
Ihre Hauptaufgaben liegen vor allem im kulturellen Bereich, in der
Erziehung ... Aber die wichtigsten politischen Fragen entscheidet
die Bundesregierung in Bonn.

- **die Partei** (political) party
- **der Bundeskanzler** Federal
  Chancellor
  neuerdings recently

- **der (Bundes-)Präsident** (Federal)
  President
- **föderativ** federal
- **die Erziehung** education

- **die Christ-Demokraten** the Christian Democrats. **CDU** stands for
  Christlich-**D**emokratische **U**nion, CSU for **C**hristlich-**S**oziale **U**nion.
  The **CSU** is the Bavarian sister party of the **CDU**.

- **die Liberalen** the liberals. The liberal party **FDP** (**F**reie **D**emokratische
  Partei is a small but important party because of its role as a possible
  coalition partner with either one or the other of the two big parties.

- **die Sozialdemokraten** the Social Democrats. **SPD** stands for **S**ozial-
  Demokratische **P**artei **D**eutschlands. Two of its most prominent
  members are Willy Brandt and Helmut Schmidt, both Federal Chancellors
  when the **SPD** was in power.

- **die Grünen** the Greens. A small but growing ecology party which emerged
  in recent years and has now some representatives in the
- **Bundestag** (Federal Parliament).

- **eine auf Umweltschutz orientierte Partei** a party with an
  environmental policy (lit. a party orientated towards the protection of the
  environment); **die Umwelt** environment, **der Schutz** protection.

  wie oft wird ... gewählt? how often are elections? **es wird gewählt** (lit.
  it is elected) is a passive construction; similar: **es wird gespielt** they play
  (lit. it is played), **es wird getanzt** there is dancing (lit. it is danced). More
  about the passive in the **Grammatik** section.

  er steht an der Spitze der Regierung he is the head of the government
  (lit. stands at the top of the government).

  er bildet das Kabinett he forms the cabinet.

- **sie besteht aus zehn Bundesländern** it consists of ten federal states.

  ihre Hauptaufgaben liegen im kulturellen Bereich their main tasks lie
  in the cultural sector.

Übungen

8 Pick the right words from the box and fill in the blanks. (Answers p.206)

a. .... ist konservativ.

b. .... ist liberal.

c. .... ist Mitte-links.

d. .... wollen eine schönere Umwelt.

e. .... ist der Chef der Regierung.

f. .... hat repräsentative Aufgaben.

g. .... hat eine föderative Struktur.

h. .... haben kulturelle Aufgaben.

i. .... entscheidet die Politik.

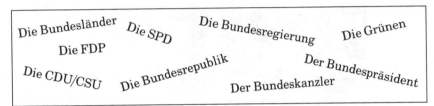

Die Bundesländer   Die SPD   Die Bundesregierung   Die Grünen

Die FDP

Die CDU/CSU   Die Bundesrepublik   Der Bundespräsident

Der Bundeskanzler

9 Here is a map of the Federal Republic with ten of its **Bundesländer**. Which capital belongs to which state? Pick the correct number from the map. (Answers on p.206)

Example: **Wiesbaden** ....

Hamburg ...1... **Mainz** ....

Bremen ....2... **Saarbrücken** ....

Kiel .... **Stuttgart** ....

Hannover .... **München** ....

Düsseldorf ....

10 Listen to the cassette, where Klaus will ask you a few questions about the Federal Republic. Andrew will prompt you.

Dialog 4: Pro und Contra

Max Also ich hab die Grünen gewählt, weil ich das Programm der Grünen besser finde – vor allem in Bezug auf die Verteidigung und in Bezug auf den Umweltschutz. Ich bin gegen Atomkraftwerke und gegen Atombewaffnung.

Karl Ich habe die CDU gewählt – auch wegen der Verteidigungspolitik. Die Bundesrepublik muß militärisch stark sein und genügend Waffen haben.

Max Ich finde, das Geld kann besser verwendet werden.

Karl Nein, ich bin der Auffassung, unsere Freiheit darf auch das nötige Geld kosten.

Max Ich finde, das Geld ist besser zu verwenden für den Hunger in der Welt, für den Umweltschutz und gegen die Arbeitslosigkeit. Das Wettrüsten ist einfach zu gefährlich, das ist der helle Wahnsinn.

»Brot für die Welt«
Postfach 476, 7000 Stuttgart 1

Brot für die Welt –
eine Organisation, die gegen
den Hunger kämpft

- **das Atomkraftwerk** nuclear power station
- **die Atombewaffnung** nuclear armament

- **die Freiheit** freedom
- **das Wettrüsten** arms race **gefährlich** dangerous

- **in Bezug auf die Verteidigung/auf den Umweltschutz** as regards defence and conservation.

- **ich bin gegen ...** I'm against ...; **ich bin für ...** I'm for ...

  die Bundesrepublik muß militärisch stark sein the Federal Republic must have a strong military presence.

  das Geld kann besser verwendet werden the money can be better spent. Here you have another sentence in the passive, see **Grammatik**.

  ich bin der Auffassung I think (lit. I am of the opinion), e.g. **ich bin anderer Auffassung** I have a different opinion.

  der helle Wahnsinn sheer insanity.

Übungen

11 Try to re-write the phrases starting with **wegen** (because of). Use **weil** (because) instead. (Answers p.206)

> *Example:* Ich habe CDU gewählt – **wegen** *der starken Verteidigungspolitik der CDU.*
> Ich habe *CDU gewählt,* **weil** *ich für die starke Verteidigungspolitik der CDU bin.*

a. Ich habe die Grünen gewählt – *wegen des Umweltprogramms der Grünen.*

....

b. Ich habe die FDP gewählt – *wegen ihrer liberalen Wirtschaftspolitik.*

....

c. Ich habe die SPD gewählt – *wegen ihrer sozialen Reformpläne.*

....

12a. Find the German equivalent for the following expressions: (Answers p.206)

a. atomic power station

					1						

b. arms race

		2							

c. conservation

		3							

d. defence policy

					4															

The letters 1–4 will give you a word much used (and abused) by politicians.

1	2	3	4

12b. **Wer sagt was? Karl oder Max?** Have a look at the statements below and decide whose opinions they are expressing. Write either **Max** or **Karl** in the boxes. (Answers p.206)

a. Die Grünen haben ein besseres Programm.

b. Ich finde die CDU gut.

c. Ich bin gegen atomare Waffen.

d. Es ist absolut notwendig, daß wir militärisch stark sind.

e. Es ist viel wichtiger, das Geld für Umweltschutz auszugeben.

f. Wir müssen bereit sein, für unsere Freiheit zu zahlen.

g. Das Wettrüsten ist wahnsinnig und gefährlich.

h. Wir sollten mehr gegen den Hunger in der Welt tun.

13 Your turn to speak. Try to express your opinions in a political argument. Andrew will prompt you. Here are a few phrases you'll need:

Ich bin gegen   Ich bin für   Ich finde ...

Wörter und Wendungen

Lifestyle/education

Ich wohne auf dem Lande/in der Stadt	I live in the country/in the city
Ich ziehe aufs Land/in die Stadt	I'm moving to the country/the city
Auf dem Land hat man ...	In the country you are ...
die Nähe zur Natur	close to nature
Kontakt zu Leuten	in contact with people
Auf dem Land ist alles ...	In the country everything is ...
persönlicher	more personal
überschaubarer	more manageable
In der Stadt kann man mehr unternehmen	In the city you can do more things
die Erziehung	education
die Kinderkrippe	crèche/day-care centre
der Kindergarten	kindergarten
die Grundschule	primary school, elementary school
das Gymnasium	grammar school, high school
die Gesamtschule	comprehensive school
die Universität	university
das Abitur	University entrance exam
das Stipendium	scholarship
Ich bin in der ersten/achten Klasse	I'm in the first/eighth year/grade
Ich möchte studieren	I would like to go to the university
der Unterricht	classes

Parties and politics

die Partei	(political) party
Ich wähle die ...	I vote for ...
CDU	the Christian Democrats
SPD	the Social Democrats
FDP	the Liberals
die Grünen	the Greens
Ich bin für/gegen ...	I am for/against ...
Umweltschutz	conservation
Atomkraftwerke	nuclear power stations
Atomwaffen	nuclear weapons
die Verteidigung	defence
das Wettrüsten	the arms race
die Bundesrepublik	Federal Republic
die Bundesregierung	Federal Government
der Bundestag	Federal Parliament
der Bundeskanzler	Federal Chancellor
der Bundespräsident	Federal President
das Bundesland	Federal State

Grammatik

The present tense

The present tense – **das Präsens** – is a flexible tense and can have different meanings. It is used:

• To describe something that is happening *now*, e.g.

Ich lese ein Buch	I read/am reading a book.
Es regnet draußen	It rains/is raining outside.
Er geht ins Kino	He goes/is going to the cinema/movies.

Whereas in most cases when something is just happening you would use the so-called continuous form in English (I am reading, it is raining, he is going, etc.) there is no such form in German. **Ich lese** means both 'I read' and 'I am reading'.

• To describe something that will happen in the *future*. It is usually obvious from the context when there is a future meaning, e.g.

Morgen fahre ich nach München	Tomorrow I will go to Munich.
Was machst du heute abend?	What are you doing this evening?
Ich gehe ins Theater	I'll be going to the theatre.

Mostly the present tense is used here to describe things that happen in the near future, but in colloquial German the present tense is also used for events which will take place in the distant future, e.g.

In 20 Jahren bin ich 60 Jahre alt.	I'll be 60 years old in 20 years' time.
In 100 Jahren sieht die Welt ganz anders aus.	The world will be quite different in 100 years time.

• To describe something that started in the past and is continuing into the present, e.g.

Ich wohne seit fünf Jahren hier.	I've been living here for five years.
Ich bin seit Weihnachten arbeitslos.	I've been unemployed since Christmas.
Er ist seit 20 Jahren Buchhalter.	He's been an accountant for 20 years.

In English you would use the perfect tense (see Unit 5) in those cases.

14 Translate the following into German: (Answers p.206)

a. He has been living in Ulm since 1955.

....

b. What are you going to do this summer?

....

c. Tomorrow we'll go to a good restaurant.

....

d. He has been president for three years.

....

e. Next week we'll go to the country.

....

f. I'm walking to the bus stop.

....

The passive

The passive is often used when you want to be impersonal about an action, e.g. **Wie wird das gemacht?** (How is it done?) instead of **Wie mache ich das?** (How do I do it?) A way around the passive is the impersonal pronoun **man** (one): **Wie macht man das?** (How does one do it?). You'll probably find it easier to use the construction based on **man**, but you should be able to recognize the passive and know how it is formed.

The passive construction is similar to that of the perfect (see **Grammatik** Unit 5), only instead of **haben** or **sein** you use **werden** plus the past participle of the main verb, e.g. **malen** (to paint):

Ich habe gemalt   I have painted (perfect)
Ich werde gemalt   I am (being) painted (passive)

Here are all the passive forms:

Ich werde gemalt	I am (being) painted
du wirst gemalt	you are (being) painted
er/sie/es wird gemalt	he/she/it is (being) painted
wir werden gemalt	we are (being) painted
ihr werdet gemalt	you are (being) painted
Sie/sie werden gemalt	You/they are (being) painted

The word order in longer sentences is also the same as for the perfect tense. The main verb goes to the end:

Der Präsident wird alle fünf Jahre gewählt.
The president is (being) elected every five years.
Walzer und Tango werden heute nicht mehr so oft getanzt.
The waltz and the tango aren't (being) danced so much today.

If you want to use the past tense of the passive, you take the imperfect of **werden**: **ich wurde gemalt, du wurdest gemalt**, etc.

Note: Do not confuse the passive with the future tense. The future is formed with **werden** plus the *infinitive*, e.g.

Ich werde ein Bild malen.   I will paint a picture.
Ein Schiff wird kommen.   A ship will come.

15 Try to translate into English: (Answers p.206)

a. Das Haus wurde 1948 gebaut. ....

b. Was wird im Kino gespielt? ....

c. Ich weiß nicht, wie das gemacht wird. ....

d. Das wurde mir nie gesagt. ....

e. Im 'Adler' wird getanzt. ....

Übungen: Lesen

16 Here is a short news item from a newspaper. Read it, then decide whether the statements below are true or false – **Richtig oder Falsch**. (Answers p.206)

> In Bonn hat der Bundestagsabgeordnete der Grünen, Vogt, mit einem zeitlich unbefristeten Fasten begonnen. Er schloß sich damit der Gruppe 'Fasten für das Leben' an. Mit dieser Aktion wollen 14 Menschen in den USA, der Bundesrepublik Deutschland, Frankreich und Kanada ein Ende des atomaren Wettrüstens erreichen.

Vocabulary:

der Bundestagsabgeordnete
   Member of Parliament
zeitlich unbefristet unlimited

fasten to fast
er schloß sich ... an he joined
erreichen to achieve

a. Mr Vogt is a member of an ecology party. [F] [R]

b. He decided not to eat at all for an unlimited period. [F] [R]

c. The group he joined is called 'Fasting for Peace'. [F] [R]

d. Only people from European countries joined the group. [F] [R]

e. Their aim is to end the nuclear arms race. [F] [R]

17 Pro und Contra Startbahn West! The extension of Frankfurt airport by building another runway (**Startbahn West**) has been the subject of much controversy in Germany. Here are two letters on that sensitive subject, sent in to a local newspaper. Frau Renner's letter is for, Herr Schranz' letter is against **Startbahn West**. Study the letters, then decide whose opinions the sentences below represent. Write either *Frau Renner* or *Herr Schranz* in the boxes. (Answers p.206)

Frau Renner

Ich bin in Frankfurt geboren und stolz darauf, daß unser Flughafen erweitert wird. Schließlich spielen wir im internationalen Flugverkehr eine führende Rolle, und diese Position wollen wir nicht verlieren. Je größer und moderner unser Flughafen ist, desto besser ist das für uns: für die Stadt Frankfurt und auch für die Bundesrepublik. Dadurch werden alte Arbeitsplätze gesichert und neue Arbeitsplätze geschaffen.

Herr Schranz

Durch den Bau der neuen Startbahn West werden riesige Wälder für immer vernichtet – ein Naturschutzgebiet, das in der BRD einmalig ist. Die Menschen, die in der Nähe des Flughafens wohnen, müssen noch mehr Lärm ertragen – und sie verlieren die Wälder, in denen sie am Wochenende Erholung fanden. Was ist wichtiger: technischer Fortschritt oder Lebensqualität?

Vocabulary:
stolz proud
erweitern to extend
sichern to secure
schaffen to create
durch den Bau by building the . . .
vernichten to destroy
das Naturschutzgebiet nature reserve
einmalig unique
der Lärm noise
ertragen to bear, put up with
die Erholung relaxation, recreation
der Fortschritt progress
die Lebensqualität quality of life

a. Wir brauchen neue und sichere Arbeitsplätze

b. Wir brauchen die Natur

c. Wir müssen uns erholen

d. Wir brauchen mehr Lebensqualität

e. Die Startbahn ist gut für die ganze Bundesrepublik

Übungen: Radio

18 Practise listening to the news – **die Nachrichten**. On the cassette Andrew will guide you step by step through the various items. Listen carefully several times, then finish the transcription below by filling in the blanks. (Answers p.213 in complete transcript.)

Vocabulary:

Tribüne der Zeit name of a news programme
das Mikrofon microphone
Wichtiges important issues
die Genfer Raketengespräche the Geneva arms talks
aufgenommen resumed

der Verhandlungstisch negotiating table
das Waldsterben the dying forests
die Lehrstelle vacancy for a trainee
schwere Kämpfe heavy fighting
der Soldat soldier
gefallen died in action

Achtzehn Uhr. Südwestfunk Baden-Baden. Tribüne ....

.... Am .... Günter Thulen, und für

.... Walter Menk. Von ihm zuerst

....

Genfer .... wieder aufgenommen.

Sowjets und .... zwei Stunden lang am

Verhandlungstisch. .... über das Ausmaß

des .... besorgt. In der

.... fehlen noch ....

.... im Libanon. Drei

.... gefallen.

Übungen: Sprechen Sie selbst

19 Make up two sentences each with **für** and **gegen**, and also use **weil**, e.g.
Ich bin für/gegen Umweltschutz, weil .... **ist.**
You'll hear some sample versions on the cassette.

20 Talk about your education in at least five sentences, e.g. what schools you
attended, did you go to the university, etc. You can listen to Klaus for
comparison.

12 Videos und Heimcomputer

You will learn

- to say what you would do with a windfall
- to assess some new gadgets in your home
- to talk about the pros and cons of modern technology

... and you'll hear some consumer news from the Federal Republic

Study guide

		Seite
	Dialog 1 + Übungen	184
	Dialog 2 + Übungen	186
	Dialog 3 + Übungen	188
	Dialog 4 + Übungen	190
	Wörter und Wendungen	192
	Grammatik	193
	Lesen	195
	Radio	197
	Sprechen Sie selbst	198

Dialog 1: Das einfache Leben

Biba   Was würden Sie machen, wenn Sie zehntausend Mark geschenkt bekämen?

Amin   Ja, zuerst einmal gehe ich davon aus, daß man mit zehntausend Mark wenig machen kann. Gehen wir einfach von hunderttausend Mark aus. Angenommen, ich hätte hunderttausend Mark. Da würde ich mir eine Insel kaufen, im Atlantik, und mal versuchen, ganz einfach zu leben – ohne Elektrizität, Waschmaschine, Radio, Fernseher, elektrischen Herd, Telefon, und was es da so alles gibt...

Biba   Würden Sie nichts vermissen?

Amin   Ja, das würd' ich dann immer noch sehen. Und ich würde mir von den hunderttausend Mark trotz alledem noch so viel übrig lassen, um gelegentlich mal nach Berlin zu fliegen, oder nach New York, um zu sehen, wie die Welt sich inzwischen weiterentwickelt hat. Wissen Sie, ganz zurückziehen will ich mich deswegen trotzdem nicht, aber ausprobieren, das wär' schon gut.

▶ **die Insel** island
    der Atlantik Atlantic Ocean
    trotz alledem despite everything

    gelegentlich occasionally
▶ **ausprobieren** (sep.) to try out

▶ **das einfache Leben** the simple life.

was würden Sie machen, wenn Sie zehntausend Mark geschenkt bekämen? what would you do if you were given ten thousand marks? This sentence is in a mood called the *subjunctive* (**Konjunktiv**); see **Grammatik** for details.

▶ Keep in mind: **was würden Sie machen, wenn ...?** what would you do if ...?

zuerst einmal gehe ich davon aus ... first of all I assume ... **von etwas ausgehen** (sep.) to assume: **davon kann man nicht ausgehen** one can't
▶ assume that; **angenommen** also means 'assumed': **angenommen, ich hätte...** let's assume I had...

▶ **ohne Elektrizität** without electricity; **der elektrische Herd** electric cooker, stove.

▶ **würden Sie nichts vermissen?** wouldn't you miss anything?

ich würde mir ... noch so viel übrig lassen, um ... I would leave sufficient funds to ...

wie die Welt sich inzwischen weiterentwickelt hat what happened to the world in the meantime; **weiterentwickeln** (sep.) lit. to develop further: **er entwickelt sich überhaupt nicht weiter** he doesn't show any signs of further development.

ganz zurückziehen will ich mich deswegen trotzdem nicht I don't want to retire completely despite all that; **sich zurückziehen** (sep.) to retire, to withdraw.

Übungen

1 Sum up Amin's dream of the simple life by filling in the appropriate words from the dialogue. (Answers p.206)

Amin würde gern das einfache Leben ....

Er würde sich eine .... im Atlantik kaufen

und versuchen, ganz .... zu leben, ohne

.... Telefon. Aber er will sich

trotzdem nicht ganz .... Gelegentlich

würde Amin nach Berlin oder New York ....

um zu sehen, was in der .... passiert ist.

2 Below you'll find some phrases from **Dialog 1** translated into English. Underline the equivalent German in the dialogue. (Answers p.206)

a. Assuming I had one hundred thousand marks . . .
b. Would you not miss anything?
c. . . . and try to live a completely simple life.
d. That would be rather good.

3 **Von der Weinflasche bis zum Porsche.** What would you buy if you were given some money? Answer Corinna's questions after Andrew's prompts.

Dialog 2: Neu auf dem Markt

Herr Bauer Das hier ist unsere neueste Küchenmaschine. Sie ist zur Zeit das Spitzenmodell auf dem Markt. Sie ist ein bewährtes Fabrikat. Sie kann nicht nur Teig kneten: Man kann auch mit ihr schnitzeln, das heißt, man kann also Möhren, Kartoffeln reiben ... Man kann entsaften, das heißt, man kann also Beeren oder Äpfel entsaften und sich daraus Getränke machen. Man kann mixen mit Milch und mit Obst ... Zudem kann man noch Fleisch drehen, das heißt, ein Fleischwolf ist mit dabei. Man kann Eis machen mit ihr, man kann Nüsse und Mandeln reiben, alles, was man also für den Hausgebrauch benötigt, ist mit dieser Maschine machbar.

- **die Küchenmaschine** food processor
- **das Spitzenmodell** top-of-the-range-model
  schnitzeln to chop (into small pieces)
  der Fleischwolf mincer
  machbar feasible, possible
  zur Zeit at the moment

  sie ist ein bewährtes Fabrikat it's a reputable make; **bewährt** lit. proven, approved.

- **man kann also Möhren, Kartoffeln reiben ...** so you can grate carrots, potatoes ... **reiben** also means 'to rub': **er reibt sich die Hände** he's rubbing his hands.

  man kann Beeren entsaften you can extract juice from berries; **die Beere** berry.

- **sie kann nicht nur Teig kneten** it's not only able to knead dough.

  zudem kann man noch Fleisch drehen besides you can mince meat; **drehen** also means 'to rotate, to turn'.

  man kann Nüsse, Mandeln reiben ... you can grind nuts, almonds ...

- **was man für den Hausgebrauch benötigt** what you need for everyday use.

Übungen

4 Das Spitzenmodell. Here is a description of the latest food processor in English. Below you'll find the German translation, but with a few extra phrases. Spot those and underline them. (Answers p.206)

> With the new Magomax you can chop fruit or vegetables. You can mix drinks, knead dough and mince meat.

> Mit dem neuen Magomax kann man Obst oder Gemüse schnitzeln, Dosen öffnen, Getränke mixen und Kuchen backen. Man kann auch Teig kneten und Fleisch drehen.

5 Alles ist machbar. But what exactly does the food processor do with nuts and almonds? Or with meat? Pick the correct verb from the box below. (Answers p.206)

a. Nüsse und Mandeln ....

b. Beeren und Äpfel ....

c. Teig ....

d. Kartoffeln und Möhren ....

e. Milch- und Obstgetränke ....

f. Fleisch ....

g. Eis ....

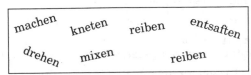

machen   kneten   reiben   entsaften

drehen   mixen   reiben

6 Now there's a chance to practise **Übung 5** again with the cassette. Corinna will give you the first part, e.g. **Nüsse und Mandeln**. You then say **Man kann Nüsse und Mandeln reiben** in the following pause. Klaus will then give you the correct version, and you go on to the next sentence.

Dialog 3: Videos, Videos

Kundin	Guten Tag. Sind Sie Verkäufer hier?
Verkäufer	Ja.
Kundin	Hm – ich hätte Interesse, mir'n Video zu kaufen, und jetzt würde ich mir gerne mal die Geräte hier anschauen.
Verkäufer	Da gibt's verschiedene Geräte. Soll's für Sie selber sein?
Kundin	Hm – ja. Für die Familie.
Verkäufer	Sie suchen speziell für die Kinder solche Geräte?
Kundin	Ja.
Verkäufer	Was wollen die denn speziell aufnehmen?
Kundin	Zum Beispiel Kindersendungen, oder Tierfilme, oder vielleicht auch mal so 'n Spielfilm.
Verkäufer	Ja, da hätten wir ein Gerät wie dieses hier. Das zeig' ich Ihnen mal. Der wird hier von oben geöffnet, da kommt die Kassette rein. Der wäre jetzt ganz gut, weil für die Kinder eigentlich 'ne einfache Programmierung genügt.
Kundin	Was kostet der?
Verkäufer	Der hat jetzt 'nen Preis von 1898. Da ist aber dann alles dabei.
Kundin	Und ... was ist mit diesem Gerät hier?
	Der kann die gleichen Funktionen ... Unterschied ist allerdings der: Er hat also diese einfache Aufnahmetaste nicht. Da wäre also der dann für die Kinder besser.

    der Tierfilm animal film
    die Kindersendung children's programme
  ◆ **die Aufnahmetaste** recording switch

  ◆ **das Videogerät** video recorder, *but* (short) **der Video** video; **das Gerät** set, also appliance, gadget: **das Fernsehgerät** TV set, **das Küchengerät** kitchen appliance.

  ◆ **ich hätte Interesse** I would be interested (lit. I would have interest); **hätte** is a subjunctive form of **haben** (see **Grammatik**).

    was wollen die denn speziell aufnehmen? what especially do they want to record? **aufnehmen** (sep.) to record, to tape; **die Aufnahme** recording.

    der (=der Video) wird hier oben geöffnet this one is opened here at the top.

    das zeig ich Ihnen mal I'll show you.

  ◆ **da kommt die Kassette rein** that's where the cassette goes.

  ◆ **der wäre jetzt ganz gut** this one would be fine; **wäre** is a subjunctive form of **sein** (see **Grammatik**): **es wäre besser, wenn ...** it would be better if ...

    weil ... 'ne einfache Programmierung genügt because a simple setting is adequate.

    (der) Unterschied ist allerdings der ... (the) difference, however, is ...

    der kann die gleichen Funktionen that one can do the same things (lit. can do the same functions); correct would have been: **der *hat* die gleichen Funktionen**.

Übungen

7 Test your vocabulary by filling in this puzzle. The letters marked 1–5 will give you a measuring unit. (Answers p.206)

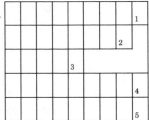

a. Sie können auch einen (*feature film*) aufnehmen.

b. Hier ist die passende (*cassette*).

c. Ich empfehle Ihnen dieses (*set*).

d. Haben Sie (*interest*) an einem Video?

e. Ja, ich bin (*sales assistant*) hier.

8 Der Super-Video. Write a blurb for the super-video by translating the advertisement below into German. (Answers p.206)

THE SUPER VIDEO

FOR YOU -
FOR THE CHILDREN -
FOR THE ENTIRE FAMILY

easy to set
simple recording switch

ideal for childrens'
programmes - films
about animals -
feature films

PRICE: DM 1900
everything included

....

....

....

....

....

....

....

....

....

....

9 Now *you*'re having a look at videos in a shop. Klaus is the sales assistant, Andrew will tell you what to say.

Dialog 4: Technologie – pro und cont

Silke Ich finde, wir haben schon viel zu viele technische Neuerungen. Wir sind viel zu weit und können das gar nicht mehr richtig gebrauchen.

Ingrid Da kann ich nicht so ganz zustimmen. Auf manchen Gebieten, finde ich, könnten wir schon technische Neuerungen gebrauchen, zum Beispiel, was die Energiegewinnung angeht. Wir müßten sparsamer und sinnvoller mit unserer Energiegewinnung umgehen, zum Beispiel Sonnenenergie und so Gebiete weiter erforschen.

Silke Ja, Sonnenenergie ist – da stimme ich dir zu – das ist ein guter Punkt. Aber das ist wieder so eine Spezialistenangelegenheit.

Günter Also, ich hab' mir schon oft Gedanken darüber gemacht, daß besonders unser Transportwesen umstrukturiert werden sollte. Das heißt, daß man mehr Nachdruck auf den öffentlichen Verkehr legen sollte und weniger auf den Verkehr mit Individualfahrzeugen.

◆ **technische Neuerungen** new technology (lit. technical innovations);
◆ **die Technologie** technology.

wir sind viel zu weit we've gone much too far.

◆ **da kann ich nicht so ganz zustimmen** I can't altogether agree with that.

◆ **die Energiegewinnung** production of energy; **gewinnen** to gain.

wir müßten sparsamer und sinnvoller mit unserer Energiegewinnung umgehen we should think of more economical and sensible ways to produce our energy.

◆ **(die) Sonnenenergie und so Gebiete weiter erforschen** to explore solar energy and (other) such areas further.

die Spezialistenangelegenheit matter for the experts; **der Spezialist** expert, specialist.

ich hab' mir schon oft Gedanken darüber gemacht ... I have thought about ...; similar: **mach' dir keine Gedanken** don't think/worry about it.

daß besonders unser Transportwesen umstrukturiert werden sollte that especially our transport system should be re-structured.

... daß man mehr Nachdruck auf den öffentlichen Verkehr legen sollte that one should put more emphasis on public transport.

mit Individualfahrzeugen with privately owned vehicles.

Übungen

10 Here are three statements containing the gist of **Silke's, Ingrid's** and **Günter's** opinions. Who believes what? (Answers p.206)

a. Die moderne Technologie ist schon viel zu weit entwickelt. $\boxed{S}\boxed{I}\boxed{G}$

b. Wir sollten ein neues Transportsystem einführen. $\boxed{S}\boxed{I}\boxed{G}$

c. Wir sind auf einigen Gebieten technologisch noch nicht weit genug. $\boxed{S}\boxed{I}\boxed{G}$

11 Underline the expressions in **Dialog 4** which correspond most closely to the ones below. (Answers p.206)

a. Damit bin ich nicht so ganz einverstanden.

b. Wir müßten unsere Energie effizienter gewinnen.

c. Da bin ich der gleichen Meinung.

d. Ich habe mir schon oft überlegt ...

e. ... daß unser Transportsystem geändert werden müßte.

f. Das wäre eine Sache für die Experten.

Eingesparte Energie kostet nichts und erzeugt auch keine Abgase.

12 In the speaking exercise you'll discuss cable television – **Kabelfernsehen** – with Klaus. Two words you might need are **die Qualität** (quality) and **Unsinn** (nonsense). Andrew will prompt you.

Wörter und Wendungen

Was würden Sie machen, wenn ...?
What would you do if ...?

Ich würde ...	I would ...
mir eine Insel kaufen	buy (myself) an island
das einfache Leben ausprobieren	try the simple life
ohne Elektrizität/Telefon leben	live without electricity/telephone
Angenommen, ich hätte ...	Let's assume I had ...
Das wäre gut/besser	That would be good/better
Würden Sie nichts vermissen?	Wouldn't you miss anything?

Ich hätte Interesse an ...
I would be interested in ...

einem Video(gerät)	a video (recorder)
einem Fernsehgerät	a TV set
einem elektrischen Herd	an electric cooker/stove
einer Küchenmaschine	a food processor
Dies hier ist ...	This (here) is ...
unser Spitzenmodell	our top of the range model
Man kann damit ...	You can ...
Möhren/Kartoffeln reiben	grate carrots and potatoes
Teig kneten	knead dough
Beeren entsaften	extract juice from berries
Hier ist die ...	Here is the ...
Kassette	cassette
Aufnahmetaste	recording switch
aufnehmen	to record

die Technologie
Technology

technische Neuerungen	new technology
technologisch	technological
die Energiegewinnung	production of energy
die Sonnenenergie	solar energy
Wir sind viel zu weit	We've gone much too far
Da kann ich dir nicht zustimmen	I can't agree with you there

Grammatik

The subjunctive

The subjunctive form of the verb gives sentences a certain 'hypothetical' character, i.e. it is used when you want to express what would or could happen if. In German the subjunctive is nearly the same as the imperfect form for verbs, except that you add an **Umlaut** when there is an **a**, **o**, or **u**, and you also add an **e** to the **er/sie/es** forms. For example, the imperfect forms of **bekommen** (to get) are **ich bekam**, **du bekamst**, etc. (I got, you got, etc.). The subjunctive forms follow the pattern below:

wenn ich bekäme	*if* I were to get
du bekämst	you were to get
er/sie/es bekäme	he/she/it were to get
wir bekämen	we were to get
ihr bekämt	you were to get
sie/Sie bekämen	they/you were to get

Wenn wir morgen das Geld bekämen...	If we were to get the money tomorrow...
Es wäre furchtbar, wenn ich Grippe bekäme.	It would be awful if I got the flu.

The most important subjunctive forms (and the ones you are most likely to use) are those of **sein**, **haben** and **können**.

sein (to be)

wenn ich wäre	*if* I were
du wärst	etc.
er/sie/es wäre	
wir wären	
ihr wärt	
sie/Sie wären	

Wenn ich reich wäre ...	If I were rich ...
Das wäre besser.	That would be better.

haben (to have)

wenn ich hätte	*if* I had
du hättest	etc.
er/sie/es hätte	
wir hätten	
ihr hättet	
sie/Sie hätten	

Wenn ich viel Geld hätte ...	If I had a lot of money ...
Hättest du das getan?	Would you have done that?
Ich hätte gerne ein Steak.	I would like (to have) a steak.

können (can)

ich könnte	I could
du könntest	etc.
er/sie/es könnte	
wir könnten	
ihr könntet	
sie/Sie könnten	

Wir könnten morgen kommen.	We could come tomorrow.
Könnte ich das noch ändern?	Could I still change that?

13 Translate into German: (Answers p.206)

a. If I had a car. ....

b. If you (**Sie**) were younger. ....

c. Let's assume I had one million marks. ....

....

d. Could I try this out? ....

e. I could eat something now. ....

With weak verbs (and in fact with most strong verbs apart from the ones above), the subjunctive is rarely used. Instead, you use **würde** plus infinitive:

Ich würde nicht so viel reden. I wouldn't talk so much.
Wenn ich mehr Geld hätte, würde ich nicht so viel arbeiten. If I had more money I wouldn't work so much.
Würden Sie bitte kommen? Would you please come?
Am liebsten würde ich jetzt nach Hause gehen. Most of all I'd like to go home now.

As **würde** is important (the equivalent of the English 'would'), here are all the forms:

ich würde	I would
du würdest	etc.
er/sie/es würde	
wir würden	
ihr würdet	
Sie/sie würden	

14 Translate into German: (Answers p.207)

a. I would drive to Paris. ....

b. I would travel to India. ....

c. Would you (**du**) please open the window? ....

....

d. If we had time, we would read more books. ....

....

e. I would go now if I were you (**Sie**). ....

....

Übungen: Lesen

15 Read this short article which appeared in the **FAZ** (**Frankfurter Allgemeine Zeitung**). The article is about a new invention shortly to be introduced in the Federal Republic. What is it and what does it do? Mark the right boxes below. (Answers p.207)

Eine neue Erfindung

BERLIN, 6. Januar (dpa). Ein Summer am Ohr soll zukünftig Autofahrer am Einschlafen hinter dem Steuer hindern. Das fünfzehn Gramm schwere Gerät, das am Ohr befestigt wird und einen Alarmton sendet, sobald der Autofahrer einzunicken beginnt, wurde am Mittwoch in Berlin vorgestellt. Die Konstrukteure beobachteten bei Untersuchungen, daß Autofahrer, die stark zu ermüden beginnen, ausnahmslos den Kopf nach vorne sinken lassen. Bei einer gewissen Neigung schalte sich der Alarmton ein, hieß es. Das in Frankreich vor vier Jahren erfundene Gerät soll in der Bundesrepublik Ende des Monats auf den Markt kommen.

Vocabulary:
der Summer buzzer
befestigen to fix, to attach
der Alarmton alarm sound
einnicken (sep.) to nod off
der Konstrukteur here: inventor
beobachten to observe
ermüden to tire
ausnahmslos without exception
eine gewisse Neigung a certain angle
sich einschalten (sep.) to trigger off
hieß es it was said

a. What's the new device called?
- [ ] Summer
- [ ] Alarmton
- [ ] Steuer

b. Where do you attach it?
- [ ] behind the wheel
- [ ] under the seat
- [ ] to your ear

c. Who would buy it?
- [ ] anybody
- [ ] motorists
- [ ] computer experts

d. What does it do?
- [ ] it buzzes
- [ ] it whistles
- [ ] it plays music

e. What's its purpose?
- [ ] making your car go faster
- [ ] stopping you from falling asleep
- [ ] keeping you entertained

f. Where was it invented?
- [ ] in West Germany
- [ ] in America
- [ ] in France

16 Video sex and violence. That's the subject of this article. Read it, then answer the questions. (Answers p.207)

Videos: Bonner Kabinett will Reformen

Filme wie 'Messerkiller' oder 'Sex mit Sechs' sollen für Kinder und Jugendliche zukünftig nicht mehr so leicht zugänglich sein. Das Kabinett in Bonn berät heute über das Problem Pornographie und Gewalt auf Videokassetten. Eine Möglichkeit wäre, daß sich die Videobranche selbst kontrolliert, das heißt, Videokassetten bekämen ein Siegel: frei ab 6 Jahren, oder auch: frei ab 18 Jahren. Ein Videoverkäufer, der diese Kontrolle ignoriert, könnte bis zu einem Jahr Gefängnis bekommen. An einem solchen Plan hat auch die Videobranche Interesse: wegen des Siegels könnten die Videopiraten nämlich ihre Kassetten nicht so leicht verkaufen. Zur Zeit verlieren die Videofirmen eine halbe Milliarde Mark pro Jahr durch Raubkopien.

Vocabulary:
zugänglich accessible
für Jugendliche for teenagers
beraten here: to discuss
die Gewalt violence
die Videobranche video trade
das Siegel seal
das Gefängnis prison
die Raubkopie illegal (pirate) copy

a. Who discusses the problem of video sex and violence?

....

b. What solution to the problem is being considered?

....

c. What could happen to someone selling such videos in spite of the new regulations?

....

d. Why would the video firms themselves probably be interested in the reforms?

....

Übungen: Radio

17 On the cassette you'll hear a **Südwestfunk** reporter's comments on successful and not so successful video games at the Berlin radio and television fair. Listen, then fill in the 'reporter's notebook' below in German. (Answers p.207)

Vocabulary:
das Videospiel video game
der Dauerbrenner (coll.) continuous bestseller
das Kriegsspiel war game
die Weltrauminvasoren invaders from outer space
drollige Kerlchen funny creatures
Sport läuft überhaupt nicht (coll.) sport (games) don't sell at all
der Dekathlon decathlon
ankommen (sep.) to appeal
raffiniert sophisticated
der Mehrkampf multi-discipline sport
die Wüste desert
ein echter Hammer (coll.) a smash hit
das macht unheimlichen Spaß that's great fun
langfristig in the long run

'out' games: ....

'in' games: ....

New successful (because sophisticated) games:

name	short description	price (if mentioned)

---

18 Now fill in the transcript of the short second part of the same interview. (Answers in complete transcript p.214)

Frage: Was ist denn mit den ...., die

mehr .... für den Spieler anbieten, also

fast schon Kleincomputer?

Antwort: Das ist eigentlich der ganz große

.... hier: ....,

Kleincomputer, und diese Geräte fangen an bei 550 Mark etwa und

gehen bis .... Mark.

Sprechen Sie selbst

19 Your turn to speak. Imagine you're going to a desert island and could take only five things with you. What would you choose? (Use **würde ... mitnehmen**.) On the cassette Corinna will tell you what she would take.

20 Describe at least two electrical appliances you own. Also mention what you would most *like* to own, and why. Klaus does it on the cassette.

Answers to exercises

Unit 1
Übung 1 *gut:* eingelegte Heringe, Ostfriesentee, Frankenwein, Schokoladeneis, Rehrücken, Schwarzwälder Kirschtorte, Coca-Cola; *scheußlich:* weiche Eier, Graupensuppe, Mokkalikör, lauwarme Milch
Übung 2 **a.** FADE **b.** HERB **c.** SÜSS **d.** WEICH **e.** HART **f.** SCHWARZ
Übung 4 **a.** essen **b.** gefroren **c.** Knoblauch **d.** gut durch **e.** kleines
Übung 5 **a.** 2 **b.** 3 **c.** 1 **d.** 5 **e.** 5
Übung 7 **a.** einen ziemlichen Reinfall erlebt **b.** zäh wie Leder **c.** die Beilagen **d.** sehr matschig **e.** was gut schmeckte **f.** ganze Stange
Übung 8 **a.** zäh **b.** frisch **c.** teuer **d.** herb **e.** scheußlich
Übung 10 **a.** BESONDERES **b.** CHINA **c.** ECKE **d.** SUPERMARKT **e.** METZGER **f.** AUSWAHL **g.** KÜHLSCHRANK **h.** MARKT **i.** BUTTER **j.** CHAMPIGNONS;
BIERGARTEN
Übung 13 **a.** zäh, zäher, am zähsten **b.** weich, weicher, am weichsten **c.** matschig, matschiger, am matschigsten **d.** klein, kleiner, am kleinsten **e.** herb, herber, am herbsten
Übung 14 **b.** kleine **c.** alten **d.** grünen **e.** französische
Übung 15 **a.** from Greece **b.** grapes and pears **c.** strawberries **d.** 0,50 to 1,20 per piece **e.** the yellow ones **f.** 1 Mark for 2–3
Übung 16 **a.** no **b.** no **c.** no **d.** no **e.** no
Übung 17 **a.** a drink **b.** a packet of crisps **c.** Deit **d.** fruit flavour **e.** fresh
Übung 18 schlank, dick, lecker, frisch, fabelhaft, knusper-knabber-knackig-frisch

Unit 2
Übung 1 **a.** Ingrid **b.** Silke **c.** Amin **d.** Silke **e.** Amin **f.** Silke **g.** Ingrid
Übung 2 **b.** am Lagerfeuer sitzen **c.** in die Disko gehen **d.** schön essen gehen **e.** Kunstschätze besichtigen **f.** nichts tun/viel lesen
Übung 4 **a.** school, kindergarten **b.** July, August **c.** the Bavarian Forest **d.** a farm **e.** expensive, friendly, good for you, trips **f.** reductions
Übung 5 **a.** yes **b.** no **c.** no **d.** no **e.** yes
Übung 7 **a.** Weihnachtslieder **b.** Hausmusik **c.** Wohngemeinschaft **d.** gemütlichen
Übung 8 **a.** F **b.** R **c.** F **d.** R **e.** F
Übung 10 **a.** gut **b.** ja **c.** mehr als zwei Stunden **d.** interessant **e.** gut
Übung 11 **a.** Idiotenhügel **b.** Sonnenbrand **c.** Skikurs
Übung 13 **a.** Wir fahren morgen weg **b.** Ich gebe viel Geld aus **c.** Das Restaurant macht um 12 Uhr auf **d.** Ich verstehe nicht, was du sagst **e.** Bitte mach die Tür zu **f.** Der Führer erklärt alles
Übung 14 **a.** guter **b.** kaltes, warmes **c.** alten **d.** gemütlichen **e.** deutschen **f.** gute
Übung 15 **a.** Traumurlaub **b.** Bildungsurlaub **c.** Kreativurlaub **d.** Ferien auf dem Bauernhof **e.** Abenteuerurlaub
Übung 16 **a.** yes **b.** no **c.** no **d.** they had a relaxed get-together in a mountain lodge **e.** much après ski
Übung 18 + 19

Norddeutschland:	Sonne	Regen	Wolken	Wind	Temperaturen
morgen	✔		✔		17–21°
Mittwoch		✔		✔	
Donnerstag	✔				
Süddeutschland:					
zuerst	✔		✔		17–21°
später		✔	✔		
Österreich/Schweiz					
erst			✔		20°
dann		✔	✔		Süden 25°

Unit 3

Übung 1 **a.** single **b.** second **c.** Intercity train **d.** DM 84

Übung 2 **a.** guten Tag **b.** eine Fahrkarte nach Wien bitte **c.** nein, hin und zurück bitte **d.** ja, bitte **e.** erster Klasse bitte

Übung 4 **a.** 9.41 **b.** München **c.** 15.20 **d.** DM 10; DM 5 **e.** eine Stunde **f.** 50% **g.** 20%

Übung 5 **a.** umsteigen **b.** Ermäßigung **c.** Zuschlag

Übung 7 **a.** PKW **b.** DM 58 **c.** günstig **d.** teurer **e.** mit Kreditkarte

Übung 8 **a.** Ich möchte ein Auto mieten **b.** Welche Typen haben Sie? **c.** Was würde ein Ford Escort kosten? **d.** Haben Sie einen Wochenpreis/eine Wochenpauschale? **e.** Haben Sie auch Automatik? **f.** Wie kann ich bezahlen? **g.** Kann ich mit Kreditkarte bezahlen?

Übung 11 **a.** to the Heidelberg castle **b.** bus **c.** (Bus)haltestelle **d.** no, just across the road **e.** every 10 minutes

Übung 13 **a.** neun **b.** neunzehn **c.** vierundvierzig **d.** einundsiebzig **e.** siebzehn **f.** fünfzig **g.** dreiunddreißig **h.** zweiundsechzig

Übung 14 **a.** 87 **b.** 93 **c.** 230 **d.** 13 **e.** 422 **f.** 666

Übung 15 **a.** 1301 **b.** 5680 **c.** 10844 **d.** 53020 **e.** 70 000 000 **f.** 7 800 000

Übung 16 **a.** Heute ist der zehnte Mai **b.** am siebenundzwanzigsten April gehen wir auf Urlaub **c.** Gestern war Freitag, der dreizehnte **d.** Ich wurde am zweiten Juli neunzehnhundertvierundvierzig geboren **e.** Wir haben am Samstag, den ersten Oktober, eine Party.

Übung 17 **a.** from 17 Sept to 19 Sept **b.** return **c.** 9 days **d.** DM 177 **e.** DM 144

Übung 18 **Kinderland.** A special attraction on the long-distance 'Königssee' express between Hamburg and Berchtesgaden is a special coach/car – only for children from 4 to 11. There's much fun here: playing, reading, going on the climbing frame and on the slide. Of course the children will be looked after.

Übung 19

Übung 20 **a.** Kaiserslautern **b.** in South Germany **c.** VW Golf Diesel (white) **d.** KL-TR71 **e.** to phone home

Übung 21 They are advised to leave the **Autobahn** at Junction Basle South/St. Jakob and to park their vehicles in the car park at St. Jakob's. There is a park and ride service into town to the trade fair.

Unit 4

Übung 1 **a.** Wetter, schön **b.** Leute, freundlich **c.** Touristen, interessant **d.** Rucksack, allein

Übung 2 **a.** Woher kommen Sie? **b.** Sind Sie hier auf Urlaub? **c.** Seit wann? **d.** Wie gefällt es Ihnen? **e.** Reisen Sie allein?

Übung 4 **a.** ADAPTER **b.** WÄRMFLASCHE **c.** DRÜBEN **d.** MUSEEN **e.** ZIMMER **f.** MORGEN **g.** GENUG --→ PENSION

Übung 5 **a.** brauchen **b.** möchten **c.** glauben **d.** haben **e.** haben ... vor

Übung 7 **a.** Herr und Frau Schmitt **b.** Herr Frauenfeld **c.** Herr und Frau Schmitt **d.** Frau Scheuermann **e.** der Babysitter **f.** Frau Frauenfeld

Übung 8 **a.** Möchten Sie einen Aperitif? **b.** Wir könnten den Wein aus Portugal probieren **c.** Ich muß meine Frau entschuldigen **d.** Darf ich Ihnen ein kleines Geschenk geben? **e.** Darf ich Sie vorstellen, Herr Frauenfeld?

Übung 10 **a.** C **b.** E **c.** A **d.** B **e.** D

Übung 11 **a.** Pastete **b.** Firma **c.** Vegetarier **d.** Salat **e.** Rezept --→ PFALZ

Übung 13 **a.** Ich tanze nicht **b.** Ich kann nicht singen **c.** Wer kann nicht schwimmen? **d.** Bist du nicht nach Bonn geflogen? **e.** Das war nicht nett **f.** Es ist nicht kalt geworden

Übung 14 **a.** Ich spreche kein Englisch **b.** Ich will keinen Wein **c.** Ich habe kein Telefon **d.** Berge? Ich sehe keine Berge

Übung 15 **a.** They worry, in case it turns out a flop **b.** Because one cannot be sure how all these people will react to each other **c.** whom to invite; where to have the party; how to entertain the guests **d.** The ones you feel you ought to invite; friends who don't like big parties **e.** Lively people who are not afraid of making the first step towards a stranger **f.** Big – but not too big. There ought to be enough space to be able to dance, but also to sit quietly in some corner for a chat **g.** The neighbours – so you better inform them about your party

Übung 16 **a.** Frau Kropf **b.** Zell **c.** 56 **d.** 4 **e.** nice breakfast **f.** coffee and cakes **g.** grill party

Übung 17 b., d., h., f., a., c., e., g.

Unit 5

Übung 1 **a.** 7,5%; 8,9% **b.** Lager- und Transport- **c.** Verkäuferinnen **d.** Lehrer und Sozialarbeiter **e.** Arbeitsamt; Arbeitslosenunterstützung; ein Jahr

Übung 2 **a.** MAURER **b.** KELLNER **c.** TISCHLER **d.** KRANKENSCHWESTER **e.** LEHRER **f.** LAGERARBEITER **g.** ZAHNARZT **h.** VERKÄUFER → **REISELEITER**

Übung 4 **a.** Haben Sie sich auch andere Berufe überlegt? **b.** Es gibt viele arbeitslose Lehrer **c.** Sind Sie mit Ihrem Beruf zufrieden? **d.** Ich komme ständig mit neuen Leuten zusammen **e.** Mein Beruf ist abwechslungsreich **f.** Ich habe manchmal Geldsorgen

Übung 5 **a.** N **b.** V **c.** V **d.** N **e.** V **f.** N

Übung 7 **Name:** Manfred Beck; **Beruf:** Buchhalter; **Arbeitet wo:** in einer großen Exportfirma; **Rente ab wann:** ab 65; **Arbeitstag:** 7–15 Uhr; **Mittagspause:** 12–1 Uhr; **Macht von gleitender Arbeitszeit Gebrauch:** nein; **Urlaub:** 4 Wochen; **Extra Urlaub:** Pfingsttage, Ostern, Weihnachtstage

Übung 8 **a.** Aufstiegsmöglichkeiten **b.** in den Ruhestand gehen/ pensioniert werden **c.** Mittagspause **d.** Kantine **e.** gleitende Arbeitszeit **f.** eine gute Rente

Übung 10 **a.** Ich wollte schnell Geld verdienen **b.** Ich habe in einer Fabrik gearbeitet, am Fließband **c.** Ich war richtig kaputt **d.** Ich ging zum Arbeitsamt **e.** Jetzt bin ich Arzthelferin **f.** Ich hab das Gefühl, daß ich etwas Wichtiges mache

Übung 11 Interesse; Arbeitsamt; Schule; Beruf; Menschen; Geld; Maschine; Idee

Übung 13 ich habe gelernt, du hast gelernt, er/sie/es hat gelernt, wir haben gelernt, ihr habt gelernt, sie/Sie haben gelernt; ich habe gekocht, du hast gekocht, er/sie/es hat gekocht, wir haben gekocht, ihr habt gekocht, sie/Sie haben gekocht; ich habe geantwortet, du hast geantwortet, er/sie/es hat geantwortet, wir haben geantwortet, ihr habt geantwortet, sie/Sie haben geantwortet

Übung 14 a. Was haben Sie am Sonntag gemacht? **b.** Ich habe Deutsch gelernt **c.** Was hast du heute abend gekocht? **d.** Ich habe dir nicht geantwortet

Übung 15 a. Ich habe Wein getrunken **b.** Haben Sie gut geschlafen? **c.** Was hast du gegessen? **d.** Er hat ein Lied gesungen **e.** Ich habe dein Buch gefunden

Übung 16 a. F **b.** R **c.** F **d.** R **e.** R **f.** R **g.** R

Übung 17 a. 4 **b.** German, Mathematics, French, English **c.** American Field Service **d.** Berlin, Aberystwyth, München **e.** teaching German **f.** writing, painting, travelling

Übung 19a. arbeitslos; Alter; Jüngere; Lust am Leben; Schönheitschirurgen

Übung 19b. a. No **b.** Yes **c.** Yes **d.** Yes **e.** No

Unit 6

Übung 1

bei Sonnenschein	bei Schnee	bei Regen
Bootfahren	Skifahren	Schwimmbad
Surfen	(Langlauf, Abfahrtsski)	Sauna
Wandern		Kegelbahn
		Tanzveranstaltung

Übung 2 a. verlängertes **b.** Ostern **c.** rechtzeitig; stark **d.** unternehmen **e.** Möglichkeiten **f.** überhaupt; Problem

Übung 4 Unkraut jäten; Hecken schneiden; Rosen düngen; Garten umgraben; Kaffee trinken; Buch lesen

Übung 5 Heide sees her parents, but they live quite far away. She always takes her two children with her. They all have coffee and cakes together and talk to each other or Heide sunbathes in her own garden, swims in the pool and reads a book. Twice a month she meets her friends for coffee and cakes.

Übung 6 a. Wir stehen spät auf **b.** Oft fahren wir ins Grüne **c.** und kehren dann in einem Gasthof ein

Übung 8

2.	Promenadenkonzert im Rosengarten	Heidelberger Mozartgruppe	'Eine kleine Nachtmusik'
3.	Kino	heißer Film, Klassiker	'M – eine Stadt sucht den Mörder'
4.	Club 87	Tanz	

Übung 9 a. toll **b.** blau **c.** Kino **d.** Tage **e.** Löwe **f.** Bier **g.** Wein **h.** Film **i.** heiß **j.** Tage; LANGWEILIG

Übung 11 a. am Sonntagmorgen **b.** am Sonntagnachmittag **c.** während der Woche **d.** seit seiner frühesten Kindheit **e.** an einem Sonntagmorgen

Übung 12 c; e;

Übung 14 a. 2.15 or 14.15 **b.** 4.45 or 16.45 **c.** 8.40 or 20.40 **d.** 3.05 or 15.05 **e.** 0.30 or 12.30 **f.** 1.30 or 13.30 **g.** 4.15 or 16.15 **h.** 9.55 or 21.55

Übung 15 a. zwölf nach fünf **b.** viertel nach acht **c.** halb zehn **d.** viertel vor eins

Übung 16 a. abends **b.** am Sonntagmorgen **c.** im Mai **d.** im Juni **e.** um zehn Uhr **f.** um halb sechs

Übung 17 a. She always comes at 7 **b.** The film will start at once **c.** Summer is here already **d.** I want to go to Berlin again **e.** I often think of Jessica

Übung 18 **b.** Jeden Sonntag geht's morgens in die Kirche **c.** Immer muß man höflich grüßen **d.** Abends sitzt die ganze Familie beim Fernsehen **e.** Kaffeekränzchen bei Tante Elsbeth – sowas Langweiliges! **f.** Mittags grillen wir im Garten – immer Würstchen!

Übung 19 **a.** Köln **b.** over 30 **c.** around 200 Marks **d.** teacher

Übung 20 Putzfrau Schmitz: gatecrashes a party and tells the guests stories about their host; Tarzan: appears in a black suit and performs a striptease

Übung 21 **a.** Lust gehabt, das zu machen **b.** ganz gut organisieren **c.** viele Leute, die Spaß dran haben **d.** feiern tun die Leute immer

Unit 7

Übung 1 **a.** Hauptbahnhof **b.** Burda **c.** Tina **d.** Buchhandlung **e.** Spiegel; BRIGITTE

Übung 2 **a.** F; **b.** F; **c.** F; **d.** R; **e.** F; **f.** R

Übung 4 **Frankfurter Allgemeine Zeitung:** überregional; konservativ· **Frankfurter Rundschau:** überregional; linksliberal

Übung 5 **a.** Es gibt nicht viele Sonntagszeitungen in der Bundesrepublik **b.** Regionalzeitungen sind wichtig für die Bevölkerung, weil sie auch Lokalnachrichten bringen **c.** Sensationsblätter haben viel Bilder und Schlagzeilen und wenig Information **d.** Die ZEIT gehört zu den Wochenblättern

Übung 7 **Henning:** Single-Hit-Parade am Sonntag; Sportreportage; nur am Wochenende. **Silke:** Regionalsendungen; Politik; aktuelle Beiträge; ganz verschieden

Übung 8 **a.** Reporter **b.** aktuelle Beiträge **c.** Wochenende **d.** Regionalsendungen **e.** Single-Hit-Parade

Übung 10 **a.** informiert **b.** verführt **c.** suche … aus **d.** laufen **e.** entscheiden

Übung 11 **b.** Sport **c.** Rundfunk **d.** Werbefernsehen **e.** Komödien

Übung 13 **a.** Regnet es? **b.** Fährt er nach Berlin? **c.** Trinkst du Wein? **d.** Haben sie Urlaub? **e.** Ist sie verheiratet?

Übung 14 **a.** Wann kommt er? **b.** Wohin gehst du? **c.** Woher kommen Sie? **d.** Warum lachst du? **e.** Wer ist die Frau da drüben? **f.** Wem sollen wir das Geld geben? **g.** Wieviel Stunden hörst du Radio? **h.** Welche Größe haben Sie? **i.** Welches Haus ist zu verkaufen?

Übung 15

a. 18.05	SPORTSCHAU	1
b. 17.02	DER GROSSE PREIS	2
c. 16.45	ENORM IN FORM	2
d. 16.15	NEUES VOM KLEIDERMARKT	1
e. 17.00	KIRCHE UND GESELLSCHAFT	1
f. 17.10	LÄNDERSPIEGEL	2
g. 14.15	SESAMSTRASSE	1

Übung 16 **a.** Spielen und Lernen **b.** DM **c.** Hobby **d.** Brigitte

Übung 17 **a.** people interested in Royalty **b.** weekly **c.** who loves all kinds of planes **d.** at the newspaper shop **e.** young women **f.** better home-making

Übung 18

Time	Which programme?	Topics for the Day
13.00	Heute Mittag (Magazin)	1. Verhandlungen über Mittelstreckenraketen 2. Massenflucht aus Beirut 3. Kinderbuchautor schreibt Schmökerlexikon
14.05	Für junge Hörer	Tagebuch eines jungen Mädchens
14.30	Radiotreff am Nachmittag	Party-Service Geschichte des Lippenstiftes

Unit 8

Übung 1 a. R b. F c. R d. R e. F f. F g. R h. R i. R k. R

Übung 2 a. Sie waren noch nie auf einem Weinfest? b. Da ist immer gute Stimmung c. Da trinkt man ein paar Viertel Wein d. Das hört sich nicht schlecht an e. Eigentlich bin ich eine Biertrinkerin f. ... der würde Ihnen auch schmecken g. Ich bin mir ganz sicher, daß Sie sich gut mit mir amüsieren werden

Übung 4 a. Was spielen Sie am Sonntag? b. Haben Sie noch Karten? c. Was kosten die Karten? d. Wann beginnt die Aufführung? e. Und was spielen Sie sonst noch diese Woche?

Übung 5 a. Liederabend b. Oper c. Rang d. Aufführung e. Mahler f. Preisgruppen; BRAHMS

Übung 7 a. Wir wollten tanzen b. Die Band war laut c. Man konnte nicht tanzen d. Wir blieben und warteten auf eine Ersatzband e. Wir bekamen unser Geld nicht zurück

Übung 8 Sequence of captions: b., d., e., a., c.

Übung 10 die schwarzen Nächte; schwarz; Eskimos; wir fuhren mit dem Auto, aber leider ... blasen; aber wir kannten niemand; Wein; um fünf; ein wenig Hunger; silbernen Eck; Wiener Würstchen

Übung 11 a. Ich hatte einen Riesenhunger b. Ich habe bis zum Umfallen getanzt c. Ich mußte ins Röhrchen blasen d. Ich habe mich als Indianer verkleidet

Übung 13 a. ich lernte b. du glaubtest c. er hörte d. wir wollten e. Sie wollten f. sie hörten

Übung 14 a. ging b. fuhren c. ließen d. traf e. gab

Übung 15 a. Ich kann gut skifahren b. Er konnte gestern abend nicht kommen c. Im Sommer will ich nach Afrika fahren d. Wir wollten am Sonntag einen langen Spaziergang machen e. Zuerst wollten sie ins Theater gehen

Übung 16 a. Sunday 10th July b. Rhine c. DM 55 d. yes e. afternoon f. Fröhlichkeit und sorgenfreie Stunden g. walk along the river or walk up to a vineyard

Übung 17 a. F b. F c. R d. R e. F f. R g. F

Übung 18 a. Medienspektakel b. sein Idol c. ein Schock d. ein Kultfilm

Übung 20 a. Kinder b. aus der ganzen Welt c. der Bundesrepublik Deutschland d. lustig e. ein Kind aus der Konserve

Übung 21 China, the GDR, Italy, Upper Volta, Scandinavian and Eastern bloc countries, the Philippines

Unit 9

Übung 1 Eierlikör, Eisbein, Käsekuchen, Kartoffeln mit Butter, Tee mit Rum

Übung 2 a. Ab: morgen b. Sie fühlt sich: schlaff, ungesund, unbeweglich c. 1. Saftkur, 2. Kaloriendiät d. 800 e. Salate, mageres Fleisch, Fisch f. Süßigkeiten, Alkohol

Übung 4 a. Muskelschmerzen b. Halsweh/schmerzen c. Fieber d. Kopfweh/schmerzen e. Durchfall f. Grippe/Schnupfen

Übung 6 Seidentuch, Shampoo, Gesichtscreme, Haarpomade, Puder

Übung 7 a. Ich möchte gerne eine kleine Reiseapotheke mitnehmen b. Können Sie mir helfen? Können Sie mich beraten? c. Sie sollten den Insektenschutz nicht vergessen d. Man kann ein Spray nehmen

Übung 9 a. Ein Lastwagen kam mir entgegen b. Plötzlich scherte ein BMW hinter dem Lastwagen aus c. Ich konnte vor Schreck nur noch das Steuer nach rechts reißen d. Der Lastwagenfahrer rief die Ambulanz e. Ich konnte aus dem Auto herauskriechen f. Die Ambulanz nahm mich und den Fahrer des BMW mit ins Krankenhaus

Übung 10 a. Sie können hier nicht parken b. Sie dürfen jetzt nicht überholen c. Sie müssen bremsen d. Bitte halten Sie! e. Sie müssen links abbiegen

Übung 12 a. Sie dürfen hier nicht parken **b.** Wir wollen jetzt gehen
c. Kannst du Französisch? **d.** Wollen Sie warten? **e.** Sie mag keinen Kaffee
f. Kann ich Ihnen helfen? **g.** Darf ich rauchen?
Übung 13 a. Ich konnte sie nicht hören **b.** Ich mußte Wasser trinken
c. Ich wollte nicht darüber sprechen **d.** Der Zug sollte um 6 Uhr abfahren
Übung 14 Sequence of captions: c., f., e., b., a., d.
Übung 15 a. R **b.** F **c.** R **d.** F **e.** R
Übung 16a = b., d., e., f.
Übung 16b a. is overweight **b.** coffee, tea **c.** calories; carbohydrates; day
after day

Unit 10

Übung 1 We have breakfast together and then my wife goes off to school.
At 9 o'clock I take my 4-year-old son to kindergarten. Then I go for a walk
with my daughter. She is 3 years old. If the weather is good we go to the zoo
or we go shopping. At lunchtime we eat out, sometimes with my wife if she
is back from work, sometimes just me and the children.
Übung 2 a. gemeinsam **b.** allein **c.** einkaufen **d.** Sohn, Tochter
e. Lehrerin **f.** Schule
Übung 4 a. Zeitung **b.** Artikel **c.** Radio **d.** Termine; ZART
Übung 5 Hausmann, Hausarbeit; Frühstück, Frühgymnastik; Nachteil,
Nachmittag
Übung 6 a. Der Wecker klingelt um 7 **b.** Ich stehe um 7 Uhr 30 auf **c.** Ich
mache Frühstück und lese die Zeitung **d.** Nach dem Frühstück mache ich
die Hausarbeit – Waschen, Staubsaugen, Aufräumen **f.** Nachmittags gehe
ich in die Bibliothek. **g.** Abends gehe ich ins Kino oder ins Theater
Übung 8 a. Ich setze mich in den Sessel **b.** Wir waschen das Geschirr ab
c. Ich helfe meiner Frau beim Kochen **d.** Ich rege mich immer schrecklich
auf **e.** Wir spielen Karten **f.** Ich trinke ein Bier **g.** Ich lege die Beine hoch
h. Es gibt Streit übers Programm; (**a.** Horst, **b.** Heide, **c.** Horst, **d.** Heide, **e.**
Heide, **f.** Horst, **g.** Horst, **h.** Heide)
Übung 10 a. after work **b.** in 1½ years **c.** English and French **d.** to speak
in a foreign language **e.** by listening to foreign radio stations **f.** when she
begins to understand things **g.** She will travel to France and England
Übung 11 a. F **b.** R **c.** R **d.** F **e.** R
Übung 13a. ich setze mich, du setzt dich, er/sie/es setzt sich, wir setzen uns,
ihr setzt euch, sie/Sie setzen sich; ich ärgere mich, du ärgerst dich, er/sie/es
ärgert sich, wir ärgern uns, ihr ärgert euch, sie/Sie ärgern sich
Übung 13b. a. Er irrt sich **b.** Ja, ich erinnere mich **c.** Ich entspanne mich
am Abend **d.** Ich amüsiere mich
Übung 14 a. sich **b.** dir **c.** mir **d.** dir **e.** mir
Übung 15 a. try something different: fruit, muesli, rye bread – it's
healthier **b.** try something that you'd never think would suit you **c.** choose
a different route **d.** you see different faces **e.** have a shower; refresh
yourself with Eau de Toilette; change into something comfortable **f.** change
it: have curls, or a punk style; cut off fringe
Übung 16 a. lots of paper – contents nil **b.** buttons on new blouses that
come off instantly **c.** new sport in the city: dog dirt slalom **d.** admission fee
to grubby toilets **e.** price tags that stick forever **f.** motor vehicles parked on
pedestrian sidewalks
Übung 18 a. love ('Ich bin von Kopf bis Fuß auf Liebe eingestellt') **b.** They
won't get very far **c.** Those wanting to try a new dish might burn their
fingers – and more **d.** to stop pursuing unattainable dreams and desires

Unit 11

Übung 1 Vorteil: Nähe zur Natur; mehr Kontakt zu den Leuten; alles ist
viel persönlicher, kleiner, überschaubarer. **Nachteil:** weite Entfernung zur
Stadt; wenig Besuch von Freunden aus der Stadt
Übung 2 a. Ich möchte mehr Kontakt zu den Leuten **b.** Das Leben auf dem
Land hat mir gut gefallen **c.** Dieser Nachteil hat sich auf die Dauer stark

ausgewirkt **d.** Ich bekomme <u>viel</u> Besuch aus der Stadt **e.** Das Leben auf dem Land ist <u>viel</u> persönlicher **f.** Viele meiner Freunde haben <u>kein</u> Auto

Übung 4

	Alter	Schule	seit wann	Pläne
Niels	7	1. Klasse Grundschule	seit einem Jahr	vielleicht studieren
Claudia	12	Gymnasium	seit zwei Jahren	Mittlere Reife, Abitur, studieren

Übung 5 a. sechs **b.** frei **c.** Hausaufgaben **d.** Studieren **e.** Regierung, Stipendium

Übung 6 a. Gymnasium **b.** Kinderkrippe **c.** Kindergarten **d.** Grundschule

Übung 8 a. Die CDU/CSU **b.** Die FDP **c.** Die SPD **d.** Die Grünen **e.** Der Bundeskanzler **f.** Der Bundespräsident **g.** Die Bundesrepublik **h.** Die Bundesländer **i.** Die Bundesregierung

Übung 9 Kiel 3, Hannover 4, Düsseldorf 5, Wiesbaden 6, Mainz 7, Saarbrücken 8, Stuttgart 9, München 10

Übung 11 a. Weil ich für das Umweltprogramm der Grünen bin **b.** Weil ich für die liberale Wirtschaftspolitik der FDP bin **c.** Weil ich für die sozialen Reformpläne der SPD bin

Übung 12a. a. ATOMKRAFTWERK **b.** WETTRÜSTEN **c.** UMWELTSCHUTZ **d.** VERTEIDIGUNGSPOLITIK; = **FREI**

Übung 12b. a. Max **b.** Karl **c.** Max **d.** Karl **e.** Max **f.** Karl **g.** Max **h.** Max

Übung 14 a. Er wohnt seit 1955 in Ulm **b.** Was machen Sie diesen Sommer? **c.** Morgen gehen wir in ein gutes Restaurant **d.** Er ist seit drei Jahren Präsident **e.** Nächste Woche fahren wir aufs Land **f.** Ich gehe zur Bushaltestelle

Übung 15 a. The house was built in 1948 **b.** What is on/playing at the cinema/the movies? **c.** I don't know how that is done **d.** I was never told that **e.** There's a dance on at the 'Adler'

Übung 16 a. R **b.** R **c.** F **d.** F **e.** R

Übung 17 a. Frau Renner **b.** Herr Schranz **c.** Herr Schranz **d.** Herr Schranz **e.** Frau Renner

Unit 12

Übung 1 ausprobieren, Insel, einfach, Elektrizität, zurückziehen, fliegen, Welt

Übung 2 a. Angenommen, ich hätte 100 000 Mark ... **b.** Würden Sie nichts vermissen? **c.** Ich würde versuchen, ganz einfach zu leben **d.** Das wär' schon gut

Übung 4 Dosen öffnen, Kuchen backen

Übung 5 a. reiben **b.** entsaften **c.** kneten **d.** reiben **e.** mixen **f.** drehen **g.** machen

Übung 7 a. SPIELFILM **b.** KASSETTE **c.** GERÄT **d.** INTERESSE **e.** VERKÄUFER; = **METER**

Übung 8 Der Super-Video – für Sie, für die Kinder, für die ganze Familie. Einfache Programmierung, einfache Aufnahmetaste. Ideal für Kindersendungen, Tierfilme, Unterhaltungsfilme. Preis: DM 1900 – alles dabei!

Übung 10 a. Silke **b.** Günter **c.** Ingrid

Übung 11 a. Da kann ich nicht so ganz zustimmen **b.** Wir müssen sparsamer und sinnvoller mit unserer Energiegewinnung umgehen **c.** Da stimme ich dir zu **d.** Ich hab mir schon oft Gedanken darüber gemacht **e.** daß unser Transportsystem umstrukturiert werden sollte **f.** Das ist eine Spezialistenangelegenheit

Übung 13 a. Wenn ich ein Auto hätte ... **b.** Wenn Sie jünger wären ... **c.** Angenommen ich hätte eine Million Mark **d.** Könnte ich das ausprobieren? **e.** Ich könnte jetzt etwas essen

Übung 14 **a.** Ich würde (mit dem Auto) nach Paris fahren **b.** Ich würde nach Indien reisen **c.** Würdest du bitte das Fenster öffnen? **d.** Wenn wir Zeit hätten, würden wir mehr Bücher lesen **e.** Ich würde jetzt gehen, wenn ich Sie wäre

Übung 15 **a.** Summer **b.** to your ear **c.** motorists **d.** it buzzes **e.** stopping you from falling asleep **f.** in France

Übung 16 **a.** The Cabinet ministers in Bonn **b.** Voluntary censorship within the video trade **c.** Prison sentence up to one year **d.** Each cassette would have a certificate so that video pirates couldn't sell their loot so easily

Übung 17

| 'out' games: | Kriegsspiele, Weltrauminvasoren |
| 'in' games: | Pacmänner und ähnliche Spiele |

New successful (because sophisticated) games:

name	short description	price (if mentioned)
Robot Tank	Kriegsspiel	
Dekathlon	Olympischer Mehrkampf	
Transamerika-Rennen	Wüste- und Stadtrennen, bei Schnee, Regen, Tag, Nacht	
Plaque-Attack	für Kinder, die ihre Zähne nicht putzen wollen	DM 140

Radio transcripts

Unit 1 Übung 17 und 18

Hallo, liebe Autofahrer! Jetzt ist Deit-Zeit! Ph – dieser Stau! Wie wär's denn mit 'ner Pause? Au Ja! Hast du Deit mitgenommen? Natürlich! Jeder bekommt sein Lieblings-Deit! Ich will Zitrone! Und ich Orange! Das erfrischt! Und hat so wenig Kalorien und viele Vitamine. Damit wir in Form bleiben – besonders du, mein Lieber, und Deine schlanke Linie. Damit der Durst nicht dick macht – Deit!

Na, was haben wir denn da? Was hat mir denn mein liebendes Weib hier hingelegt? Das wollen wir doch gleich mal probieren! Donnerwetter! Die schmecken ja richtig lecker! Und richtig frisch! Was denn – wie heißen diese Chips? Chips-frisch – von Pfanni-frisch? Na, das ist ja fabelhaft! Gerda, du bist ein Schatz. Hmm . . . das muß ich mir ja unbedingt merken: Chips-frisch von Pfanni-frisch – die schmecken ja wirklich knusper-knabber-knackig-frisch – fabelhaft!

Unit 1 Übung 19

Die Milupa-Mütterberatung informiert: Kinder haben oft Durst, das wissen wir, und sie brauchen die richtigen Getränke. Milupa hat jetzt Teegetränke mit neuer Rezeptur. Sie sind leicht, aber ausreichend gesüßt, und sie schmecken großen und kleinen Kindern.

Unit 2 Übung 17

Sie haben Ihren Sommerurlaub noch nicht gebucht? Dann kommen Sie bitte mal ganz dicht an den Apparat! Wir geben Ihnen einen Geheimtip. Fliegen Sie mit Neckermann nach Süd-Dalmatien. Dort in der Region um Dubrovnik erwartet Sie eine herrliche, sonnige Urlaubswelt, und mittendrin die bekannte Klubanlage Admiral. Hier braucht der Urlaub nicht mehr als 609 Mark zu kosten – Flugreise und Halbpension inbegriffen. Informationen gibt's in allen Reisebüros mit den Zeichen von Neckermann-Reisen.

Unit 2 Übung 18

SWF 3 – Wetter . . . Reisewetterbericht, gültig bis Donnerstag. Norddeutschland: Morgen heiter bis wolkig und kein Regen, am Mittwoch regnet's dann aber und ist ziemlich windig. Ab Donners-tag wieder freundlicher, 17 bis 21 Grad. Süddeutschland: Heiter bis wolkig und trocken, später überwiegend veränderlich bewölkt und etwas Regen, Höchsttemperaturen 17 bis 21 Grad.

Unit 2 Übung 19

Österreich, Schweiz: Erst aufgelockerte Bewölkung, dann auf der Alpennordseite vielfach starke Bewölkung und zeitweise Regen, 20 Grad, im Süden bis 25 Grad.

Unit 3 Übung 19

In einer halben Minute dreizehn Uhr neun. SWF 3 Radiodienst aus

Baden-Baden mit Meldungen zur Verkehrslage. A6 Mannheim Richtung Heilbronn: Zwischen Bad Rappenau und Heilbronn-Neckarsulm Unfall, 5 bis 6 km Stau. A8 Stuttgart Richtung München zwischen Aichelberg und Merklingen Baustelle, 6 bis 7 km Stau.

Unit 3 Übung 20

Und ein Reiseruf: Herr Friedrich Trappe, Herr Friedrich Trappe aus Kaiserslautern, zur Zeit unterwegs in Süddeutschland mit einem weißen VW Golf Diesel, amtliches Kennzeichen KL-TR 71 wird gebeten, zu Hause anzurufen.

Unit 3 Übung 21

Besuchern der Fachmessen in der Schweizer Mustermesse wird empfohlen, die Autobahn über den Anschluß Basel-Süd/St. Jakob zu verlassen und ihr Fahrzeug im Parkhaus St. Jakob abzustellen. Es besteht ein Park-and-Ride-Dienst zur Schweizer Mustermesse.

Unit 3 Übung 22

In zwanzig Sekunden 19 Uhr 5. SWF 3 Radiodienst aus Baden-Baden: Keine Meldungen über Verkehrsbehinderungen.

Unit 4 Übung 16

Jetzt sind wir bei unserem Geburtstagskind des Tages – das sollte sein: die liebe Frau Kropf – ist das richtig? – in Zell? – Ja, das ist richtig. – Frau Kropf, einen schönen guten Morgen erst mal. – Guten Morgen, Herr Metzler. – ... und allerherzlichsten Glückwunsch zu Ihrem – danke – ach, das ist ja lächerlich, den Geburtstag – 'ne Oma mit – wie alt werden Sie heute? 56? – 56! – Nee, ich find' das nett, so 'ne junge Oma. Wieviel Enkel haben Sie? – Vier. – Vier Enkelkinder hab' ich. – Vier Enkelkinder schon! – Ja. – Und jetzt erzählen Sie mal 'n bißchen: Wie wird denn die Oma gefeiert heute? Das muß doch 'n großes Fest werden. – Ja, am Nachmittag gibt es Kaffee, und am Abend gibt's dann 'n schönes Abendbrot mit Grillbraten und verschiedene Salate ... Ich hab' heute morgen auch schon schön den Tisch gedeckt gekriegt, mit frischen Brötchen ... – Sehen Sie, das ist wichtig, nicht? An so 'nem Tag da soll man mal wirklich von vorne bis hinten richtig verwöhnt werden. – Ja. – So, und am Nachmittag kommen dann meine Kinder mit Enkelkindern. – Das wird ein richtiges Familienfest werden? – Das wird 'n Familienfest, ja.

Unit 4 Übung 17

Überschrift: Hochzeit mit Hindernissen. Eigentlich wollte der Engländer Ken in diesem Frühjahr heiraten. Aber er brach sich am Polterabend ein Bein, und aus der Hochzeit wurde nix. Jetzt versuchte er es zum zweiten Mal. Er nahm einen großen Anlauf zum Standesamt und brach sich wieder ein Bein – dasselbe wie beim ersten Mal. Ergebnis: Die Hochzeit wird verschoben, der Bräutigam liegt mindestens noch drei Monate im Streckverband. Die Braut nimmt's gelassen auf. Wir wünschen Hals- und Beinbruch fürs nächste Mal.

Unit 5 Übung 18

What a feeling ... Sie träumt den Traum von der großen Karriere. Doch selbst wenn ein Traum nur einmal wahr wird, verändert er das Leben für immer. Flashdance. Sie tanzt sich ganz nach oben in Flashdance – die Diskosensation aus den USA. Ein Film voller Träume und heißer Musik. Flashdance. Ein Film, der in die Beine geht. Jetzt im Kino. Und die Flashdance-Hits gibt's jetzt auch auf LP und Kassette.

Unit 5 Übung 19a

Ich habe ein Problem. Von und mit Alexander Borell. – Ich habe hier den Brief einer Hörerin, sie ist 53 Jahre alt. Und sie schreibt: Ich bin seit einem Jahr arbeitslos. Von Beruf bin ich Hotelkauffrau und Serviermeisterin. Mein Problem ist, wenn ich mich bewerbe, mein Alter. Ich lese dann immer: Wir haben uns für eine Jüngere entschieden. Das ist auf die Dauer so deprimierend, daß ich die Lust am Leben schon verloren habe. Ich muß arbeiten, weil ich allein bin. – Auch die Männer im Inserat wollen immer jüngere Frauen. Ich sehe noch gut aus und bin auch sehr attraktiv, allerdings habe ich ein paar Fältchen. Nun kämpfe ich seit Wochen mit mir, ob ich zu einem Schönheitschirurgen gehen soll. Aber aus meinem ganzen Bekanntenkreis höre ich nur negative Antworten. Was ich tun soll? Ich weiß es nicht, und bitte um Ihre Antwort.

Unit 5 Übung 19b

Liebe Hörerin, ich würde auf gar keinen Fall zu einem Schönheitschirurgen gehen. Denn sehen Sie, wie Sie aussehen oder nicht aussehen – in Ihren Papieren steht, daß Sie 53 Jahre alt sind, und das ist sicherlich ein viel wichtigeres Problem. Denn ob Sie nun ein bißchen geliftet sind oder nicht, Sie bleiben 53. Aber ich glaube, Sie fangen irgendwas falsch an. Wenn Sie bei einer Bewerbung zum Beispiel gleich hingehen und sagen: Ich bin zwar nicht mehr ein junges Mädchen, ich habe aber auch keine Flausen mehr im Kopf und ich weiß, was Arbeit ist und ich kann was, dann würde das sicher manchem Menschen, der andere einstellt, wahrscheinlich imponieren und sagen: Die hat eigentlich recht. – Und was dann mit den Männern in den Inseraten ist, das braucht Sie gar nicht zu kümmern. Machen Sie's doch mal umgekehrt: Geben Sie doch mal ein Inserat auf und schreiben Sie offen, daß eine Hausfrau, 53 Jahre alt, einen Lebensgefährten sucht, daß es dabei nicht um Geld geht, sondern um Zuneigung und Freundschaft undsoweiter. Dann melden sich Männer, die an einer Frau in reifen Jahren interessiert sind. Ich wünsche Ihnen von Herzen in beiden Problemen großen Erfolg.

Unit 6 Übung 19

Hauptsache, es macht Spaß und die Leute können darüber lachen! Dann ist die Party gerettet. Kein Problem für die Firma Knallbonbon in Köln – über 30 Attraktionen zur Partyverschönerung hat sie im Angebot. Wer will, der kann sich zum Beispiel einen Schornsteinfeger, ein Revue-Girl, einen Clown, eine Putzfrau und vieles mehr mieten, und die tragen dann zur Stimmung während der heimischen Fete bei. Dieser Spaß kostet pro Nummer so um 200

Mark. Und die Firma Knallbonbon, die gibt es seit März. Chefin ist die ehemalige Lehrerin Jutta Lüssen, und Petra Korn wollte von ihr wissen, was da sonst noch alles läuft.

Unit 6 Übung 20

Wir haben mehrere Renner – zum Beispiel die Putzfrau Schmitz, die in eine Gesellschaft platzt und aus dem Leben desjenigen erzählt, für den sie bestimmt ist. Tarzan, der kühle Blonde, entblättert sich – beziehungsweise, er kommt im schwarzen Anzug, mit Hut, weißen Handschuhen, todschick, in eine Gesellschaft und entblättert sich zu Tarzan. Es ist für die Damen besonders ansprechend, diese Nummer.

Unit 6 Übung 21

Und woher hatte sie den Nerv, in unserer Zeit der wirtschaftlichen Rezession solch einen Service aufzuziehen? – Ich hab' Lust gehabt, das zu machen, und ich kann ganz gut organisieren. Ich kenne viele Leute, die Spaß dran hatten, das mit mir zusammen zu machen. Und eben: das war der nächste Gedanke – kann man das jetzt zu dieser Zeit machen, und ich habe mir gesagt: Klar! Feiern tun die Leute immer, egal zu welcher Zeit.

Unit 7 Übung 17

Sieben Tage, Sieben Tage ist die beste für dich, keine Frage ... Ja, wirklich! Wieder beste Unterhaltung für sieben glückliche Tage erleben Sie in der Zeitschrift 'Sieben Tage'. Lesen Sie diese Woche in 'Sieben Tage': Königin Silvia in Angst. Erleidet Carl Gustav das gleiche Schicksal wie Prinz Klaus? Holen Sie sich die neue 'Sieben Tage' bei Ihrem Zeitschriftenhändler. 'Sieben Tage' gibt's jetzt immer montags neu.

Flugzeuge sind voller faszinierender Technik und Elektronik. Das wöchentliche Sammelwerk 'Aero' beschreibt sie jetzt alle. 'Aero' hat ein großes Kapitel der Flugzeuge von A–Z. Als Star der Woche bring Heft eins den Senkrechtstarter Harrier. Neben einem Porträt der Swiss Air beschreibt 'Aero' in Heft eins die Grundlagen der Luftkampfmanöver. 'Aero' ist ein komplettes Sammel- und Nachschlagewerk der zivilen und militärischen Luftfahrt. Aero – Heft eins jetzt bei Ihrem Zeitschriftenhändler.

Karina Seite 6: Die neue Mode, edel, lässig und romantisch. Karina Seite 12: Pullover zum Selberstricken in den Farben der Natur. Karina Seite 124: 101 Ideen – Wohnen für wenig Geld. Karina Seite 84: Das ABC der zärtlichen Liebe, das große neue Thema in Karina. Karina – die Zeitschrift für junge Frauen. Jetzt überall im Handel.

Unit 7 Übung 18

13 Uhr – das aktuelle Magazin 'Heute Mittag'. Folgende Themen sind unter anderem geplant: Letzte Chance: Großmächte verhandeln in Genf über Mittelstreckenraketen. Große Angst – Massenflucht aus Beirut. Viel Spaß – Kinderbuchautor schreibt Schmökerlexikon. 14.05 Uhr – für junge Hörer: Ihr seid zwar älter, aber sonst? heißt das Tagebuch eines jungen Mädchens, aus dem Sybille Nikolai heute wieder vorlesen wird. Radiotreff am Nach-

mittag: Um 14.30 lernen Sie einen ausgefallenen Party-Service kennen. Und wir haben eine Kosmetikerin zu Gast, die über die einhundertjährige Geschichte des Lippenstiftes berichtet.

Unit 8 Übung 19

Popshop unterwegs. Die Sommerpause ist vorbei, es geht wieder los. SWF 3, Popshop unterwegs. Am zehnten September, in Griesheim in der Hegelsberghalle, von 18 bis 22 Uhr, und mit dabei, live aus München, die 'Münchener Freiheit'. Also nicht vergessen, kommenden Samstag, 10. September, Griesheim, Hegelsberghalle, von 18 bis 22 Uhr. SWF 3 Popshop unterwegs. So, und wer noch wissen will, wo Griesheim liegt, da gibt's nämlich mehrere Griesheim in der ganzen Republik – das liegt bei Erbarmstadt – Darmstadt.

Unit 8 Übung 20 + 21

Filmfestival – neuntes internationales Kinderfilmfestival im Kommunalen Kino in Frankfurt. Bis 16. September sind da noch Kinderfilme zu sehen, aus Obervolta, der Volksrepublik China, der DDR, Italien, aus skandinavischen und Ostblockländern, von den Philippinen. Hanne Huntemann berichtet über den ersten Tage des Kinderfilmfestivals.

Als bundesdeutscher Beitrag läuft am kommenden Donnerstag, morgens um neun, 'Konrad aus der Konservenbüchse'. Ein witziger, phantasievoller Film, in dem ein sogenanntes Instant-Kind per Konserve bei einer völlig überraschten, etwas flippigen Malerin abgeliefert wird.

Unit 9 Übung 16a

Sie sehen zwar gut erholt aus – doch, doch, aber Sie haben auch ganz schön charmant zugelegt. Spaghetti, Carbonara, Tortellini. . . . Aha, jetzt aber blitzschnell ran an die BRIGITTE-Blitzdiät. Dafür ist es nie zu spät. Nie? Nie – denn blitzschnell schwinden alle Urlaubspfunde. Mit dem BRIGITTE-Einkaufszettel blitzschnell den Sieben-Tage-Vorrat einkaufen. Täglich fünf leckere Mahlzeiten mit insgesamt 800 Kalorien blitzschnell zubereiten – und blitzschnell nehmen Sie das ab, was im Urlaub so gut schmeckte. Spaghetti, Carbonara, Tortellini ... Also blitzschnell die neue BRIGITTE kaufen. Denn Sie wollen doch nicht auf Ihren Urlaubspfunden sitzenbleiben. – Die Blitzdiät – jetzt in der neuen BRIGITTE.

Unit 9 Übung 16b

Sag mal, wußtest du eigentlich, daß jeder zweite Bundesbürger übergewichtig ist? – Ja, und weil ich nicht dazu gehören will, süß' ich meinen Kaffee und Tee und die vielen Süßspeisen nur noch mit Natreen. – Und warum? – Weil Natreen ohne Kalorien und ohne Kohlenhydrate süßt. So spar' ich Tag für Tag viele Kalorien.

Unit 9 Übung 17

Die meisten Unfälle passieren in der Stadt. Und so ein Aufprallunfall mit Tempo 50 – das ist wie ein Sturz aus 12 Meter Höhe. Diese Wucht können Sie gar nicht mit Ihren Armen abfangen. Das kann nur der Sicherheitsgurt. Darum, Partner, fahren Sie mit Gurt – gerade auch in der Stadt.

Unit 10 Übung 17

Radiotreff am Nachmittag: Das Thema des Tages.

Und jetzt haben wir's auch noch amtlich. Eine Studie zur Situation der Frau im Auftrag des baden-württembergischen Sozialministeriums hat es an den Tag gebracht: Nur acht Prozent der Männer sind bereit, sich mit ihren Frauen die Hausarbeit zu teilen. Und dabei sind noch die Familien mitgezählt, in denen die Frau ganztags arbeitet. Wie ist es, meine Herren: Wollen Sie nicht, oder können Sie nicht? Ist das alte Rollenklischee noch so drin: Frau Gemahlin wäscht und wuselt, und der Herr Gemahl legt mal gnädig Hand an den Staubsauger, zum Beispiel. Das ist nämlich des deutschen Hausmannes liebstes Gerät. Geschirrspülen geht auch noch, aber Putzen, nee! Da hört die Gleichberechtigung auf. Frage an Sie: Hört die Gleichberechtigung wirklich beim Putzen auf, oder soll der Mann gleichberechtigt den Haushalt machen? Ja oder nein?

Unit 10 Übung 18

Was sagen die Sterne? Das Horoskop von Merkurius.

Für Mittwoch, den 7. September. Widder: Ihre Devise heißt für morgen: Ich bin von Kopf bis Fuß auf Liebe eingestellt. Und daran halten Sie sich. Und sonst an gar nichts. Waage: Wenn Sie morgen fremdgehen wollen, dann kommen Sie nicht weit. Bleiben Sie daheim bei Hausmannskost. Skorpion: Sie haben ebenfalls Appetit auf fremde Töpfe. Vorsicht! Sie könnten sich nicht nur die Finger verbrennen. Wassermann: Sie schwimmen in einem Meer von unerfüllbaren Wünschen. Kommen Sie an Land und betrachten Sie sich die Welt mal etwas trockener.

Unit 11 Übung 18

Achtzehn Uhr. Südwestfunk Baden-Baden. Tribüne der Zeit. Am Mikrofon Günter Thulen, und für die Nachrichten Walter Menk. Von ihm zunächst Wichtiges in Schlagzeilen: Genfer Raketengespräche wieder aufgenommen. Sowjets und Amerikaner zwei Stunden lang am Verhandlungstisch. Kabinett über das Ausmaß des Waldsterbens besorgt. In der Bundesrepublik fehlen noch 97 000 Lehrstellen. Schwere Kämpfe im Libanon: Drei amerikanische Soldaten gefallen.

Unit 12 Übung 17

SWF 3 – Radiokiosk. Internationale Funkausstellung in Berlin, unter anderem mit dem Dauerbrenner Videospiele. Wolfgang Schmidt in Berlin: Was ist denn da in, was ist out?

Ja, guten Tag Herr Deike, es ist eigentlich 'ne Überraschung. Out sind bei Videospielen die Kriegesspiele und die Weltrauminvasoren. In sind dafür immer noch die Pacmänner und andere drollige Kerlchen dieser Art. Und Sport läuft überhaupt nicht, weil die Spiele zu wenig Möglichkeiten bieten. Wenn Neuheiten überhaupt ankommen, dann müssen sie schon sehr, sehr raffiniert sein. So'n Top-Spiel ist Robot-Tank. Das ist natürlich 'n Kriegsspiel, aber eins von der etwas feineren Sorte. Oder Dekathlon, eine Art olympischer Mehrkampf, das ist entwickelt von David Crane, einem Superstar unter den Spiel-Designern. Oder das Trans-Amerika-Rennen mit Schnee-, Regen-, Tag-, Nacht-, Wüste- und Stadtrennen, das ist'n echter Hammer, das macht unheimlichen Spaß, da zu sitzen und an den Knöpfen zu drücken und zu spielen. Und Plaque-Attack, das könnte was werden für Eltern, die Probleme haben mit den Kindern, wenn sie keine Zähne putzen wollen. Da geht's nämlich um gesunde Zähne, die von bösen Bakterien bedroht werden. Es kostet 140 Mark, und das ist ganz schön teuer.

Unit 12 Übung 18

Was ist denn mit den Geräten, die mehr Kreativität für den Spieler anbieten, also fast schon Kleincomputer? Das ist eigentlich der ganz große Trend hier; Heimcomputer, Kleincomputer, und diese Geräte fangen an bei 550 Mark etwa und gehen bis zweitausend Mark.

Strong verbs

Infinitive	English	Present	Imperfect	Perfect
bekommen	*to get*	bekommt	bekam	hat bekommen
bieten	*to offer*	bietet	bot	hat geboten
bitten	*to ask*	bittet	bat	hat gebeten
bleiben	*to stay*	bleibt	blieb	ist geblieben
brechen	*to break*	bricht	brach	hat gebrochen
empfehlen	*to recommend*	empfiehlt	empfahl	hat empfohlen
essen	*to eat*	ißt	aß	hat gegessen
fahren	*to drive*	fährt	fuhr	ist gefahren
fallen	*to fall*	fällt	fiel	ist gefallen
finden	*to find*	findet	fand	hat gefunden
fliegen	*to fly*	fliegt	flog	ist geflogen
geben	*to give*	gibt	gab	hat gegeben
gefallen	*to please*	gefällt	gefiel	hat gefallen
gewinnen	*to win*	gewinnt	gewann	hat gewonnen
halten	*to stop*	hält	hielt	hat gehalten
heißen	*to call*	heißt	hieß	hat geheißen
helfen	*to help*	hilft	half	hat geholfen
kommen	*to come*	kommt	kam	ist gekommen
lassen	*to let*	läßt	ließ	hat gelassen
laufen	*to run*	läuft	lief	ist gelaufen
leihen	*to lend*	leiht	lieh	hat geliehen
lesen	*to read*	liest	las	hat gelesen
liegen	*to lie*	liegt	lag	hat gelegen
nehmen	*to take*	nimmt	nahm	hat genommen
riechen	*to smell*	riecht	roch	hat gerochen
rufen	*to call*	ruft	rief	hat gerufen
scheinen	*to shine*	scheint	schien	hat geschienen
schlafen	*to sleep*	schläft	schlief	hat geschlafen
schneiden	*to cut*	schneidet	schnitt	hat geschnitten
schreiben	*to write*	schreibt	schrieb	hat geschrieben
schwimmen	*to swim*	schwimmt	schwamm	ist geschwommen
sehen	*to see*	sieht	sah	hat gesehen
singen	*to sing*	singt	sang	hat gesungen
sitzen	*to sit*	sitzt	saß	hat gesessen
sprechen	*to speak*	spricht	sprach	hat gesprochen
stehlen	*to steal*	stiehlt	stahl	hat gestohlen
steigen	*to climb*	steigt	stieg	ist gestiegen
sterben	*to die*	stirbt	starb	ist gestorben
tragen	*to carry*	trägt	trug	hat getragen
treffen	*to meet*	trifft	traf	hat getroffen
trinken	*to drink*	trinkt	trank	hat getrunken
vergessen	*to forget*	vergißt	vergaß	hat vergessen
vergleichen	*to compare*	vergleicht	verglich	hat verglichen
verlieren	*to lose*	verliert	verlor	hat verloren
waschen	*to wash*	wäscht	wusch	hat gewaschen
werfen	*to throw*	wirft	warf	hat geworfen
ziehen	*to pull*	zieht	zog	hat gezogen

List of grammar

Vocabulary

The *plural* of nouns is given in brackets, e.g.

Abend(e) add **e**: **Abende**

Aktion(en) add **en**: **Aktionen**

Apotheke(n) add **n**: **Apotheken**

Freundin(nen) add **nen**: **Freundinnen**

Fahrplan(¨e) add **e** and stem vowel takes *Umlaut*: **Fahrpläne**

Dorf(¨er) add **er** and vowel takes *Umlaut*: **Dörfer**

Chef(s) add **s**: **Chefs**

Vater(¨) no change except for *Umlaut*: **Väter**

Kellner(–) no change at all

Fluß(¨sse) add **e**, modify vowel to *Umlaut* and ß to **ss**: **Flüsse**

Gymnasium(ien) irregular plural: **Gymnasien**

If nothing is given in brackets, there is no plural for that particular word or the plural is hardly ever used:

Butter butter

If (*pl.*) appears in brackets, the word is used in the plural only:

Ferien (*pl.*) holiday, vacation

The *gender* of nouns is given after the plural brackets:
m. = masculine (**der**), *f.* = feminine (**die**), *n.* = neuter (**das**)

The translation given in the vocabulary refers exclusively to the contexts in which the word appears and must not be taken as its 'meaning' in all cases. For more complete guidance you should consult a larger bilingual dictionary

German–English

ab off; from
abbiegen to turn
Abend(e), m. evening
Abendessen(–), n. dinner
Abendgymnasium(ien), n. evening
  college
aber but
abfahren to leave
Abfahrt(en), f. departure
Abfahrtsski, m. downhill skiing
abgehen to come off
abhängen to depend
abholen to pick up, to collect
Abitur(e), n. A-level, diploma
ablegen to take off (one's coat, etc.)
abliefern to deliver
abnehmen to lose weight
abreiben to rub down
abschließen to lock up
abschmecken to taste for seasoning
abstellen to leave (cars, etc.); to turn off
  (engine, etc.)
Abteil(e), n. compartment
abwaschen to wash up
Abwechslung(en), f. change, variety
abwechslungsreich diversified, varied
ach oh, well
Ackersalat(e), m. field salad
Adapter(–), m. adapter
Ägypten Egypt
Aktion(en), f. action
aktiv active
Akkordarbeit(en), f. piecemeal work
aktuell topical
akzeptieren to accept
Alarmton(¨e), m. alarm sound
alkoholisch alcoholic
allein(e) alone
allerdings though, but
alles Gute all the best
Allgemeinbildung, f. general
  education
Alltagstrott, m. daily routine
Alpennordseite(n), f. north side of the
  Alps
also so, that is to say
alt old
Alter, n. age
altmodisch old-fashioned
Ambulanz(en), f. ambulance
Amerika America
am liebsten best of all
amtlich official
amüsant amusing
amüsieren to enjoy, to amuse
am wenigsten least of all
anbieten to offer
Anbieter(–), m. supplier
an den Tag bringen to bring to light
ändern to change
anders else, different
anfangen to start

Anfänger(–), m. beginner
Anfängerkurs(e), m. beginner's course
Angebot(e), n. offer
Anglistik, f. English (language and
  literature)
Angst(¨e), f. fear
anhören to sound, to listen
ankommen to arrive; to appeal
Ankunft, f. arrival
Anlauf(¨e), m. dash, run-up
anprobieren to try on
Anregung(en), f. suggestion,
  inspiration
anreisen to arrive
anrufen to telephone
anschauen to watch
anschaulich clear
anschließen to join
anschließend after that
Anschluß(¨sse), m. motorway exit,
  junction
ansehen to look at
ansprechend appealing
Anstellung(en), f. job, position
anstrengend exhausting
Antiseptikum(ka), n. antiseptic
antworten to answer
Anzug(¨e), m. suit
anzünden to light
Apéritif(s), m. apperitif
Apotheke(n), f. pharmacy
Apotheker(–), m. pharmacist
Appetit(e), m. appetite
April, m. April
Arbeit(en), f. work
arbeiten to work
Arbeiter(–), m. worker (m.)
Arbeiterin(nen), f. worker (f.)
Arbeitgeber(–), m. employer
Arbeitsamt(¨er), n. labour exchange
Arbeitslage(n), f. job situation
arbeitslos unemployed
Arbeitslosenunterstützung(en), f.
  unemployment benefit, social security
Arbeitsmarkt(¨e), m. job market
Arbeitsplatz(¨e), m. place of work
Arbeitstag(e), m. working day
Ärger, m. trouble
ärgern to annoy
(sich) ärgern to get angry
Art(en), f. sort
Artikel(–), m. article
Arzt(¨e), m. doctor (m.)
Ärztin(nen), f. doctor (f.)
Arzthelferin(nen), f. doctor's assistant (f.)
Atlantik, m. Atlantic Ocean
Atombewaffnung(en), f. nuclear
  armament
Atomkraftwerk(e), n. nuclear power
  station
Attraktion(en), f. attraction
attraktiv attractive

auch also
aufbewahren to keep
auf die Dauer in the long run
aufeinander reagieren to relate to each other
Auffassung(en), *f.* opinion
Aufführung(en), *f.* performance
auflockern to intersperse, to loosen up
aufhören to stop
Aufnahme(n), *f.* recording
Aufnahmetaste(n), *f.* recording switch
aufnehmen to resume; to record
Aufprall(e), *m.* impact
aufräumen to tidy up
aufstehen to get up
Aufstieg(e), *m.* rise
Aufstiegsmöglichkeit(en), *f.* promotion prospect
Auftrag(¨e), *m.* commission
aufzählen to number
aufziehen to start; to wind up
Auge(n), *n.* eye
Augentropfen (pl.), *f.* eye drops
August, *m.* August
ausbeißen to break; to take a bite out of s.th.
Ausbildung(en), *f.* education, training
Ausbildungskurs(e), *m.* training course
ausbrechen to escape
Ausflug(¨e), *m.* excursion, trip
ausgeben to spend
ausgefallen unique
ausgehen to go out
Ausgleich(e), *m.* balance
ausländisch foreign
Ausmaß(e), *n.* extent
ausnahmslos without exception
ausprobieren to try out
ausreichend sufficient
ausruhen to rest
ausscheren to pull out
aussehen to look like
außerdem besides
ausstatten to appoint, to furnish
ausstellen to issue; to exhibit
Ausstellung(en), *f.* exhibition
Auswahl(en), *f.* selection
auswirken to matter
Auto(s), *n.* car
Autobahn(en), *f.* motorway, freeway
Auto fahren to drive
Autofahrer(–), *m.* driver (*m.*)
Automatik, *f.* automatic
Autor(en), *m.* author (*m.*)
Autovermietung(en), *f.* car hire

backen to bake
Badewanne(n), *f.* bath-tub
Badezimmer(–), *n.* bathroom
Bahnfahrt(en), *f.* railway journey
Bakterie(n), *f.* germ
Banane(n), *f.* banana
Bank(¨e), *f.* bench
Bank(en), *f.* bank
bar cash
Bau, *m.* construction

Bauernhof(¨e), *m.* farm
Baustelle(n), *f.* road works; building site
Bayrischer Wald, *m.* Bavarian Forest
beachten to consider
Beamte(n), *m.* clerk; civil servant (*m.*)
Beamtin(nen), *f.* clerk; civil servant (*f.*)
Bedeutung(en), *f.* meaning; importance
bedrohen to threaten
beeilen to hurry
Beere(n), *f.* berry
befestigen to fix
beginnen to begin
Beilage(n), *f.* side dish
Bein(e), *n.* leg
beinahe nearly
Beispiel(e), *n.* example
bekannt well-known
Bekanntenkreis(e), *m.* circle of friends
Bekanntgabe(n), *f.* announcement
bekommen to get, to receive
beliebig any at all
Belüftungsanlage(n), *f.* air condition
beobachten to observe
bequem comfortable
beraten to advise
Bereich(e), *m.* region, sector
Berg(e), *m.* mountain
Beruf(e), *m.* job, profession
Berufsleben(–), *n.* professional life
Berufsplan(¨e), *m.* career plan
besichtigen to view
besitzen to own
besonders special
bestehen to consist
bestellen to book, to order
besuchen to visit
Besucher(–), *m.* visitor (*m.*)
Besucherin(nen), *f.* visitor (*f.*)
betreffen to affect
betreuen to look after
Bett(en), *n.* bed
Bevölkerung(en), *f.* population
bewährt proved
beweglich supple, fit
bewerben to apply
bewölkt cloudy
bezahlen to pay
Bibliothek(en), *f.* library
Bier(e), *n.* beer
Bild(er), *n.* picture
Bildungsurlaub(e), *m.* educational holiday
billig cheap
Binde(n), *f.* bandage
Birne(n), *f.* pear
bisher yet
bißchen a bit
bitte please; you're welcome
bitten to ask for
blasen to blow
Blatt(¨er), *n.* leaf; sheet; (news)paper
blau blue
Blaukraut, *n.* red cabbage
bleiben to stay
Blickfeld(er), *n.* field of vision

blitzschnell in a flash
Blume(n), *f.* flower
Blumenkohl, *m.* cauliflower
blutig rare; bloody
Bohne(n), *f.* bean
Bootfahren, *n.* boating
böse nasty
Boulevardpresse (pl.), *f.* popular press
braten to fry
Bratensatz, *m.* meat juice
Brathähnchen(–), *n.* roast chicken
brauchen to need
Braut(¨e), *f.* bride
Bräutigam(e), *m.* bridegroom
brechen to break
bremsen to brake
brennen to burn
Brief(e), *m.* letter
bringen to bring
Brombeere(n), *f.* blackberry
Brot(e), *n.* bread
Brötchen(–), *n.* bread roll
Brücke(n), *f.* bridge
brutal cruel, brutal
brutto gross
Buch(¨er), *n.* book
buchen to book
Bücherregal(e), *n.* bookshelf
Buchhalter(–), *m.* accountant (*m.*)
Buchhandlung(en), *f.* book-shop
Bundesbürger(–), *m.* citizen of the Federal Republic
Bundeskanzler(–), *n.* Federal Chancellor
Bundesland(¨er), *n.* Federal State
Bundesliga(en), *f.* Federal (football) league
Bundespräsident(en), *m.* Federal President
Bundesrepublik Deutschland, *f.* Federal Republic of Germany
Bundestag, *m.* Federal Parliament
Bundestagsabgeordnete(n), *m.*, *f.* Member of Parliament
Burg(en), *f.* castle
Büro(s), *n.* office
Bus(se), *m.* bus
Busch(¨e), *m.* bush
Butter, *f.* butter

CDU = Christlich-Demokratische Union Christian Democrats
Champignon(s), *m.* button mushroom
Chance(n), f. chance
Chef(s), *m.* boss (*m.*)
Chefin(nen), *f.* boss (*f.*)
China China
Chips (pl.), *f.* crisps, potato chips
Cineast(en), *m.* movie buff
CSU = Christlich-Soziale Union Bavarian Christian Democrats

damenhaft ladylike
danke thank you
dann then
daran at it
darauf achten to take care, to watch

Darmgrippe, *f.* gastric flu
dasselbe the same
Dauerbrenner(–), *m.* continuous bestseller
dauern to last
dazu with it
dazurechnen to include
Decke(n), *f.* blanket
decken to set, to lay
demnächst in the near future
deprimieren to depress
Desinfektionsmittel(–), *n.* disinfectant
Deutsch, *n.* German
Deutsche Bundesbahn German Federal Railways
Deutschsprachiger Dienst German Service
Devise(n), *f.* motto
Dezember, *m.* December
Diät(en), *f.* diet
dicht close
dick fat
Dienst(e), *m.* service
Diesel diesel driven car
dieselbe the same
direkt direct
Donnerstag(e), *m.* Thursday
Dorf(¨er), *n.* village
dort there
Dose(n), *f.* tin, can
drehen to turn
drollig funny
düngen to fertilize
dünsten to steam, to stew
durch well done; through
Durchfall(¨e), *m.* diarrhoea
dürfen may, must
Durst, *m.* thirst
Dusche(n), *f.* shower

Ecke(n), *f.* corner
ehemalig former
Ei(er), *n.* egg
Eierlikör(e), *m.* egg flip, egg liqueuer
eigentlich really, actually
einfach easy, simple; single
eingelegt pickled
einkaufen to shop
Einkaufszettel(–), *m.* shopping list
einkehren to go to a pub/tavern
einladen to invite
Einladung(en), *f.* invitation
Einmachgurke(n), *f.* gherkin
einmalig single, unique
einnicken to nod off
einschalten to switch on
(sich) einschalten to trigger off
einschließlich including
einstellen to employ
Einzelheit(en), *f.* detail
einverstanden agreed
einzig only
Eis, *n.* ice, ice cream
Eisbein(e), *n.* pig's trotter
Eisenbahn(en), *f.* railway
Eissalat(e), *m.* iceberg lettuce
Elektrizität, *f.* electricity

Elektronik(en), f. electronic
Eltern (pl.), f. parents
empfehlen to advise
Ende(n), n. end
enden to end
Energiegewinnung(en), f. production of energy
Engländer(–), m. Englishman
englisch English
Enkelkind(er), n. grandchild
Entdecker(–), m. explorer
Ente(n), f. duck
entfernt distant
Entfernung(en), f. distance
entsaften to extract juice
entscheiden to decide
Entscheidung(en), f. decision
Entschlackung(en), f. purification
entschließen to decide
entschuldigen to excuse, to apologize
entspannen to relax
entweder - oder either - or
entwickeln to develop
Erdbeere(n), f. strawberry
erfahren to find out
Erfindung(en), f. invention
Erfolg(e), m. success
erforschen to research
erfrischen to refresh
erhalten to receive
erholen to rest
Erholung(–), f. relaxation
Erkältung(en), f. cold
erklären to explain
erleben to experience
erleiden to suffer
ermäßigen to reduce
Ermäßigung(en), f. reduction
ermüden to retire
erreichen to achieve
Ersatzband(s), f. replacement band
ertragen to bear
Erwachsene(n), m. adult
erwarten to await, to expect
erweitern to extend
erzählen to tell
Erziehung, f. upbringing, education
Eskimo(s), m. Eskimo
essen to eat
Essen(–), n. food
etwas something
ewig eternal
Experiment(e), n. experiment
explodieren to explode
Exportfirma(men), f. export firm
extra additional

fabelhaft phantastic
Fabrik(en), f. factory
Fabrikat(e), n. manufactured product
Fachmesse(n), f. trade fair
fade bland
fahren to drive, to go, to travel
Fahrer(–), m. driver (m.)
Fahrkartenschalter(–), m. ticket office
Fahrpreis(e), m. fare
Fahrstrecke(n), f. route

Fahrtrichtung(en), f. direction
Fahrzeug(e), n. vehicle
fallen to die in action; to fall
falsch wrong
Falte(n), f. wrinkle
Familie(n), f. family
Familienepidemie(n), f. family epidemic
Familienfest(e), n. family occasion
Farbauflösung(en), f. colour separation
Farbe(n), f. colour
Fasching, m. carnival
fasten to fast
faszinierend fascinating
faul lazy
FDP = Freie Demokratische Partei Liberal Party
Feierabend(e), m. time after work
feiern to celebrate
fein nice; delicate, fine
Fenster(–), n. window
Fensterplatz(¨e), m. window seat
Ferien (pl.) holidays, vacation
Feriensonderzug(¨e), m. special holiday train
Fern-Express(e), m. long-distance train
Fernsehen, n. television
Fernsehgerät(e), n. television set
fest steady
Fest(e), n. party, feast
Fete(n), f. party
fettarm low in fat
Feuerwerk(e), n. fireworks
Fieber(–), n. fever, temperature
finanziell financial
finanzieren to finance
finden to find
Firma(men), f. firm, company
Fisch(e), m. fish
Flause(n), f. nonsense
Fleisch, n. meat
Fleischwolf, m. mincer
fliegen to fly
Fließband(¨er), n. production line
Flughafen(¨), m. airport
Flugverkehr, m. air traffic
Flugzeug(e), n. aeroplane
Fluß(¨sse), m. river
föderativ federal
Forelle(n), f. trout
Form(en), f. shape; in Form fit
Fortschritt(e), m. progress
fragen to ask
Frankenwein(e), m. wine from Franconia
fränkisch Franconian
Frankreich France
Französisch, n. French (language)
Frau(en), f. wife; woman
Frauenzeitschrift(en), f. women's magazine
Fräulein(–), n. Miss
frei freelance; free; im Freien open-air
Freiheit(en), f. freedom
Freitag(e), m. Friday

freiwillig voluntary
fremdgehen to stray
(sich) freuen to be delighted, to enjoy
o.s.
Freund(e), *m.* friend, boy friend
Freundin(nen), *f.* girl friend
freundlich friendly
Freundschaft(en), *f.* friendship
frisch fresh
Frisur(en), *f.* hair-do
froh glad
Fröhlichkeit(en), *f.* fun, gaiety
früh early
früher at one stage; earlier
frühestens at the earliest date
Frühgymnastik(en), *f.* morning
exercise
Frühjahr, *n.* spring
frühstücken to have breakfast
füllen to fill
Funkausstellung(en), *f.* radio
exhibition
Fuß(¨e), *m.* foot
Fußball (¨e), *m.* football
Fußball *m.* soccer
Fußballplatz(¨e), *m.* soccer pitch

ganz whole
ganztags full-time
garantieren to guarantee
Gärtner(–), *m.* gardener (*m.*)
Gast(¨e), *m.* guest
Gasthof(¨e), *m.* inn, pub
geben to give
geboren born
Gebrauch machen to make use
Geburtstag(e), *m.* birthday
Geburtstagskind(er), *n.* birthday boy/
girl
Gedanke(n), *m.* thought
gefährlich dangerous
gefallen to like
Gefängnis(se), *n.* prison
Geflügel, *n.* poultry
gefrieren to freeze
gefroren frozen
Gefühl(e), *n.* feeling
gegen towards
Gegenteil(e), *n.* opposite
Gehalt(¨er), *n.* salary
Geheimtip(s), *m.* hot tip
gehen to go
Gehweg(e), *m.* pavement, sidewalk
Geist(er), *m.* ghost
gelassen aufnehmen to take it in one's
stride
Geld(er), *n.* money
Geldsorgen (pl.) money worries
Gelee(s), *n.* gel
gelegentlich occasional
gelten to be valid
Geltungstag(e), *m.* validity date
Gemälde(–), *n.* painting
gemeinsam together
Gemüse(–), *n.* vegetable
Gemüsegarten(¨), *m.* kitchen garden
gemütlich cosy

Gemütlichkeit, *f.* cosiness
genau exact
genug enough
genügen to be sufficient
geradeaus straight on
Gerät(e), *n.* appliance
Germanistik, *f.* German
gern with pleasure
Geschäft(e), *n.* shop
gescheit clever
Geschenk(e), *n.* present
Geschichte, *f.* history
Geschirr, *n.* dishes
Geschwister (pl.), *f.* brother(s) and
sister(s)
Gesellschaft(en), *f.* society; party
Gesichtscreme, *f.* face cream
Gespenst(er), *n.* phantom, ghost
gestern yesterday
gesund healthy
Gesundheit, *f.* health
Getränk(e), *n.* drink
Gewalt(en), *f.* violence, force
gewinnen to win
Gewinner(–), *m.* winner
gießen to pour
Glas(¨er), *n.* glass
glauben to think, to believe
gleich right away
Gleichberechtigung, *f.* equality
gleichzeitig at the same time
gleitende Arbeitszeit(en), *f.* flexitime
glücken to turn out well
Glückspilz(e), *m.* lucky thing
gnädig gracious
Graben(¨), *m.* ditch
Gramm (pl.), *m.* gram
gratulieren to congratulate
Graupensuppe(n), *f.* barley soup
Griechenland Greece
Grillbraten(–), *m.* grilled meat
Grippe(n), *f.* flu
groß big
Größe(n), *f.* size
Großmacht(¨e), *f.* super power
Großraumwagen(–), *m.* saloon car
Grundlage(n), *f.* basis
Gruppe(n), *f.* group
grün green
Grund(¨e), *m.* reason
Grundschule(n), *f.* primary school
Grünen (pl.), *f.* the Greens, ecologists
grüßen to greet
günstig good value
Gurke(n), *f.* cucumber
gut good; **was Gutes** something good
(i.e. special)
Güteklasse(n), *f.* quality (range)
Guten Abend good evening
Gymnasium(ien), *n.* grammar school,
high school

haben to have
Haferschleim, *m.* porridge
halb half
Halbpension, *f.* half-board
Hals- und Beinbruch best of luck

Halsweh(e), *n.* sore throat
halten to stop, to keep
Haltestelle(n), *f.* stop
Handballplatz("e), *m.* handball pitch
im Handel on sale
Handschuh(e), *m.* glove
hart hard
hassen to hate
Haupt("er), *n.* head
Hauptaufgabe(n), *f.* main task
Hauptbahnhof("e), *m.* main station
Hauptfach("er), *m.* main subject
Hauptsache(n), *f.* main point
Hauptstadt("e), *f.* capital
Haus("er), *n.* house
Hausarbeit(en), *f.* housework
Hausaufgabe(n), *f.* homework
zu Hause bleiben to stay at home
Hausfrau(en), *f.* housewife
Hausgebrauch, *m.* everyday use
Hausmann("er), *m.* househusband
Hausmannskost (pl.), *f.* plain fare
Hausmusik, *f.* music in the home
Hecke(n), *f.* hedge
Heiliger Abend, *m.* Christmas Eve
Heimcomputer(–), *m.* home (personal)
  computer
heimisch at home
heiraten to get married
heiß hot
heißen to mean
heiter fair; jolly
Held(en), *m.* hero
helfen to help
herauskriechen to crawl out
herausnehmen to take out
herb dry
Herbst(e), *m.* autumn
Herd(e), *m.* stove, cooker
Hering(e), *m.* herring
herrlich delightful
Herz(en), *n.* heart
herzlichen
  Glückwunsch congratulations
heute today
hier here
hier drüben over here
Hilfsarbeiter(–), *m.* unskilled labourer
Himmel(–), *m.* sky
Hindernis(se), *n.* hitch, obstacle
hinfahren to go somewhere
hinfallen to fall
hinkommen to get there
hinlegen to put down
hinschauen to look at
Hintergrund("e), *m.* background
Hobby(s), *n.* hobby
Hochstraße(n), *f.* mountain road
Höchsttemperatur(en), *f.* highest
  temperature
Hochzeit(en), *f.* wedding
hoffen to hope
höflich polite
Höhepunkt(e), *m.* highlight
holen to get, to fetch
Holz("er), *n.* wood
Hörer(–), *m.* listener (*m.*)

Hörerin(nen), *f.* listener (*f.*)
Horoskop(e), *n.* horoscope
Hose(n), *f.* trousers
Hotelkauffrau(en), *f.* hotel
  manageress
Hühnchen(–), *n.* baby chicken
Hundehaufen(–), *m.* dog turd
Hunger, *m.* hunger
Hungerkur(en), *f.* fast
Hut("e), *m.* hat

Idee(n), *f.* idea
Idiot(en), *m.* idiot
ignorieren to ignore
Imbißhalle(n), *f.* snack bar
immer always
imponieren to impress
improvisieren to improvise
inbegriffen included
Indien India
Individualfahrzeug(e), *n.* privately
  owned vehicle
Informationsschalter(–), *m.*
  information desk
informieren to inform
inklusiv inclusive
innen inside
insbesondere especially
Insektenschutz, *m.* insect repellent
Insel(n), *f.* island
Inserat(e), *n.* advertisement (classified)
insgesamt all together
intensiv intensive
interessant interesting
interessieren to be interested
Interview(s), *n.* interview
irgend etwas something
irgendwelche some sort of
irgendwie somehow
ironisch ironical
irren to err
italienisch Italian

Jägerschnitzel(–), *n.* special kind of
  Schnitzel
Jahr(e), *n.* year
Jahresurlaub(e), *m.* annual holiday
Jahreszeit(en), *f.* time of the year,
  season
jährlich yearly
jäten to weed
jede, jeder each
je früher desto besser the sooner the
  better
je nachdem depending on
jetzt now
Johannisbeere(n), *f.* red currant
Journalist(en), *m.* journalist
Jugendliche(n), *f. m.* youth
jugoslawisch Yugoslavian
Juli, *m.* July
jung young

Kabelfernsehen, *n.* cable television
Kabinett(e), *n.* cabinet
Kaffee, *m.* coffee
Kaffeekränzchen(–), *n.* coffee circle

Kalbsleber, *f.* calf's liver
Kalorie(n), *f.* calorie
kalt cold
kämpfen to fight
Kandiszucker, *m.* rock candy
Kaninchen(–), *n.* rabbit
Kantine(n), *f.* canteen
Kapelle(n), *f.* band; chapel
kaputt exhausted; broken; spoiled, ruined
Karriere(n), *f.* career
Karottensalat(e), *m.* carrot salad
Karte(n), *f.* ticket
Karten spielen to play cards
Kartoffel(n), *f.* potato
Käse(–), *m.* cheese
Käsekuchen(–), *m.* cheese-cake
Kassette(n), *f.* cassette
Kassiererin(nen), *f.* cashier (*f.*)
Kater(–), *m.* hangover; tomcat
Kaufmann(leute), *m.* merchant; shop keeper
Kegelbahn(en), *f.* bowling alley
Kellner(–), *m.* waiter
Kellnerin(nen), *f.* waitress
Kennzeichen(–), *n.* registration number
Kerlchen(–), *n.* creature
Kerze(n), *f.* candle
Kilo(s), *n.* kilogram
Kilometergeld(er), *n.* rate per kilometre
Kind(er), *n.* child
Kindergarten(¨), *n.* kindergarten
Kinderkrippe(n), *f.* crêche
Kindersendung(en), *f.* children's programme
Kino(s), *n.* cinema, movie house
Kirche(n), *f.* church
Klapptisch(e), *m.* folding-table
Klasse(n), *f.* class
klassisch classical
Klassiker(–), *m.* classic
klauen to nick
Kleid(er), *n.* dress
Kleidermarkt(¨e), *m.* clothes market
klein small
Kletterleiter(n), *f.* climbing frame
klimatisieren to climatize
klingen to sound
Klubanlage(n), *f.* holiday compound
knackig crunchy
Knallbonbon(s), *n.* cracker
knallvoll very crowded
kneten to knead
Knoblauch, *n.* garlic
Knödel(–), *m.* dumpling
Knopf(¨e), *m.* button
knusprig crispy
Koalitionspartner(–), *m.* coalition partner
kochen to cook
Kohlehydrat(e), *n.* carbohydrate
Kollege(n), *m.* colleague (*m.*)
komisch funny, strange
kommen to come
kommerzialisieren to commercialize

kommunal communal
Komödie(n), *f.* comedy
kompliziert complicated
König(e), *m.* king
können can, to be able to
konservativ conservative
Konservenbüchse(n), *f.* tin, can
Konstrukteur(e), *m.* inventor; constructor
Konsum, *m.* consumption
kontrollieren to control
Kopf(¨e), *m.* head
Kopfweh(e), *n.* headache
Kosmetikerin(nen), *f.* beautician
kosten to cost
Krach(e, also ¨e), *m.* noise; quarrel
krank sick, ill
Krankenhaus(¨er), *n.* hospital
Krankenschwester(n), *f.* nurse
Krankenwagen(–), *m.* ambulance
Krankheit(en), *f.* illness
Kreis(e), *m.* circle
Kraut(¨er), *n.* herb
Kreativität(en), *f.* creativity
Kreditkarte(n), *f.* credit card
Krieg(e), *m.* war
Kriegsspiel(e), *n.* war game
kritisch critical
Küche(n), *f.* kitchen
Kuchen(–), *m.* cake
Küchenapfel(¨), *m.* cooking apple
Küchenmaschine(n), *f.* food processor
kühlen to cool
Kühlschrank(¨e), *m.* fridge
Kult(e), *m.* cult
kulturell cultural
Kummer(–), *m.* trouble
Kunde(n), *m.* customer
Kunst(¨e), *f.* art
Kunstschatz(¨e), *m.* art treasure
Kur(en), *f.* course of treatment, cure
Kürbis(se), *m.* pumpkin
kürzlich recently

lachen to laugh
lächerlich funny, strange, ridiculous
Lagerarbeiter(–), *m.* storeman
Lagerfeuer(–), *n.* campfire
Land, *n.* countryside
Land(¨er), *n.* country, state
landen to land
Landstraße(n), *f.* country road
lang long
Langeweile, *f.* boredom
langfristig in the long run
Langlauf(¨e), *m.* cross-country skiing
(sich) langweilen to be bored
langweilig boring
Lärm, *m.* noise
lässig casual
Lastwagen(–), *m.* lorry, truck
laut noisy
lauwarm lukewarm
Leben(–), *n.* life
Lebensgefährte(n), *m.* companion, partner
Lebenslauf(¨e), *m.* curriculum vitae

lecker delicious
Leder(–), n. leather
legen to lay, to put
Lehrer(–), m. teacher (m.)
Lehrerin(nen), f. teacher (f.)
Lehrstelle(n), f. vacancy for a trainee
leicht light
Leichtathletik, f. athletics
leider unfortunately
leid tun to feel sorry for
Leselampe(n), f. reading lamp
lesen to read
letzte last
Leute (pl.), f. people
liberal liberal
Liberalen (pl.), f. Liberals
Liebe(n), f. love
Lieben (pl.) loved ones
liebend loving
lieber rather
Lieblingssportart(en), f. favourite
  kind of sport
Lied(er), n. song
Liederabend(e), m. song recital
liegen to lie
Liegepolster(–), n. cushion
Liegewagen(–), m. couchette
Limonade(n), f. lemonade
Linie(n), f. line
links left
linksliberal liberal to left-wing
Lippenstift(e), m. lipstick
Liste(n), f. list
Literatur(en), f. literature
LKW = Lastkraftwagen(–), m. lorry
Locke(n), f. curl
Löffel(–), m. spoon
Lokalnachrichten (pl.), f. local news
Lücke(n), f. gap
Luft(¨e), f. air
Luftfahrt(en), f. aviation
Luftkampfmanöver(–), n. air
  manoeuvre
Luftzwischenfall(¨e), m. aerial
  incident
Lust am Leben love of life
lustig funny

machbar feasible, possible
machen to do, to make
Mädchen(–), n. girl
Magenschmerz(en), m. stomach pain
mager lean
Mal(e), m. time(s); fünf mal five times
Maler(–), m. painter (m.)
Malerin(nen), f. painter (f.)
manchmal sometimes
Mandel(n), f. almond
Mango(s), f. mango
Mann(¨er), m. man, husband
Margarine, f. margarine
Markt(¨e), m. market
Maschine(n), f. machine
Massenflucht, f. mass exodus
Mathematik, f. mathematics
matschig soggy
Maurer(–), m. bricklayer

Meer(e), n. sea
Mehrkampf, m. multi discipline sport
Meinung(en), f. opinion
Meinungsumfrage(n), f. opinion poll
meist in most cases
meistens mostly
melden to answer; to report
Meldung(en), f. news
Menge(n), f. amount
Mensch(en), m. man, people
Mensch ärgere dich nicht ludo
Metzger(–), m. butcher
Miete(n), f. rent
mieten to rent, to hire
Mikrofon(e), n. microphone
Milch, f. milk
militärisch military
Milliarde(n), f. milliard, billion
mindestens at least
Minute(n), f. minute
mischen to mix
mitnehmen to take along
Mittag(e), m. noon, mid-day
mittags lunchtime
Mittagspause(n), f. lunch break
Mittel(–), n. means
Mittelstreckenrakete(n), f. medium
  range missile
mittendrin in the middle
Mittlere Reife, f. O-levels, school
  leaving certificate
Mittwoch, m. Wednesday
mitzählen to include
mixen to mix
mobil mobile
Mode(n), f. fashion
modern modern
mögen to like
möglich possible
Möglichkeit(en), f. possibility
Möhre(n), f. carrot
Mokkalikör(e), m. mocha liqueur
mollig plump
Moment(e), m. moment
Monat(e), m. month
monatlich monthly
Mondaufgang(¨e), m. moonrise
Monduntergang(¨e), m. moon sets
Mörder(–), m. murderer (m.)
Morgen(–), m. morning
morgen tomorrow
morgens in the morning
Morgenstunde(n), f. morning hour
Moskau Moscow
Motor(en), m. motor
Motto(s), n. theme, motto
müde tired
munter wide awake
Museum(en), n. museum
Musik (pl.), f. music
Muskel(n), m. muscle
Muskelschmerz(en), m. sore muscles
Müsli(s), n. muesli
müssen must, to have to
Mutter(¨), f. mother
Mütterberatung(en), f. mothers'
  advisory service

Nachbar(n), *m.* neighbour
nachdenken to think about
Nachdruck, *m.* emphasis
Nachmittag(e), *m.* afternoon
nachmittags in the afternoon
nächste next, nearest
Nacht("e), , *f.* night
Nachteil(e), *m.* disadvantage
Nachtreise(n), *f.* night journey
nah near, nearby
Nähe, *f.* proximity
na ja well, you see
nämlich actually, namely, you see, you know
Natur(en), *f.* nature
natürlich of course
Naturschutzgebiet(e), *n.* nature reserve
neben next to, beside
nebenher at the same time
negativ negative
Neger(–), *m.* negro
nehmen to take
Neigung(en), *f.* angle
Nektarine(n), *f.* nectarine
Nerv(en), *m.* nerve
Neuerung(en), *f.* innovation
Niederschlag("e), *m.* rainfall, precipitation
niemand nobody
noch also
Norddeutschland Northern Germany
normal normal, ordinary
normalerweise normally
notwendig necessary
Notwendigkeit(en), *f.* necessity
Nudelsuppe(n), *f.* noodle soup
Nummer(n), *f.* act, party piece; number
Nuß("sse), *f.* nut

Obervolta Upper Volta
Obst, *n.* fruit
offen open
öffentlich public
öffnen to open
oft often
Ohr(en), *n.* ear
Oktober, *m.* October
Ölscheich(e), *m.* oil sheik
olympisch Olympic
Oma(s), *f.* granny, grandma
Oper(n), *f.* opera
organisieren to organize
Orgelkonzert(e), *n.* organ recital
originell ingenious, original
Ostblockland("er), *n.* East European country
Ostern (pl.), *n.* Easter
Österreich Austria
Ostfriesentee, *m.* East Frisian tea

Palast("e), *m.* palace
Panoramafenster(–), *n.* panorama window
Papier(e), *n.* document; paper
Paprikaschote(n), *f.* capsicum
parken to park

Parkett(e), *n.* dance floor
Parkhaus("er), *n.* multi-storey car park
Partei(en), *f.* (political) party
Partner(–), *m.* partner
passen to suit; to fit
passend fitting
passieren to happen
Pastete(n), *f.* pie, pâté
pauschal flat rate
Pension(en), *f.* boarding-house
pensioniert werden to retire
Pensionswirtin(nen), *f.* landlady
Person(en), *f.* person
persönlich personal
pfeffern to pepper
Pferd(e), *n.* horse
Pfingsten(–), *n.* Whitsun
Pfirsich(e), *m.* peach
Pflaster(–), *n.* elastoplast
Pfund(e), *n.* pound
Philosophie(n), *f.* philosophy
Pilz(e), *m.* mushroom
PKW = Personenkraftwagen(–), *m.* car
Plan("e), *m.* plan
planen to plan
Platz("e), *m.* space
platzen to burst
plaudern to chat
plötzlich suddenly
Politik(en), *f.* politics
Polizei, *f.* police
Polterabend(e), *m.* wedding-eve
Pomade(n), *f.* pomade
Pommes Frites (pl.), *f.* chips
Pony(s), *m.* fringe
Pornographie, *f.* pornography
Portugal Portugal
Postbote(n), *m.* postman
Preis(e), *m.* prize; cost, price
Preisgruppe(n), *f.* price-range
preisgünstig reasonable
Preisschild(er), *n.* price-tag
Premiere(n), *f.* première
Presse, *f.* press
prima excellent, great
Prinzip(ien), *n.* principle
Privatklinik(en), *f.* private clinic
pro per
probieren to taste; to try
Problem(e), *n.* problem
Produkt(e), *m.* product
Produzent(en), *m.* producer (*m.*)
Produzentin(nen), *f.* producer (*f.*)
Programmierung(en), *f.* programme
Promenadenkonzert(e), *n.* promenade concert
promenieren to take a stroll
Prozent(e), *n.* per cent
Puder(–), *n.* powder
Pute(n), *f.* turkey
putzen to clean
Putzfrau(en), *f.* cleaner (*f.*)

Qualität(en), *f.* quality
Quark, *m.* curd cheese

quer durch right through

Radieschen(–), *n.* radish
Radio(s), *n.* radio, wireless
Radiodienst(e), *m.* radio service
raffiniert sophisticated
Rang(¨e), *m.* circle, tier (theat.)
Rasiersteckdose(n), *f.* razor point
Ratespiel(e), *n.* guessing game
Raubkopie(n), *f.* illegal copy
rauchen to smoke
Raum(¨e), *m.* room
reagieren to react
rechts right
rechtzeitig in time
Reform(en), *f.* reform
Regel(n), *f.* norm; **in der Regel** as a rule
Regierung(en), *f.* government
Regierungssystem(e), *n.* form of government
regional regional
Regionalsendung(en), *f.* regional programme
Regisseur(e), *m.* director (theat. etc.) (*m.*)
regnen to rain
Rehrücken(–), *m.* saddle of venison
reiben to grate; to rub
reif mature
Reinfall(¨e), *m.* flop, fiasco
reinkommen to get into
Reise(n), *f.* journey
Reiseapotheke(n), *f.* medical kit for travelling
Reisebüro(s), *n.* travel agency
Reiseführer(–), *m.* guide (*m.*)
reisen to travel
Reiseruf(e), *m.* radio message
Reisesessel(–), *m.* Pullman seat
Reiseveranstalter(–), *m.* tour operator
Reisewagen(–), *m.* coach
Reiseziel(e), *n.* destination
reiten to ride
relativ relative
Renner(–), *m.* favourite
Rente(n), *f.* pension
Reportage(n), *f.* report
Reporter(–), *m.* reporter (*m.*)
repräsentativ representative
Restaurant(s), *n.* restaurant
retten to save
Rettich(e), *m.* white radish
Rezept(e), *f.* recipe
Rezeptur(en), *f.* recipe, ingredients
Rezession(en), *f.* recession
richtig right, proper
Richtung(en), *f.* towards; direction
Riese(n), *m.* giant
riesig gigantic
Rindfleisch, *n.* beef
Rohr(e), *n.* tube, pipe
Rollenklischee(s), *n.* role cliché
romantisch romantic
rosarot pink
Rose(n), *f.* rose
Rosenkohl, *n.* Brussels sprouts
rosig rosy

rösten to roast
Routine, *f.* routine
Rückfahrt(en), *f.* return journey
Rucksack(¨e), *m.* rucksack
rufen to call
Ruhestand, *m.* retirement
ruhig quiet
Rumpsteak(s), *n.* rumpsteak
Rundfunk, *m.* radio
Rüstungsgespräch(e), *n.* arms talks
Rutschbahn(en), *f.* slide

Sache(n), *f.* matter, thing
Saftkur(en), *f.* fruit-juice diet
sagen to say
Sahne, *f.* cream
Salat(e), *m.* salad
Salz, *n.* salt
salzen to salt
Sammelwerk(e), *n.* partwork
Samstag(e), *m.* Saturday
Sänger(–), *m.* singer (*m.*)
Sängerin(nen), *f.* singer (*f.*)
Sanktion(en), *f.* sanction
Sauna(s), *f.* sauna
schaffen to manage, to create
scharf spicy
Schatz(¨e), *m.* treasure
schauen to look
scheinen to shine
schenken to give away
scheußlich horrible, terrible
Schicksal(e), *n.* fate
Schienenstrecke(n), *f.* rail track
Schiff(e), *n.* ship
Schild(er), *n.* sign
schimpfen to complain
schlachten to slaughter
schlafen to sleep
schlaff listless; limp
Schlagsahne, *f.* whipped cream
Schlagzeile(n), *f.* headline
schlank slim
schlecht bad
Schloß(¨sser), *n.* castle; lock
schlüpfen to slip
schmecken to taste
Schmerz(en), *m.* pain
schmutzig dirty
Schnee, *m.* snow
schneiden to cut
schneien to snow
schnell fast, quick
Schnellzug(¨e), *m.* express train
Schnitt(e), *m.* cut
Schnitzel(–), *n.* escalope, *schnitzel*
schnitzeln to chop
Schnupfen(–), *m.* runny nose
Shock(s), *m.* shock
Schokoladeneis, *n.* chocolate ice-cream
Scholle(n), *f.* plaice
schon already
schön beautiful, nice
Schönheitschirurg(en), *m.* plastic surgeon
Schornsteinfeger(–), *m.*

chimneysweep
Schreck(en), *m.* fright
schreiben to write
Schritt(e), *m.* step, move
Schulabschluß("sse), *m.* final school examination
Schule(n), *f.* school
Schutz, *m.* protection
schwarz black
Schwarzbrot(e), *n.* black (rye) bread
Schwarzwälder Kirschtorte(n), *f.* Black Forest Gateaux
Schweineschnitzel(–), *n.* pork *schnitzel*
Schweiz, *f.* Switzerland
Schweizer Mustermesse Swiss Trade Fair
Schwester(n), *f.* sister
schwierig difficult
Schwierigkeit(en), *f.* difficulty
Schwimmbad("er), *n.* swimming-pool
schwimmen to swim
SDP = Sozialdemokratische Partei Deutschlands Social Democrats
See(n), *m.* lake
Segelfliegen, *n.* gliding
sehen to see
sehr very
Seide(n), *f.* silk
sein to be
seitdem since
Seite(n), *f.* side; page
Seitengang("e), *m.* side corridor
selbst even; self
selbstgemacht home-made
selbstverständlich of course
senden to broadcast; to send
Sendung(en), *f.* programme, broadcast
Senf, *m.* mustard
Senfgurke(n), *f.* pickled cucumber
Senfsoße(n), *f.* mustard sauce
Senkrechtstarter(–), *m.* vertical take-off aircraft
Sensationsblatt("er), *m.* tabloid
September, *m.* September
Serviermeisterin(nen), *f.* head waitress
Sessel(–), *m.* armchair
sicher safe
Sicherheitsgurt(e), *m.* safety belt
sichern to secure
Sicht, *f.* view
Siegel(–), *n.* seal
singen to sing
sinnvoll sensible; meaningful
Situation(en), *f.* situation
sitzen to sit
sitzenbleiben to get stuck; to remain seated
skandinavisch Scandinavian
skifahren to ski
Skihütte(n), *f.* skiing hut; mountain lodge
Skikurs(e), *m.* skiing lesson
Skilehrer(–), *m.* skiing instructor
Skiurlaub(e), *m.* skiing trip
Skorpion, *m.* Scorpio

sofort at once
sogar even
Sohn("e), *m.* son
Soldat(en), *m.* soldier
sollen shall, to be supposed to
Sommer(–), *m.* summer
Sommerferien (pl.), *f.* summer holidays/vacation
Sommerpause(n), *f.* summer break
Sonne(n), *f.* sun
Sonnenaufgang("e), *m.* sunrise
Sonnenbrand, *m.* sunburn
Sonnenenergie(n), *f.* solar energy
Sonnenuntergang("e), *m.* sunset
Sonnenschutzmittel(–), *n.* sun protection cream
Sonntag(e), *m.* Sunday
Sonntagszeitung(en), *f.* Sunday paper
Sorge(n), *f.* worry, care
sorgen to worry
sorgenfrei carefree
Sorte(n), *f.* type, species
sortieren to work out; to classify
Sortiment(e), *n.* collection
Soße(n), *f.* sauce
sowieso anyway
Sozialarbeiter(–), *m.* social worker (*m.*)
Sozialministerium(ien), *n.* Ministry of Social Affairs
spannend exciting
sparen to save, to economize
sparsam economical
Spaß("e), *m.* fun; joke
spät late
später later
spazierengehen to go for a walk
Spaziergang("e), *m.* walk
Speiselokal(e), *n.* restaurant
Spezialist(en), *m.* expert, specialist
Spezialistenangelegenheit(en), *f.* matter for the experts
Spezialität(en), *f.* speciality
speziell specific(ally)
Spiegel(–), *m.* mirror
spielen to play
Spieler(–), *m.* player (*m.*)
Spinat, *m.* spinach
Spitzenmodell(e), *n.* top model, top of the range
Sport, *m.* sport, games
Sportart(en), *f.* kind of sport
Sportschau(en), *f.* sports programme
Sprachkurs(e), *m.* language course
Sprachlabor(e), *n.* language laboratory
sprechen to speak
Staatsexamen(–), *n.* state exam (equivalent to an M.A.)
Stadt("e), *f.* town
Städtetour(en), *f.* city tour
Stand("e), *m.* stall
Standesamt("er), *n.* registry office
ständig constantly
Stange(n), *f.* pole
stark heavy; strong
Stau(e), *m.* (traffic) jam
staubsaugen to vacuum, to hoover

Staubsauger(–), *m.* vacuum cleaner
stehen to stand
Stelle(n), *f.* job, situation, vacancy
stets always
Steuer(–), *n.* steering wheel
Stimmung(en), *f.* atmosphere, mood
Stipendiatin(en), *f.* holder of a
  scholarship (*f.*)
Stipendium(ien), *n.* scholarship
stolz proud
Strand("e), *m.* beach
Strecke(n), f. route
Streckennetz(e), *n.* rail network
Streit(e), *m.* quarrel
stricken to knit
Struktur(en), *f.* structure
Stück(e), *n.* piece
Student(en), *m.* student (*m.*)
Studie(n), *f.* study
studieren to study
Stunde(n), *f.* hour
Sturz("e), *m.* fall
suchen to seek, to look for
Süddalmatien Southern Dalmatia
süddeutsch South German
Süddeutschland Southern Germany
Summer(–), *m.* buzzer
Supermarkt("e), *m.* supermarket
Suppenhuhn("er), *n.* boiling chicken
süß sweet
Süßspeise(n), *f.* sweet

Tag(e), *m.* day
tagelang for days
Tagesablauf("e), *m.* daily routine
Tagesausflug("e), *m.* day trip
Tageskarte(n), *f.* daily menu
Tagesreise(n), *f.* a day's journey
Tagessatz("e), *m.* daily rate
Tagesthema(men), *m.* topic of the day
Tageszeit(en), *f.* time of day
täglich daily
Tankstelle(n), *f.* petrol/gas station
Tante(n), *f.* aunt
tanzen to dance
Tanzlokal(e), *n.* dance hall
Tanzschule(n), *f.* dance school
Tanzveranstaltung(en), *f.* dance
Tasche(n), *f.* pocket, bag
Tauchen, *n.* scuba diving
Technik(en), *f.* technique
Technik, *f.* technical science
Technologie, *f.* technology
technologisch technological
Tee(s), *m.* tea
Teig(e), *m.* dough
Teil(e), *n.* part, portion; zum Teil
  partly
teilen to share
Telefon(e), *n.* telephone
telefonieren to telephone
Tennis spielen, *n.* to play tennis
Teppichboden("), *m.* fitted carpet
Termin(e), *m.* appointment,
  engagement
teuer expensive
Theater(–), *n.* theatre

Theaterkasse(n), *f.* box office
Tier(e), *n.* animal
Tierfilm(e), *m.* animal film
Tisch(e), *m.* table
Tischler(–), *m.* carpenter (*m.*)
Tochter("), *f.* daughter
todschick terribly chic
toll super, great, exciting
Tomate(n), *f.* tomato
Topf("e), *m.* pot
Tourenkarte(n), *f.* touring ticket
Tourist(en), *m.* tourist
trampeln to trample
trampen to hitchhike
Transportarbeiter(–), *m.* transport
  worker (*m.*)
Transportmittel(–), *n.* means of
  transport
Transportwesen, *n.* transport system
transsibirisch Trans-Siberian
Traube(n), *f.* grape
Traum("e), *m.* dream
Traumurlaub(e), *m.* dream holiday
traurig sad
treffen to meet
trinken to drink
Triumph(e), *m.* triumph
trocken dry
trotz despite
trotzdem in spite of
Tür(en), *f.* door
Typ(en), *m.* type
typisch typical

üben to practise
über over
überall everywhere
überhaupt at all
überholen to overtake, to pass
überlegen to think, to consider
übermorgen day after tomorrow
überraschen to surprise
überregional national
überschaubar manageable
(sich) überschlagen to turn over
Überschrift(en), *f.* title
übertreiben to exaggerate
überwiegend mainly
überzeugen to convince
übrigens by the way
Ufer(–), *n.* shore
umfallen to fall over
umfassend comprehensive
umgekehrt the other way around
umgraben to dig
Umstand("e), *m.* circumstance
umsteigen to change (trains, etc.)
umstrukturieren re-structure
Umweg(e), *m.* diversion
Umwelt(en), *f.* environment
unbefristet unlimited
unerfüllbar unfulfilled
Unfall("e), *m.* accident
ungesund unhealthy
Universität(en), *f.* university
Unkraut("er), *n.* weed
Unsicherheit(en), *f.* insecurity

Unsinn, *m.* nonsense
unter among; under
unterhalten to entertain; to amuse
(sich) unterhalten to converse
Unterhaltung(en), *f.* entertainment;
conversation
Unterhaltungsfilm(e), *m.* light feature
film
unternehmen to undertake
Unterricht(e), *m.* lesson
unterrichten to teach
Unterschied(e), *m.* difference
unterstützen to support
unterwegs travelling, on the move
unverheiratet single
uralt ancient
Urlaub(e), *m.* holiday, vacation
Urlaubsgebiet(e), *n.* holiday area
Urlaubsort(e), *m.* holiday resort
Urlaubsplan(¨e), *m.* holiday plan
utopisch utopian

Vegetarier(–), *m.* vegetarian (*m.*)
Vegetarierin(nen), *f.* vegetarian (*f.*)
veränderlich changeable
Verbandzeug, *n.* bandages
verbessern to improve
Verbraucher(–), *m.* consumer
verbrennen to burn
Verdacht(e), *m.* suspicion
verderben to spoil
verdienen to earn
verführen to seduce
vergessen to forget
verhandeln to negotiate
Verhandlung(en), *f.* negotiation
Verhandlungstisch(e), *m.* negotiating
table
verkaufen to sell
Verkäufer(–), *m.* shop-assistant (*m.*)
Verkäuferin(nen), *f.* shop-assistant (*f.*)
Verkehr, *m.* traffic
Verkehrsbehinderung(en), *f.* (traffic)
hold-up
Verkehrslage(n), *f.* traffic conditions
Verkehrsmeldung(en), *f.* traffic news
Verkehrsstau(e), *m.* traffic jam
verkleiden to dress up
verlassen to leave
verletzen to injure
verlieren to lose
vermissen to miss
vernichten to destroy
Verpackung(en), *f.* wrapping
verrückt crazy
versäumen to miss
verschieben to postpone
verschieden different, diverse
verschwinden to disappear
verstehen to understand
verstellbar adjustable
Verteidigung(en), *f.* defence
Verteidigungspolitik(en), *f.* defence
policy
verwenden to use
verwöhnen to spoil
Video(s), *n.* video

Videobranche, *f.* video trade
Videogerät(e), *n.* video recorder
Videospiel(e), *n.* video game
viel besser much better
vielleicht possibly, perhaps
Viertel(–), *n.* quarter
Volkshochschule(n), *f.* adult
education centre
völlig totally, completely
von vorne bis hinten throroughly;
from beginning to end
vor allen Dingen first of all, above all
voraussetzen to assume
vorbereiten to prepare
vorgestern day before yesterday
vorhaben to plan
vorher before
vorhersagen to predict
(sich) vorkommen to feel like
vor kurzem recently
Vormittag(e), *m.* late morning
vormittags in the morning
Vorrat(¨e), *m.* provision
Vorschlag(¨e), *m.* suggestion
vorstellen to introduce; to imagine
Vorstellung(en), *f.* performance
Vorteil(e), *m.* advantage
vorwiegend predominant
Vorzugskarte(n), *f.* special (cheap)
ticket

Waage, *f.* Libra
wachsen to grow
wackeln to wobble
Waffe(n), *f.* weapon
wählen to elect, to vote
Wahnsinn, *m.* insanity
wahr werden to come true
Wald(¨er), *m.* wood, forest
Waldsterben, *n.* dying of the forests
Walzer(–), *m.* waltz
Wand(¨e), *f.* wall
wandern to hike
wann when
warm warm
Wärmflasche(n), *f.* hot-water bottle
warten to wait
warum why
was what
waschen to wash
Waschraum(¨e), *m.* cloak room,
lavatory
Wasser(–), *n.* water
Wassermann, *m.* Aquarius
Wassermelone(n), *f.* watermelon
wechseln to change
Wecker(–), *m.* alarm-clock
Weg(e), *m.* way
wegen because of
wegfahren to go away
Weib(er), *n.* spouse (*f.*), wife
weich soft
Weihnachten, *n.* Christmas
Weihnachtsbaum(¨e), *m.* Christmas
tree
Weihnachtsgans(¨e), *f.* Christmas
goose

Weihnachtslied(er), Christmas carol
Weihnachtstag(e), *m.* Christmas Day
Wein(e), *m.* wine
Weinberg(e), *m.* vineyard
Weinfest(e), *n.* wine festival
Weinflasche(n), *f.* winebottle
Weinlokal(e), *n.* wine bar
weiß white
Weißkraut, *n.* white cabbage
welche/r/s which
Welt(en), *f.* world
Weltrauminvasor(en), *m.* space invader
wenig little; **zu wenig** too little
wer/wem/wen who/m
Werbefernsehen, *n.* TV commercials
werden to become
Werk(e), *n.* work
Wertsachen (pl.) valuables
Wetter, *n.* weather
Wettrüsten, *n.* arms race
wichtig important
widerlich disgusting
Widder, *m.* Aries
wie how
wieder again
wieviel how much
Winter(–), *m.* winter
Winterferien, *f.* winter holiday
wirklich really
wissen to know
witzig funny
wo where
Wochenblatt(¨er), *n.* weekly paper
Wochenende(n), *n.* weekend
wochenlang for weeks
Wochenpauschale(n), *f.* weekly rate
woher where from
wohin where to
wohnen to live
Wohngemeinschaft(en), *f.* group of people living communally sharing a house or an apartment
Wohnmobil(e), *n.* mobile home
Wohnung(en), *f.* flat, apartment
Wolke(n), *f.* cloud
wollen to want
Wucht(en), *f.* force
Wunde(n), *f.* wound

Wunder(–), *n.* wonder
wunderbar wonderful
(sich) wundern to be amazed
Wunsch(¨e), *m.* wish
Würstchen(–), *n.* sausage
Wüste(n), *f.* desert

zäh tough
Zahl(en), *f.* number, figure
Zahlungsmittel(–), *n.* means of payment
Zahn(¨e), *m.* tooth
Zahnarzt(¨e), *m.* dentist (*m.*)
Zahnärztin(nen), *f.* dentist (*f.*)
zart tender
zärtlich tender, loving
zeigen to show
Zeit(en), *f.* time; **zur Zeit** at this moment
Zeitschrift(en), *f.* magazine
Zeitschriftenhändler(–), *m.* newsagent
Zeitung(en), *f.* newspaper
zeitweise at times
zerknittert creased
ziemlich rather
Zigarette(n), *f.* cigarette
Zimmer(–), *n.* room
zirka about
Zitrone(n), *f.* lemon
zivil civilian
zubreiten to prepare
Zucchini (pl.) courgettes
zuerst at first
zufrieden contented, satisfied
Zug(¨e), *m.* train
zugänglich accessible
Zuneigung(en), *f.* affection
zurückzahlen to pay back
zurückziehen to retire, to withdraw
zusammen together
zusammenkommen to meet
zusätzlich additional
Zuschlag(¨e), *m.* surcharge
zustimmen to agree
zweimal twice
Zwetschge(n), *f.* plum
Zwiebel(n), *f.* onion
zwischen between

English–German

(to be) able to **können**
about **zirka, ungefähr**
above all **vor allen Dingen**
accept **akzeptieren**
accessible **zugänglich**
accident **Unfall(¨e),** *m.*
accountant **Buchhalter(–),** *m.*
achieve **erreichen**
act **Nummer(n),** *f.;* **Akt(e)** *m.*
action **Aktion(en),** *f.*
active **aktiv**
actually **nämlich, eigentlich**
adapter **Adapter(–),** *m.*
additional **zusätzlich, extra**
adjustable **verstellbar**
adult **Erwachsene(n),** *m.*
advantage **Vorteil(e),** *m.*
advertisement **Inserat(e),** *n.*
advise **empfehlen, beraten**
aeroplane **Flugzeug(e),** *n.*
affect **betreffen**
affection **Zuneigung(en),** *f.*
afternoon **Nachmittag(e),** *m.*
after that **anschließend**
again **wieder**
age **Alter,** *n.*
agree **zustimmen**
air **Luft(¨e),** *f.*
air condition **Belüftungsanlage(n),** *f.*
air manoeuvre **Luftkampfmanöver(–),** *n.*
airport **Flughafen(¨),** *m.*
air traffic **Flugverkehr,** *m.*
alarm-clock **Wecker(–),** *m.*
alarm sound **Alarmton(¨e),** *m.*
alcoholic **alkoholisch**
A-level **Abitur(e),** *n.*
all the best **alles Gute**
almond **Mandel(n),** *f.*
alone **alleine**
already **schon**
also **noch, auch**
altogether **insgesamt**
always **stets, immer**
(to be) amazed **sich wundern**
ambulance **Krankenwagen(–),** *m.;*
  Ambulanz(en), *f.*
America **Amerika**
among **unter**
amount **Menge(n),** *f.*
amuse **(sich) amüsieren, unterhalten**
amusing **amüsant**
ancient **uralt; antik**
angle **Neigung(en),** *f.,* **Winkel(–),** *m.*
animal **Tier(e),** *n.*
animal film **Tierfilm(e),** *m.*
annual holiday **Jahresurlaub(e),** *m.*
announcement **Bekanntgabe(n),** *f.*
annoy **ärgern**
answer **melden, antworten**
antiseptic **Antiseptikum(ka),** *n.*
any at all **beliebig**
anyway **sowieso**

apéritif **Apéritif(s),** *m.*
apologize **entschuldigen**
appeal **ankommen, appellieren**
appealing **ansprechend**
appetite **Appetit(e),** *m.*
appliance **Gerät(e),** *n.*
apply **bewerben**
appointment **Termin(e),** *m.*
April **April,** *m.*
Aquarius **Wassermann,** *m.*
Aries **Widder,** *m.*
armchair **Sessel(–),** *m.*
arms race **Wettrüsten,** *n.*
arms talks **Rüstungsgespräch(e),** *n.*
arrival **Ankunft,** *f.*
arrive **anreisen, ankommen**
art **Kunst(¨e),** *f.*
article **Artikel(–),** *m.*
art treasure **Kunstschatz(¨e),** *m.*
ask **fragen**
ask for **bitten**
assume **voraussetzen, annehmen**
at all **überhaupt**
at first **zuerst**
athletics **Leichtathletik,** *f.*
at home **heimisch, zu Hause**
at it **daran**
Atlantic Ocean **Atlantik,** *m.*
at least **mindestens**
atmosphere **Stimmung(en),** *f.*
at once **sofort**
at one stage **früher**
at the earliest date **frühestens**
at the same time **nebenher,**
  gleichzeitig
at this moment **zur Zeit**
at times **zeitweise**
attraction **Attraktion(en),** *f.*
attractive **attraktiv**
aubergine **Aubergine(n),** *f.*
August **August,** *m.*
aunt **Tante(n),** *f.*
Austria **Österreich**
author **Autor(en),** *m.*
automatic **Automatik,** *f.*
autumn **Herbst(e),** *m.*
aviation **Luftfahrt(en),** *f.*
await **erwarten**

background **Hintergrund(¨e),** *m.*
bad **schlecht**
bag **Tasche(n),** .
bake **backen**
balance **Ausgleich(e),** *m.*
banana **Banane(n),** *f.*
band **Kapelle(n),** *f.*
bandage **Binde(n),** *f.*
bandages **Verbandzeug,** *n.*
bank **Bank(en),** *f.*
barley soup **Graupensuppe(n),** *f.*
basis **Grundlage(n),** *f.*
bathroom **Badezimmer(–),** *n.*

bath tub **Badewanne(n)**, *f.*
Bavarian Christian Democrats
 Christlich-Soziale Union = CSU
Bavarian Forest **Bayrischer Wald**, *m.*
be **sein**
beach **Strand(¨e)**, *m.*
bean **Bohne(n)**, *f.*
bear **ertragen**
beautician **Kosmetikerin(nen)**, *f.*
beautiful **schön**
because of **wegen**
become **werden**
bed **Bett(en)**, *n.*
beef **Rindfleisch**, *n.*
beer **Bier(e)**, *n.*
before **vorher**
begin **beginnen**
beginner **Anfänger(–)**, *m.*
beginner's course Anfängerkurs(e), *m.*
believe **glauben**
bench **Bank(¨e)**, *f.*
berry **Beere(n)**, *f.*
besides **außerdem**
best of all **am liebsten**
best of luck **Hals- und Beinbruch**
between **zwischen**
big **groß**
birthday **Geburtstag(e)**, *m.*
birthday child **Geburtstagskind(er)**, *n.*
a bit **bißchen**
bite (out) **ausbeißen**
black **schwarz**
blackberry **Brombeere(n)**, *f.*
black bread **Schwarzbrot(e)**, *n.*
Black Forest Gateaux **Schwarzwälder**
 Kirschtorte(n), *f.*
bland **fade**
blanket **Decke(n)**, *f.*
bloody **blutig**
blow **blasen**
blue **blau**
boarding-house **Pension(en)**, *f.*
boating **Bootfahren**, *n.*
boiling chicken **Suppenhuhn(¨er)**, *n.*
book **Buch(¨er)**, *n.*
book **buchen, bestellen**
bookshelf **Bücherregal(e)**, *n.*
book-shop **Buchhandlung(en)**, *f.*
(to be) bored (**sich**) **langweilen**
boredom **Langeweile**, *f.*
boring **langweilig**
born **geboren**
boss **Chef(s)**, *m.*, **Chefin(nen)**, *f.*
bowling alley **Kegelbahn(en)**, *f.*
box office **Theaterkasse(n)**, *f.*
boyfriend **Freund(e)**, *m.*
brake **bremsen**
bread **Brot(e)**, *n.*
bread roll **Brötchen(–)**, *n.*
break **brechen**
(to have) breakfast **frühstücken**
bricklayer **Maurer(–)**, *m.*
bride **Braut(¨e)**, *f.*
bridegroom **Bräutigam(e)**, *m.*
bridge **Brücke(n)**, *f.*
bring **bringen**
bring to light **an den Tag bringen**

broadcast **senden**
broken **kaputt**
brother(s) and sister(s) **Geschwister**
 (pl.), *f.*
Brussels sprouts **Rosenkohl**, *m.*
building site **Baustelle(n)**, *f.*
burn **verbrennen, brennen**
burst **platzen**
bus **Bus(se)**, *m.*
bush **Busch(¨e)**, *m.*
but **aber**
butcher **Metzger(–)**, *m.*
butter **Butter**, *f.*
button **Knopf(¨e)**, *m.*
button mushroom **Champignon(s)**, *m.*
buzzer **Summer(–)**, *m.*
by the way **übrigens**

cabinet **Kabinett(e)**, *n.*
cable television **Kabelfernsehen**, *n.*
cake **Kuchen(–)**, *m.*
calf's liver **Kalbsleber**, *f.*
call **rufen**
calorie **Kalorie(n)**, *f.*
camp-fire **Lagerfeuer(–)**, *n.*
can **Dose(n)**, *f.*
can **können**
candle **Kerze(n)**, *f.*
canteen **Kantine(n)**, *f.*
capital **Hauptstadt(¨e)**, *f.*
car **Auto(s)**, *n.*,
 Personenkraftwagen(–), *m.* = PKW
carbohydrate **Kohlehydrat(e)**, *n.*
care **Sorge(n)**, *f.*
career **Karriere(n)**, *f.*
career plan **Berufsplan(¨e)**, *m.*
carefree **sorgenfrei**
car hire **Autovermietung(en)**, *f.*
carnival **Fasching**, *m.*
carpenter **Tischler(–)**, *m.*
carrot **Möhre(n)**, *f.*
carrot salad **Karottensalat(e)**, *m.*
cash **bar**
cashier (*f.*) **Kassiererin(nen)**, *f.*
cassette **Kassette(n)**, *f.*
castle **Schloß(¨sser)**, *n.*, **Burg(en)**, *f.*
casual **lässig**
cauliflower **Blumenkohl**, *m.*
celebrate **feiern**
chance **Chance(n)**, *f.*
change **Abwechslung(en)**, *f.*
change **wechseln, ändern, umsteigen**
changeable **veränderlich**
chat **plaudern**
cheap **billig**
cheese **Käse(–)**, *m.*
cheese-cake **Käsekuchen(–)**, *m.*
child **Kind(er)**, *n.*
children's programme
 Kindersendung(en), *f.*
chimneysweep **Schornsteinfeger(–)**, *m.*
China **China**
chips **Pommes Frites** (pl.), *f.*
chocolate ice-cream **Schokoladeneis**, *n.*
chop **schnitzeln**
chop **Kotelett(s)**, *n.*
Christian Democrats **Christlich-**

Demokratische Union = CDU
Christmas **Weihnachten**
Christmas carol **Weihnachtslied(er)**, *n.*
Christmas Day **Weihnachtstag(e)**, *m.*
Christmas Eve **Heiliger Abend**, *m.*
Christmas goose **Weihnachtsgans(¨e)**, *f.*
Christmas tree **Weihnachtsbaum(¨e)**, *m.*
church **Kirche(n)**, *f.*
cigarette **Zigarette(n)**, *f.*
cinema **Kino(s)**, *n.*
circle **Kreis(e)**, *m.*
circle (theat.) **Rang(¨e)**, *m.*
circle of friends **Bekanntenkreis(e)**, *m.*
circumstance **Umstand(¨e)**, *m.*
Citizen of the Federal Republic
  Bundesbürger(–), *m.*
civilian **zivil**
class **Klasse(n)**, *f.*
classic **Klassiker(–)**, *m.*
classical **klassisch**
classify **sortieren**
clean **putzen**
clean **sauber**
cleaner *(f.)* **Putzfrau(en)**, *f.*
clear **anschaulich**
clerk **Beamte(n)**, *m.*, **Beamtin(nen)**, *f.*
clever **gescheit**
to climatize **klimatisieren**
climbing frame **Kletterleiter(n)**, *f.*
cloak room **Waschraum(¨e)**, *m.*
close **dicht**
cloud **Wolke(n)**, *f.*
cloudy **bewölkt**
coach **Reisewagen(–)**, *m.*
coalition partner **Koalitionspartner**
  (–), *m.*
coffee **Kaffee**, *m.*
coffee circle **Kaffeekränzchen(–)**, *n.*
cold **kalt**
cold **Erkältung(en)**, *f.*
colleague **Kollege(n)**, *m.*
collection **Sortiment(e)**, *n.*
colour **Farbe(n)**, *f.*
colour separation **Farbauflösung(en)**, *f.*
come **kommen**
comedy **Komödie(n)**, *f.*
come off **abgehen**
come true **wahr werden**
comfortable **bequem**
commercialize **kommerzialisieren**
commission **Auftrag(¨e)**, *m.*
communal **kommunal**
communism **Kommunismus**, *m.*
companion **Lebensgefährte(n)**, *m.*
company **Firma(men)**, *f.*
compartment **Abteil(e)**, *n.*
complain **schimpfen; (sich) beklagen**
completely **völlig**
complicated **kompliziert**
comprehensive **umfassend**
congratulate **gratulieren**
congratulations **Herzlichen**
  Glückwunsch (Herzliche ¨e)
conservative **konservativ**
consider **überlegen, beachten**
consist **bestehen**
constantly **ständig**

construction **Bau**, *m.*
constructor **Konstrukteur(e)**, *m.*
consumer **Verbraucher(–)**, *m.*
consumption **Konsum**, *m.*
contented **zufrieden**
contribution **Beitrag(¨e)**, *m.*
control **kontrollieren**
converse **sich unterhalten**
convince **überzeugen**
cook **kochen**
cooker **Herd(e)**, *m.*
cooking apple **Küchenapfel(¨)**, *m.*
cool **kühlen**
corner **Ecke(n)**, *f.*
cosiness **Gemütlichkeit**, *f.*
cost **Preis(e)**, *m.*
cost **kosten**
cosy **gemütlich**
cottage cheese **Quark** (pl.), *m.*
couchette **Liegewagen(–)**, *m.*
country road **Landstraße(n)**, *f.*
countryside **Land**, *n.*
courgettes **Zucchini** (pl.), *f.*
cracker **Knallbonbon(s)**, *n.*
crawl out **herauskriechen**
crazy **verrückt**
cream **Sahne**, *f.*
creased **zerknittert**
create **schaffen**
creativity **Kreativität(en)**, *f.*
creature **Kerlchen(–)**, *n.*
crèche **Kinderkrippe(n)**, f.
credit card **Kreditkarte(n)**, *f.*
crisps **Chips** (pl.), *f.*
crispy **knusprig**
critical **kritisch**
cross-country skiing **Langlauf(¨e)**, *m.*
cruel **brutal**
crunchy **knackig**
cucumber **Gurke(n)**, *f.*
cult **Kult(e)**, *m.*
cultural **kulturell**
curl **Locke(n)**, *f.*
curriculum vitae **Lebenslauf(¨e)**, , *m.*
cushion **Liegepolster(–)**, *n.*
customer **Kunde(n)**, *m.*
cut **Schnitt(e)**, *m.*
cut **schneiden**

daily **täglich**
daily menu **Tageskarte(n)**, *f.*
daily rate **Tagessatz(¨e)**, *m.*
daily routine **Tagesablauf(¨e)**, *m.*,
  Alltagstrott, *m.*
dance **Tanzveranstaltung(en)**, *f.*
dance **tanzen**
dance floor **Parkett(e)**, n.
dance hall **Tanzlokal(e)**, *n.*
dance school **Tanzschule(n)**, *f.*
dangerous **gefährlich**
dash **Anlauf(¨e)**, *m.*
daughter **Tochter(¨)**, *f.*
day **Tag(e)**, *m.*
day after tomorrow **übermorgen**
day before yesterday **vorgestern**
day journey **Tagesreise(n)**, *f.*
December **Dezember**, *m.*

decide entschließen, entscheiden
decision Entscheidung(en), f.
defence Verteidigung(en), f.
defence politics
  Verteidigungspolitik(en), f.
delicate fein
delicious lecker
be delighted sich freuen
delightful herrlich
deliver abliefern
dentist Zahnarzt(¨e), m.,
  Zahnärztin(nen), f.
departure Abfahrt(en), f.
depend abhängen
depending on je nachdem
depress deprimieren
desert Wüste(n), f.
disinfectant Desinfektionsmittel(–), n.
despite trotz
destination Reiseziel(e), n.
destroy vernichten
detail Einzelheit(en), f.
develop entwickeln
diarrhoea Durchfall(¨e), m.
die in action fallen
diesel driven car Diesel
diet Diät(en), f.
difference Unterschied(e), m.
different verschieden, anders
difficult schwierig
difficulty Schwierigkeit(en), f.
dig umgraben
dinner Abendessen(–), n.
direct direkt
direction Richtung(en), f.
direction of journey
  Fahrtrichtung(en), f.
director (theat.) Regisseur(e), m.
dirty schmutzig
disadvantage Nachteil(e), m.
disappear verschwinden
disgusting widerlich
dishes Geschirr(e), n.
distance Entfernung(en), f.
distant entfernt
ditch Graben(¨), m.
diverse verschieden
diversified abwechslungsreich
diversion Umweg(e), m.
do machen, tun
doctor Arzt(¨e), m., Ärztin(nen), f.
doctor's assistant Arzthelferin(nen), f.
document Papier(e), n.
dog dirt Hundehaufen(–), m.
door Tür(en), f.
dough Teig(e), m.
downhill skiing Abfahrtsski, m.
drama Theaterstück(e), n.
dream Traum(¨e), m.
dream holiday Traumurlaub(e), m.
dress Kleid(er), n.
dress up verkleiden
drink Getränk(e), n.
drink trinken
drive Auto fahren, fahren
driver Fahrer(–), m., Autofahrer(–), m.
dry trocken, herb

duck Ente(n), f.
dumpling Knödel(–), m.

each jede, jeder
ear Ohr(en), n.
earlier früher
early früh
earn verdienen
Easter Ostern (pl.), n.
East European country
  Ostblockland(¨er), n.
East Frisian tea Ostfriesentee, m.
easy einfach
eat essen
ecologists Grünen (pl.)
economical sparsam
education Ausbildung(en), f.
educational holiday
  Bildungsurlaub(e), m.
egg Ei(er), n.
egg flip Eierlikör(e), m.
egg liqueur Eierlikör(e), m.
Egypt Ägypten
either – or entweder – oder
elastoplast Pflaster(–), n.
elect wählen
electricity Elektrizität, f.
electronic Elektronik(en), f.
emphasis Nachdruck, m.
employ einstellen
employer Arbeitgeber(–), m.
end Ende(n), n.
end enden
engagement Termin(e), m.
English englisch
Englishman Engländer(–), m.
enjoy o.s. sich freuen
enough genug
entertain unterhalten
entertainment Unterhaltung(en), f.
environment Umwelt(en), f.
equality Gleichberechtigung, f.
err irren
escape ausbrechen
Eskimo Eskimo(s), m.
especially insbesondere
eternal ewig
even selbst, sogar
evening Abend(e), m.
evening classes Volkshochschule(n), f.
evening college
  Abendgymnasium(ien), n.
everyday use Hausgebrauch, m.
everywhere überall
exact genau
exaggerate übertreiben
example Beispiel(e), n.
excellent prima
exciting toll, spannend
excursion Ausflug(¨e), m.
excuse entschuldigen
exhausted kaputt, erschöpft
exhausting anstrengend
exhibition Ausstellung(en), f.
expect erwarten
expensive teuer
experience erleben

experiment **Experiment(e)**, *n.*
expert **Spezialist(en)**, *m.*
explain **erklären**
explode **explodieren**
explorer **Entdecker(–)**, *m.*
export firm **Exportfirma(men)**, *f.*
express train **Schnellzug(¨e)**, *m.*
extend **erweitern**
extract juice **entsaften**
extent **Ausmaß(e)**, *n.*
eye **Auge(n)**, *n.*
eye drops **Augentropfen** (pl.), *f.*

face cream **Gesichtscreme**, *f.*
factory **Fabrik(en)**, *f.*
fair **heiter**
fall **Sturz(¨e)**, *m.*
fall **fallen, hinfallen**
fall over **umfallen**
family **Familie(n)**, *f.*
family epidemic **Familienepidemie(n)**, *f.*
family occasion **Familienfest(e)**, *n.*
fare **Fahrpreis(e)**, *m.*
farm **Bauernhof(¨e)**, *m.*
fascinating **faszinierend**
fashion **Mode(n)**, *f.*
fast **schnell**
fast **Hungerkur(en)**, *f.*
fast **fasten**
fat **dick**
fate **Schicksal(e)**, *n.*
favourite **Renner(–)**, *m.*
favourite kind of sport
  Lieblingssportart(en), *f.*
fear **Angst(¨e)**, *f.*
feasible **machbar**
federal **föderativ**
Federal Chancellor **Bundeskanzler(–)**, *m.*
Federal League **Bundesliga(gen)**, *f.*
Federal Parliament **Bundestag** (pl.), *m.*
Federal President
  Bundespräsident(en), *m.*
Federal Republic of Germany
  Bundesrepublik Deutschland, *f.*
Federal State **Bundesland(¨er)**, *n.*
feeling **Gefühl(e)**, *n.*
feel like **sich vorkommen**
feel sorry for **leid tun**
fertilize **düngen**
fetch **holen**
fever **Fieber(–)**, *n.*
fiasco **Reinfall(¨e)**, *m.*
field of vision **Blickfeld(er)**, *m.*
field salad **Ackersalat(e)**, *m.*
fight **kämpfen**
fill **füllen**
film **Film(e)**, *m.*
final school examination
  Schulabschluß(¨sse), *m.*
finance **finanzieren**
financial **finanziell**
find **finden**
find out **erfahren**
fireworks **Feuerwerk(e)**, *n.*
firm **Firma(men)**, *f.*
first of all **vor allen Dingen**

fish **Fisch(e)**, *m.*
fit **in Form, beweglich**
fitted carpet **Teppichboden(¨)**, *m.*
fitting **passend**
fix **befestigen**
flat **Wohnung(en)**, *f.*
flat rate **pauschal**
flexitime **gleitende Arbeitszeit(en)**, *f.*
flop **Reinfall(¨e)**, *m.*
flower **Blume(n)**, *f.*
flu **Grippe(n)**, *f.*
fly **fliegen**
folding-table **Klapptisch(e)**, *m.*
food **Essen(–)**, *n.*
food processor **Küchenmaschine(n)**, *f.*
foot **Fuß(¨e)**, , *m.*
football **Fußball(¨e)**, *m.*
force **Wucht(en)**, *f.*
for days **tagelang**
foreign **ausländisch**
forest **Wald(¨er)**, *m.*
forget **vergessen**
former **ehemalig**
form of Government
  Regierungssystem(e), *n.*
for weeks **wochenlang**
France **Frankreich**
Franconian **fränkish**
freedom **Freiheit(en)**, *f.*
freelance **frei(beruflich)**
freeze **gefrieren**
French **Französisch**, *n.*
fresh **frisch**
Friday **Freitag(e)**, *m.*
fridge **Kühlschrank(¨e)**, *m.*
friend **Freund(e)**, *m.*
friendly **freundlich**
friendship **Freundschaft(en)**, *f.*
fright **Schreck(en)**, *m.*
fringe **Pony**, *m.*
from beginning to end **von vorne bis
  hinten**
fruit **Obst**, *n.*
fruit-juice diet **Saftkur(en)**, *f.*
fry **braten**
full-time **ganztags**
fun **Spaß(¨sse)**, *m.*, **Fröhlichkeit(en)**, *f.*
funny **lächerlich, lustig**
furnish **ausstatten**

gaiety **Fröhlichkeit(en)**, *f.*
games **Sport**, *m.*
gap **Lücke(n)**, *f.*
gardener **Gärtner(–)**, *m.*
garlic **Knoblauch**, *n.*
gastric flu **Darmgrippe**, *f.*
gel **Gelee(s)**, *n.*
general education **Allgemeinbildung**, *f.*
germ **Bakterie(n)**, *f.*
German **deutsch**
German Federal Railways **Deutsche
  Bundesbahn**
German Service **Deutschsprachiger
  Dienst**
get **holen, bekommen**
get into **reinkommen**
get married **heiraten**

get stuck **sitzenbleiben,
 hängenbleiben**
get there **hinkommen**
get up **aufstehen**
gherkin **Einmachgurke(n)**, *f.*
ghost **Geist(er)**, *m.*
giant **Riese(n)**, *m.*
gigantic **riesig**
girl **Mädchen(–)**, *n.*
girl friend **Freundin(nen)**, *f.*
give **geben**
give away **schenken**
glad **froh**
glass **Glas(¨er)**, *n.*
gliding **Segelfliegen**, *n.*
glove **Handschuh(e)**, *m.*
go **gehen**
go away **wegfahren**
go for a walk **spazierengehen**
good **gut**
good evening **Guten Abend**
good value **günstig**
go out **ausgehen**
go somewhere **hinfahren**
go to a pub **einkehren**
government **Regierung(en)**, *f.*
gracious **gnädig; anmutig**
gram **Gramm** (pl.), *n.*
grammar school **Gymnasium(ien)**, *n.*
grandchild **Enkelkind(er)**, *n.*
granny **Oma(s)**, *f.*
grape **Traube(n)**, *f.*
grate **reiben**
great **toll, prima**
Greece **Griechenland**
green **grün**
(the) Greens **die Grünen** (pl.)
greet **grüßen**
grilled meat **Grillbraten(–)**, *m.*
gross **brutto**
group **Gruppe(n)**, *f.*, **Gesellschaft(en)**, *f.*
grow **wachsen**
guarantee **garantieren**
guessing game **Ratespiel(e)**, *n.*
guest **Gast(¨e)**, *m.*
guide **Reiseführer(–)**, *m.*

hair-do **Frisur(en)**, *f.*
half **halb**
half-board **Halbpension**, *f.*
handball pitch **Handballplatz(¨e)**, *m.*
hangover **Kater(–)**, *m.*
happen **passieren**
hard **hart**
hat **Hut(¨e)**, *m.*
hate **hassen**
have **haben**
have to **müssen**
head **Kopf(¨e)**, *m.*, **Haupt(¨er)**, *n.*
headache **Kopfweh(e)**, *n.*
headline **Schlagzeile(n)**, *f.*
head-waitress **Serviermeisterin(nen)**, *f.*
health **Gesundheit**, *f.*
healthy **gesund**
heart **Herz(en)**, *n.*
heavy **stark, schwer**
hedge **Hecke(n)**, *f.*

help **helfen**
herb **Kraut(¨er)**, *n.*
hero **Held(en)**, *m.*
herring **Hering(e)**, *m.*
highest temperature
 Höchstemperatur(en), *f.*
highlight **Höhepunkt(e)**, *m.*
hike **wandern**
hire **mieten**
history **Geschichte**, *f.*
hitch **Hindernis(se)**, *n.*
hitchhike **trampen**
hobby **Hobby(s)**, *n.*
holiday **Urlaub(e)**, *m.*
holiday area **Urlaubsgebiet(e)**, *n.*
holiday compound **Klubanlage(n)**, *f.*
holiday plan **Urlaubsplan(¨e)**, *m.*
holiday resort **Urlaubsort(e)**, *m.*
home (personal) computer
 Heimcomputer(–), *m.*
home-made **selbstgemacht**
homework **Hausaufgabe(n)**, *f.*
hope **hoffen**
horrible **scheußlich**
horse **Pferd(e)**, *n.*
hospital **Krankenhaus(¨er)**, *n.*
hot **heiß**
hotel manageress **Hotelkauffrau(en)**, *f.*
hot tip **Geheimtip(s)**, *m.*
hot-water bottle **Wärmflasche(n)**, *f.*
hour **Stunde(n)**, *f.*
house **Haus(¨er)**, *n.*
househusband **Hausmann(¨er)**, *m.*
housewife **Hausfrau(en)**, *f.*
housework **Hausarbeit(en)**, *f.*
how **wie**
how much **wieviel**
hunger **Hunger**, *m.*
hurry **(sich) beeilen**
husband **(Ehe-) Mann(¨er)**, *m.*

ice **Eis**, *n.*
iceberg lettuce **Eissalat(e)**, *m.*
icecream **Eis**, *n.*
idea **Idee(n)**, *f.*
idiot **Idiot(en)**, *m.*
ignore **ignorieren**
ill **krank**
illegal copy **Raubkopie(n)**, *f.*
illness **Krankheit(en)**, *f.*
imagine **(sich) vorstellen**
impact **Aufprall(e)**, *m.*
important **wichtig**
impress **imponieren**
improve **verbessern**
improvise **improvisieren**
in a flash **blitzschnell**
include **mitzählen, dazurechnen**
included **inbegriffen**
including **einschließlich**
inclusive **inklusiv**
India **Indien**
inform **informieren**
information desk
 Informationsschalter(–), *m.*
ingenious **originell**
injure **verletzen**

in most cases **meist**
inn **Gasthof(¨e)**, *m.*
innovation **Neuerung(en)**, *f.*
insanity **Wahnsinn**, *m.*
insect repellent **Insektenschutz**, *m.*
insecurity **Unsicherheit(en)**, *f.*
inside **innen**
in spite of **trotzdem**
intensive **intensiv**
(to be) interested **(sich) interessieren**
interesting **interessant**
interview **Interview(s)**, *n.*
in the long run **langfristig, auf die Dauer**
in the middle **mittendrin**
in the morning **morgens, vormittags**
in the near future **demnächst**
in time **rechtzeitig**
introduce **vorstellen**
invention **Erfindung(en)**, *f.*
invitation **Einladung(en)**, *f.*
invite **einladen**
ironical **ironisch**
island **Insel(n)**, *f.*
issue **ausstellen**
Italian **italienisch**

job **Anstellung(en)**, *f.*, **Stelle(n)**, *f.*, **Beruf(e)**, *m.*
job market **Arbeitsmarkt(¨e)**, *m.*
job situation **Arbeitslage(n)**, *f.*
join **(sich) anschließen, beitreten**
joke **Spaß(¨sse)**, *m.*
journalist **Journalist(en)**, *m.*
journey **Reise(n)**, *f.*
July **Juli**, *m.*
junction **Anschluß(¨sse)**, *m.*

keep **(sich) halten, aufbewahren**
kilogram **Kilo(s)**, *n.*
kindergarten **Kindergarten(¨)**, *m.*
king **König(e)**, *m.*
kitchen **Küche(n)**, *f.*
kitchen garden **Gemüsegarten(¨)**, *m.*
knead **kneten**
knit **stricken**
know **wissen**

labour exchange **Arbeitsamt(¨er)**, *n.*
ladylike **damenhaft**
lake **See(n)**, *m.*
land **landen**
landlady **Pensionswirtin(nen)**, *f.*
language course **Sprachkurs(e)**, *m.*
language laboratory **Sprachlabor(e)**, *n.*
last **letzte,r,s**
last **dauern**
late **spät**
late morning **Vormittag(e)**, *m.*
later **später**
laugh **lachen**
lavatory **Waschraum(¨e)**, *m.*, **Toilette(n)**, *f.*
lay **decken, legen, liegen**
lazy **faul**
leaf **Blatt(¨er)**, *n.*
lean **mager**

least of all **am wenigsten**
leather **Leder(–)**, *n.*
leave **verlassen, abstellen, abfahren**
left **links**
leg **Bein(e)**, *n.*
lemon **Zitrone(n)**, *f.*
lemonade **Limonade(n)**, *f.*
lesson **Unterricht(e)**, *m.*
letter **Brief(e)**, *m.*
liberal **liberal**
Liberal Party **Freie Demokratische Partei = FDP**
Liberals **Liberale** (pl.)
liberal to left-wing **linksliberal**
Libra **Waage**, *f.*
library **Bibliothek(en)**, *f.*
life **Leben(–)**, *n.*
light **leicht**
light **anzünden**
light feature film **Unterhaltungsfilm(e)**, *m.*
like **so, wie**
like **mögen, gefallen**
line **Linie(n)**, *f.*
lipstick **Lippenstift(e)**, *m.*
list **Liste(n)**, *f.*
listen **anhören**
listener **Hörer(–)**, *m.*, **Hörerin(nen)**, *f.*
listless **schlaff**
literature **Literatur(en)**, *f.*
little **wenig**
live **wohnen**
local news **Lokalnachrichten** (pl.), *f.*
lock up **abschließen**
long **lang**
long-distance train **Fern-Express(e)**, *m.*
look **schauen, sehen**
look after **betreuen**
look at **hinschauen, ansehen**
look for **suchen**
look like **aussehen**
loosen-up **auflockern**
lorry **Lastwagen(–)**, *m.* = **LKW**
lose **verlieren**
lose weight **abnehmen**
love **Liebe**, *f.*
loved ones **Lieben** (pl.)
love of life **Lust am Leben**
loving **liebend**
low in fat **fettarm**
lucky dog **Glückspilz(e)**, *m.*
ludo **Mensch ärgere dich nicht!**
lukewarm **lauwarm**
lunch break **Mittagspause(n)**, *f.*
lunch-time **mittags**
luxury rail motor coach **Komforttriebwagen(–)**, *m.*

machine **Maschine(n)**, *f.*
magazine **Zeitschrift(en)**, *f.*
mainly **meistens, überwiegend**
main point **Hauptsache(n)**, *f.*
main station **Hauptbahnhof(¨e)**, *m.*
main subject **Hauptfach(¨er)**, *n.*
main task **Hauptaufgabe(n)**, *f.*
make **machen**
make use **Gebrauch machen**

man **Mensch(en)**, *m.*, **Mann(¨er)**, *m.*
manage **schaffen; leiten**
manageable **überschaubar**
mango **Mango(s)**, *f.*
manufactured product **Fabrikat(e)**, *n.*
margarine **Margarine**, *f.*
market **Markt(¨e)**, *m.*
mass exodus **Massenflucht** (pl.), *f.*
mathematics **Mathematik**, *f.*
matter **Sache(n)**, *f.*
matter **auswirken; eine Rolle spielen**
matter for the experts
  Spezialistenangelegenheit(en), *f.*
mature **reif**
may **dürfen**
mean **heißen; bedeuten**
meaning **Bedeutung(en)**, *f.*
meaningful **sinnvoll**
means **Mittel(–)**, *n.*
means of payment **Zahlungsmittel(–)**, *n.*
means of transport **Transportmittel(–)**, *n.*
meat **Fleisch**, *n.*
meat juice **Bratensatz**, *m.*
medical kit for travelling
  Reisapotheke(n), *f.*
medium range missile
  Mittelstreckenrakete(n), *f.*
meet **treffen, zusammenkommen**
Member of Parliament
  Bundestagsabgeordnete(n), *m.*
merchant **Kaufmann(leute)**, *m.*
microphone **Mikrofon(e)**, *n.*
military **militärisch**
milk **Milch**, *f.*
milliard **Milliarde(n)**, *f.*
mincer **Fleischwolf**, *m.*
Ministry of social affairs
  Sozialministerium(ien), *n.*
minute **Minute(n)**, *f.*
mirror **Spiegel(–)**, *m.*
Miss **Fräulein(–)**, *n.*
miss **vermissen, versäumen**
mix **mischen, mixen**
mobile **mobil**
mobile home **Wohnmobil(e)**, *n.*
mocha liqueur **Mokkalikör(e)**, *m.*
modern **modern**
moment **Moment(e)**, *m.*
money **Geld(er)**, *n.*
money worries **Geldsorgen** (pl.), *f.*
month **Monat(e)**, *m.*
monthly **monatlich**
mood **Stimmung(en)**, *f.*
moonrise **Mondaufgang(¨e)**, *m.*
morning **Morgen(–)**, *m.*
morning exercise **Frühgymnastik(en)**, *f.*
morning hour **Morgenstunde(n)**, *f.*
Moscow **Moskau**
mother **Mutter(¨)**, *f.*
mother's advisory service
  Mütterberatung(en), *f.*
motor **Motor(en)**, *m.*
motorway **Autobahn(en)**, *f.*
motorway exit **Anschluß(¨sse)**, *m.*
motto **Devise(n)**, *f.*
mountain **Berg(e)**, *m.*
mountain road **Hochstraße(n)**, *f.*

move **Schritt(e)**, *m.*
movie buff **Cineast(en)**, *m.*
much better **viel besser**
muesli **Müsli(s)**, *n.*
multi discipline sport **Mehrkampf**, *m.*
multi storey car park **Parkhaus(¨er)**, *n.*
murderer **Mörder(–)**, *m.*
muscle **Muskel(n)**, *m.*
museum **Museum(een)**, *m.*
mushroom **Pilz(e)**, *m.*
music **Musik** (pl.), *f.*
music in the home **Hausmusik**, *f.*
must **müssen**
mustard **Senf**, *m.*
mustard sauce **Senfsoße(n)**, *f.*

namely **nämlich**
nasty **böse**
national **überregional**
nature **Natur(en)**, *f.*
nature reserve **Naturschutzgebiet(e)**, *n.*
near **nah**
nearby **nah**
nearest **nächste**
nearly **beinahe**
necessary **notwendig**
nectarine **Nektarine(n)**, *f.*
need **brauchen**
negative **negativ**
negotiate **verhandeln**
negotiating table
  Verhandlungstisch(e), *m.*
negotiation **Verhandlung(en)**, *f.*
negro **Neger(–)**, *m.*
neighbour **Nachbar(n)**, *m.*
nerv **Nerv(en)**, *m.*
news **Meldung(en)**, *f.*, **Nachrichten** (pl.)
newsagent **Zeitschriftenhändler(–)**, *m.*
newspaper **Zeitung(en)**, *f.*
next **nächste**
nice **schön, fein**
nick **klauen**
night **Nacht(¨e)**, *f.*
night journey **Nachtreise(n)**, *f.*
nobody **niemand**
nod off **einnicken**
noise **Lärm**, *m.*, **Krach(e** also ¨**e)**, *m.*
noisy **laut**
nonsense **Flause(n)**, *f.*, **Unsinn**, *m.*
noodle soup **Nudelsuppe(n)**, *f.*
noon **Mittag(e)**, *m.*
norm **Regel(n)**, *f.*
normal **normal**
normally **normalerweise**
Northern Germany **Norddeutschland**
northside of the Alps
  Alpennordseite(n), *f.*
now **jetzt**
nuclear armament
  Atombewaffnung(en), *f.*
nuclear power station
  Atomkraftwerk(e), *n.*
number **Zahl(en)**, *f.*, **Nummer(n)**, *f.*
number **aufzählen**
nurse **Krankenschwester(n)**, *f.*
nut **Nuß(¨sse)**, *f.*

observe **beobachten; beachten**
occasional **gelegentlich**
October **Oktober**, *m.*
of course **natürlich,**
    selbstverständlich
offer **Angebot(e)**, *n.*
offer **anbieten**
office **Büro(s)**, *n.*
official **amtlich**
often **oft**
oh **ach nee, ach**
oil sheik **Ölscheich(e)**, *m.*
old **alt**
old-fashioned **altmodisch**
O-levels **Mittlere Reife**, *f.*
Olympic **olympisch**
onion **Zwiebel(n)**, *f.*
only **einzig**
on sale **im Handel**
on the move **unterwegs**
open **offen**
open **öffnen**
open-air **im Freien**
opera **Oper(n)**, *f.*
opinion **Meinung(en)**, *f.*,
    Auffassung(en), *f.*
opinion poll **Meinungsumfrage(n)**, *f.*
opposite **Gegenteil(e)**, *n.*
order **bestellen**
ordinary **normal**
organ recital **Orgelkonzert(e)**, *n.*
organize **organisieren**
over **über**
over here **hier drüben**
overtake **überholen**
own **besitzen**

pain **Schmerz(en)**, *m.*
painter **Maler(–)**, *m.*, **Malerin(nen)**, *f.*
painting **Gemälde(–)**, *n.*
palace **Palast(¨e)**, *m.*
panorama window
    Panoramafenster(–), *n.*
parents **Eltern** (pl.), *f.*
park **Park(s)**, *m.*
park **parken**
part **Teil(e)**, *n.*
partly **zum Teil**
partner **Partner(–)**, *m.*
partwork **Sammelwerk(e)**, *n.*
party (political) **Partei(en)**, *f.*
party **Fete(n)**, *f.*, **Fest(e)**, *n.*
party piece **Nummer(n)**, *f.*
pâté **Pastete(n)**, *f.*
pavement **Gehweg(e)**, *m.*
to pay **bezahlen**
to pay back **zurückbezahlen**
peach **Pfirsich(e)**, *m.*
pear **Birne(n)**, *f.*
pension **Rente(n)**, *f.*
people **Leute** (pl.), *f.*
pepper **pfeffern**
per **pro**
per cent **Prozent(e)**, *n.*
performance **Vorstellung(en)**, *f.*,
    Aufführung(en), *f.*
perhaps **vielleicht**

person **Person(en)**, *f.*
personal **persönlich**
petrol station **Tankstelle(n)**, *f.*
phantastic **fabelhaft**
phantom **Gespenst(er)**, *n.*
pharmacist **Apotheker(–)**, *m.*
pharmacy **Apotheke(n)**, *f.*
philosophy **Philosophie(n)**, *f.*
pickled **eingelegt**
pickled cucumber **Senfgurke(n)**, *f.*
pick up **abholen**
picture **Bild(er)**, *n.*
pie **Pastete(n)**, *f.*
piece **Stück(e)**, *n.*
piecemeal work **Akkordarbeit(en)**, *f.*
pig's trotter **Eisbein(e)**, *n.*
pink **rosarot, rosa**
place of work **Arbeitsplatz(¨e)**, *m.*
plaice **Scholle(n)**, *n.*
plain fare **Hausmannskost** (pl.), *f.*
plan **Plan(¨e)**, *m.*
plan **vorhaben, planen**
plastic surgeon
    Schönheitschirurg(en), *m.*
play **Theaterstück(e)**, *n.*
play **spielen**
play cards **Karten spielen**, *n.*
player **Spieler(–)**, *m.*
play tennis **Tennis spielen**, *n.*
please **bitte**
plum **Zwetschge(n)**, *f.*
plump **mollig**
pocket **Tasche(n)**, *f.*
pole **Stange(n)**, *f.*
police **Polizei**, *f.*
polite **höflich**
politics **Politik(en)**, *f.*
pomade **Pomade(n)**, *f.*
popular press **Boulevardpresse** (pl.), *f.*
population **Bevölkerung(en)**, *f.*
pork steak **Schweineschnitzel(–)**, *n.*
pornography **Pornographie(n)**, *f.*
porridge **Haferschleim**, *m.*
portion **Teil(e)**, *n.*, **Portion(en)**, *f.*
Portugal **Portugal**
position **Anstellung(en)**, *f.*
possibility **Möglichkeit(en)**, *f.*
possible **möglich, machbar**
possibly **vielleicht**
postman **Postbote(n)**, *m.*
postpone **verschieben**
pot **Topf(¨e)**, *m.*
potato **Kartoffel(n)**, *f.*
poultry **Geflügel**, *n.*
pound **Pfund(e)**, *n.*
pour **gießen**
powder **Puder(–)**, *n.*
practice **üben**
predict **vorhersagen**
predominant **vorwiegend**
première **Premiere(n)**, *f.*
prepare **vorbereiten, zubereiten**
present **Geschenk(e)**, *n.*
press **Presse** (pl.), *f.*
price-range **Preisgruppe(n)**, *f.*
price-tag **Preisschild(er)**, *n.*
primary school **Grundschule(n)**, *f.*

principle **Prinzip(ien)**, *n.*
prison **Gefängnis(se)**, *n.*
private clinic **Privatklinik(en)**, *f.*
privately owned vehicle
  Individualfahrzeug(e), *n.*
prize **Preis(e)**, *m.*
problem **Problem(e)**, *n.*
producer **Produzent(en)**, *m.*,
  Produzentin(nen), *f.*
product **Produkt(e)**, *n.*
production line **Fließband("er)**, *n.*
production of energy
  Energiegewinnung(en), *f.*
profession **Beruf(e)**, *m.*
professional life **Berufsleben(–)**, *n.*
programme **Sendung(en)**, *f.*,
  Programmierung(en), *f.*
progress **Fortschritt(e)**, *m.*
promenade concert
  Promenadenkonzert(e), *n.*
promotion **Aufstiegsmöglichkeit(en)**, *f.*
proper **richtig**
prospect **Aufstiegsmöglichkeit(en)**, *f.*
protection **Schutz**, *m.*
proud **stolz**
proved **bewährt**
provide **zur Verfügung stellen**
provision **Vorrat("e)**, *m.*
proximity **Nähe**, *f.*
pub **Gasthof("e)**, *m.*
public **öffentlich**
pullman seat **Reisesessel(–)**, *m.*
pull out **ausscheren**
pumpkin **Kürbis(se)**, *m.*
purification **Entschlackung(en)**, *f.*
put down **hinlegen**

quality **Güteklasse(n)**, *f.*,
  Qualität(en), *f.*
quarrel **Streit(e)**, *m.*
quarter **Viertel(–)**, *n.*
quick **schnell**
quiet **ruhig**

rabbit **Kaninchen(–)**, *n.*
radio **Radio(s)**, *n.*, **Rundfunk**, *m.*
radio message **Reiseruf(e)**, *m.*
radio service **Radiodienst(e)**, *m.*
radish **Radieschen(–)**, *n.*
rail network **Streckennetz(e)**, *n.*
railway journey **Bahnfahrt(en)**, *f.*
rain **regnen**
rainfall **Niederschlag("e)**, *m.*
rare **blutig**
rate per kilometre **Kilometergeld(er)**, *n.*
rather **lieber, ziemlich**
razor point **Rasiersteckdose(n)**, *f.*
react **reagieren**
read **lesen**
reading lamp **Leselampe(n)**, *f.*
really **eigentlich, wirklich**
reason **Grund("e)**, *m.*
reasonable **preisgünstig**
receive **bekommen, erhalten**
recently **vor kurzem, kürzlich**
recession **Rezession(en)**, *f.*
recipe **Rezept(e)**, *n.*

record **aufnehmen**
recording **Aufnahme(n)**, *f.*
recording switch **Aufnahmetaste(n)**, *f.*
red cabbage **Blaukraut**, *n.*
red currant **Johannisbeere(n)**, *f.*
reduce **ermäßigen**
reduction **Ermäßigung(en)**, *f.*
reform **Reform(en)**, *f.*
refresh **erfrischen**
region **Bereich(e)**, *m.*,
  Schienenstrecke(n), *f.*
regional **regional**
regional programme
  Regionalsendung(en), *f.*
registration number **Kennzeichen(–)**, *n.*
registry office **Standesamt("er)**, *n.*
relate to each other **aufeinander**
  reagieren
relative **relativ**
relax **entspannen**
relaxation **Erholung(–)**, *f.*
rent **Miete(n)**, *f.*
rent **mieten**
replacement band **Ersatzband(s)**, *f.*
report **Reportage(n)**, *f.*
report **melden**
reporter **Reporter(–)**, *m.*
representative **repräsentativ**
research **erforderschen**
rest **erholen, ausruhen**
restaurant **Speiselokal(e)**, *n.*,
  Restaurant(s), *n.*
re-structure **umstrukturieren**
resume **aufnehmen**
retire **(sich) zurückziehen,**
  pensionieren
retirement **Ruhestand**, *m.*
return journey **Rückfahrt(en)**, *f.*
ride **reiten**
ridiculous **lächerlich**
right **rechts, richtig**
right away **gleich**
right through **quer durch**
rise **Aufstieg(e)**, *m.*
river **Fluß("sse)**, *m.*
road works **Baustelle(n)**, *f.*
roast **rösten**
roasting chicken **Brathähnchen(–)**, *n.*
rock candy **Kandiszucker**, *m.*
role cliché **Rollenklischee(s)**, *n.*
romantic **romantisch**
room **Raum("e)**, *m.*, **Zimmer(–)**, n.
rose **Rose(n)**, *f.*
rosy **rosig**
route **Strecke(n)**, *f.*, **Fahrstrecke(n)**, *f.*
routine **Routine**, *f.*
rub down **abreiben**
rucksack **Rucksack("e)**, *m.*
ruined **kaputt**
(as a) rule **in der Regel**
rumpsteak **Rumpsteak(s)**, *n.*
runny nose **Schnupfen(–)**, *m.*
run-up **Anlauf("e)**, *m.*

sad **traurig**
saddle of venison **Rehrücken(–)**, *m.*
safe **Safe(s)**, *m.*

safe **sicher**
safety belt **Sicherheitsgurt(e)**, *m.*
salad **Salat(e)**, *m.*
salary **Gehalt("er)**, *n.*
saloon car **Großraumwagen(–)**, *m.*
salt **Salz**, *n.*
salt **salzen**
the same **dasselbe, dieselbe**
sanction **Sanktion(en)**, *f.*
satisfied **zufrieden**
Saturday **Samstag(e)**, *m.*
sauce **Soße(n)**, *f.*
sauna **Sauna(s)**, *f.*
sausage **Würstchen(–)**, *n.*
save **retten; sparen**
say **sagen**
Scandinavian **skandinavisch**
scholarship **Stipendium(ien)**, *n.*
school **Schule(n)**, *f.*
Scorpio **Skorpion**, *m.*
scuba diving **Tauchen**, *n.*
sea **Meer(e)**, *n.*
seal **Siegel(–)**, *n.*
season **Jahreszeit(en)**, *f.*
sector **Bereich(e)**, *m.*
secure **sichern**
seduce **verführen**
see **sehen**
seek **suchen**
selection **Auswahl(en)**, *f.*
self **selbst**
sell **verkaufen**
send **senden**
sensible **sinnvoll, vernünftig**
September **September**, *m.*
service **Dienst(e)**, *m.*
set **decken**
shall **sollen**
shape **Form(en)**, *f.*
share **teilen**
sheet **Blatt("er)**, *n.*
shine **scheinen**
ship **Schiff(e)**, *n.*
shock **Schock(s)**, *m.*
shop **Geschäft(e)**, *n.*
shop **einkaufen**
shop-assistant **Verkäufer(–)**, *m.*,
   Verkäuferin(nen), *f.*
shopping list **Einkaufszettel(–)**, *m.*
shore **Ufer(–)**, *n.*
show **zeigen**
shower **Dusche(n)**, *f.*
sick **krank**
side **Seite(n)**, *f.*
side corridor **Seitengang("e)**, *m.*
side dish **Beilage(n)**, *f.*
sign **Schild(er)**, *n.*
silk **Seide(n)**, *f.*
simple **einfach**
since **seitdem**
sing **singen**
singer **Sänger(–)**, *m.*, **Sängerin(nen)**, *f.*
single **einmalig, unverheiratet,**
   einfach
sister **Schwester(n)**, *f.*
sit **sitzen**
situation **Stelle(n)**, *f.*, **Situation(en)**, *f.*

size **Größe(n)**, *f.*
ski **skifahren**
skiing instructor **Skilehrer(–)**, *m.*
skiing holiday **Skiurlaub(e)**, *m.*
skiing hut **Skihütte(n)**, *f.*
skiing lesson **Skikurs(e)**, *m.*
sky **Himmel(–)**, *m.*
slaughter **schlachten**
sleep **schlafen**
slide **Rutschbahn(en)**, *f.*
slim **schlank**
slip **schlüpfen**
small **klein**
smoke **rauchen**
snack bar **Imbißhalle(n)**, *f.*
snow **Schnee**, *m.*
snow **schneien**
so **also**
soccer **Fußball** (pl.), *m.*
soccer pitch **Fußballplatz("e)**, *m.*
Social Democrats
   Sozialdemokratische Partei
   Deutschlands = SDP
social worker **Sozialarbeiter(–)**, *m.*
soft **weich**
soggy **matschig**
solar energy **Sonnenenergie(n)**, *f.*
soldier **Soldat(en)**, *m.*
somebody **jemand**
somehow **irgendwie**
some sort of **irgendwelche**
something **irgend etwas, etwas**
something good **was Gutes**
something special **was Besonderes**
sometimes **manchmal**
son **Sohn("e)**, *m.*
song **Lied(er)**, *n.*
song recital **Liederabend(e)**, *m.*
soon **bald**
sophisticated **raffiniert**
sore muscle **Muskelschmerz(en)**, *m.*
sore throat **Halsweh(e)**, *n.*
sort **Art(en)**, *f.*
sort out **sortieren**
sound **klingen, anhören**
Southern Dalmatia **Süd Dalmatien**
Southern Germany **Süddeutschland**
South German **süddeutsch**
space **Platz("e)**, *m.*
space invader **Weltrauminvasor(en)**, *m.*
speak **sprechen**
special **besonders**
specialist **Spezialist(en)**, *m.*
speciality **Spezialität(en)**, *f.*
special ticket (cheap) **Vorzugskarte(n)**, *f.*
species **Sorte(n)**, *f.*
specific **speziell**
spend **ausgeben**
spicy **scharf**
spinach **Spinat**, *m.*
spoil **verderben; verwöhnen**
spoiled **kaputt**
spoon **Löffel(–)**, *m.*
sport **Sport**, *m.*
sports programme **Sportschau(en)**, *f.*
spouse **Weib(er)**, *n.*
spring **Frühjahr**, *n.*

stall **Stand(¨e)**, *m.*
stand **stehen**
star **Stern(e)**, *m.*
start **aufziehen, anfangen**
state exam (M.A.) **Staatsexamen(–)**, *n.*
stay **bleiben**
stay at home **zu Hause bleiben**
steady **fest**
steak **Steak(s)**, *n.*
steam **dünsten**
steering-wheel **Steuer(–)**, *n.*
step **Schritt(e)**, *m.*
stew **dünsten**
stomach pain **Magenschmerz(en)**, *m.*
stop **Haltestelle(n)**, *f.*
stop **halten, aufhören**
storeman **Lagerarbeiter(–)**, *m.*
stove **Herd(e)**, *m.*
straight on **geradeaus**
strawberry **Erdbeere(n)**, *f.*
stray **fremdgehen**
strong **stark**
structure **Struktur(en)**, *f.*
student **Student(en)**, *m.*
study **Studie(n)**, *f.*
study **studieren**
success **Erfolg(e)**, *m.*
suddenly **plötzlich**
suffer **erleiden**
sufficient **ausreichend**
(to be) sufficient **genügen**
suggestion **Anregung(en)**, *f.*,
  Vorschlag(¨e), *m.*
suit **Anzug(¨e)**, *m.*
suit **passen**
summer **Sommer(–)**, *m.*
summer break **Sommerpause(n)**, *f.*
summer holidays vacation
  Sommerferien (pl.), *f.*
sun **Sonne(n)**, *f.*
sunburn **Sonnenbrand**, *m.*
Sunday **Sonntag(e)**, *m.*
Sunday paper **Sonntagszeitung(en)**, *f.*
sun protection cream
  Sonnenschutzmittel(–), *n.*
sunrise **Sonnenaufgang(¨e)**, *m.*
sunset **Sonnenuntergang(¨e)**, *m.*
super **toll**
supermarket **Supermarkt(¨e)**, *m.*
super power **Großmacht(¨e)**, *f.*
supple **beweglich**
supplier **Anbieter(–)**, *m.*
support **unterstützen**
to be supposed to **sollen**
surcharge **Zuschlag(¨e)**, *m.*
surprise **überraschen**
suspicion **Verdacht(e)**, *m.*
sweet **Süßspeise(n)**, *f.*
sweet **süß**
swim **schwimmen**
swimming-pool **Schwimmbad(¨er)**, *n.*
Swiss Trade Fair **Schweizer
  Mustermesse**
switch on **einschalten**
Switzerland **Schweiz**, *f.*

table **Tisch(e)**, *m.*

tabloid **Sensationsblatt(¨er)**, *n.*
take **nehmen**
take along **mitnehmen**
take a stroll **promenieren**
take care **darauf achten**
take in one's stride **gelassen
  aufnehmen**
take off **ablegen**
take out **herausnehmen**
taste **schmecken, probieren**
tea **Tee(s)**, *m.*
teach **unterrichten**
teacher **Lehrer(–)**, *m.*, **Lehrerin(nen)**,
  f.
technical science **Technik** (pl.), *f.*
technique **Technik(en)**, *f.*
technological **technologisch**
technology **Technologie**, *f.*
telephone **Telefon(e)**, *n.*
telephone **telefonieren, anrufen**
television **Fernsehen**, *n.*
television set **Fernsehgerät(e)**, *n.*
tell **erzählen**
tender **zärtlich, zart**
terrible **scheußlich**
terribly chic **todschick**
thank you **danke**
that is to say **also**
theatre **Theater(–)**, *n.*
theme **Motto(s)**, *n.*
then **dann**
the other way around **umgekehrt**
there **dort**
the sooner the better **je früher desto
  besser**
thing **Sache(n)**, *f.*
think **überlegen, glauben, denken**
think about **nachdenken**
thirst **Durst**, *m.*
this **hier**
thoroughly **von vorne bis hinten**
though **allerdings**
thought **Gedanke(n)**, *m.*
threaten **bedrohen**
through **durch**
Thursday **Donnerstag(e)**, *m.*
ticket **Karte(n)**, *f.*
ticket office **Fahrkartenschalter(–)**, *m.*
tidy up **aufräumen**
time **Zeit(en)**, *f.*, **Mal(e)**, *n.*
time after work **Freierabend(e)**, *m.*
time of day **Tageszeit(en)**, *f.*
time of the year **Jahreszeit(en)**, *f.*
tin **Konservenbüchse(n)**, *f.*, **Dose(n)**, *f.*
tire **ermüden**
tired **müde**
title **Überschrift(en)**, *f.*
today **heute**
together **gemeinsam, zusammen**
topical **aktuell**
tomato **Tomate(n)**, *f.*
tomcat **Kater(–)**, *m.*
tomorrow **morgen**
too little **zu wenig**
tooth **Zahn(¨e)**, *m.*
topic of the day **Tagesthema(men)**, *n.*
top model **Spitzenmodell(e)**, *n.*

top of the range **Spitzenmodell(e)**, *n.*
totally **völlig**
tough **zäh**
touring ticket **Tourenkarte(n)**, *f.*
tourist **Tourist(en)**, *m.*
tour operator **Reiseveranstalter(–)**, *m.*
towards **Richtung(en)**, *f.*, **gegen**
town **Stadt(¨e)**, *f.*
trade fair **Fachmesse(n)**, *f.*
traffic **Verkehr**, *m.*
traffic conditions **Verkehrslage(n)**, *f.*
traffic jam **Stau(e)**, *m.*,
    Verkehrsstau(e), *m.*
traffic news **Verkehrsmeldung(en)**, *f.*
train **Zug(¨e)**, *m.*, **Eisenbahn(en)**, *f.*
training course **Ausbildungskurs(e)**, *m.*
trample **trampeln**
transport system **Transportwesen**, *n.*
transport worker
    Transportarbeiter(–), *m.*
Trans-Siberian **transsibirisch**
travel **reisen**
travel agency **Reisebüro(s)**, *n.*
travelling **unterwegs**
treasure **Schatz(¨e)**, *m.*
trigger off **sich einschalten**
trip **Ausflug(¨e)**, , *m.*
triumph **Triumph(e)**, *m.*
trouble **Ärger** (pl.), *m.*, **Kummer(–)**, *m.*
trousers **Hose(n)**, *f.*
trout **Forelle(n)**, *f.*
truck **Lastwagen(–)**, *m.*
try **probieren**
try on **anprobieren**
try out **probieren, ausprobieren**
tube **Rohr(e)**, *n.*
turkey **Pute(n)**, *f.*, **Truthahn(¨e)**, *m.*
turn **abbiegen**
turn out well **glücken**
turn over **(sich) überschlagen**
TV commercials **Werbefernsehen**, *n.*
twice **zweimal**
type **Typ(en)**, *m.*, **Sorte(n)**, *f.*
typical **typisch**

understand **verstehen**
undertake **unternehmen**
unemployed **arbeitslos**
unemployment benefit
    Arbeitslosenunterstützung(en), *f.*
unfortunately **leider**
unfulfilled **unerfüllbar**
unhealthy **ungesund**
unique **einmalig, ausgefallen**
university **Universität(en)**, *f.*
unlimited **unbefristet**
unskilled labourer **Hilfsarbeiter(–)**, *m.*
upbringing **Erziehung**, *f.*
Upper Volta **Obervolta**
use **verwenden**
utopian **utopisch**

vacancy **Stelle(n)**, *f.*
vacancy for trainee **Lehrstelle(n)**, *f.*
vacation **Urlaub**, *m.* **Ferien** (pl.)
vacuum **staubsaugen**
vacuum cleaner **Staubsauger(–)**, *m.*

(to be) valid **gelten**
validity date **Geltungstag(e)**, *m.*
valuables **Wertsache(n)**, *f.*
varied **abwechslungsreich**
variety **Abwechslung(en)**, *f.*
vegetable **Gemüse(–)**, *n.*
vegetarian **Vegetarierin(nen)**, *f.*
vehicle **Fahrzeug(e)**, *n.*
vertical take-off **Senkrechtsstarter(–)**, *m.*
very **sehr**
very crowded **knallvoll**
video **Video(s)**, *n.*
video game **Videospiel(e)**, *n.*
video recorder **Videogerät(e)**, *n.*
video trade **Videobranche**, *f.*
view **Sicht**, *f.*
view **besichtigen**
village **Dorf(¨er)**, *n.*
vineyard **Weinberg(e)**, *m.*
violence **Gewalt(en)**, *f.*
visit **besuchen**
visitor **Besucher(–)**, *m.*,
    Besucherin(nen), *f.*
voluntary **freiwillig**

wait **warten**
waiter **Kellner(–)**, *m.*
waitress **Kellnerin(nen)**, *f.*
walk **Spaziergang(¨e)**, *m.*
wall **Wand(¨e)**, *f.*
waltz **Walzer(–)**, *m.*
want **wollen**
war **Krieg(e)**, *m.*
war game **Kriegsspiel(e)**, *n.*
warm **warm**
wash **waschen**
wash up **abwaschen**
watch **anschauen**
water **Wasser(–)**, *n.*
watermelon **Wassermelone(n)**, *f.*
way **Weg(e)**, *m.*
weapon **Waffe(n)**, *f.*
weather **Wetter**, *n.*
wedding **Hochzeit(en)**, *f.*
wedding-eve **Polterabend(e)**, *m.*
Wednesday **Mittwoch(e)**, *m.*
weed **Unkraut(¨er)**, *n.*
weed **jäten**
weekend **Wochenende(n)**, *n.*
weekly paper **Wochenblatt(¨er)**, *n.*
weekly rate **Wochenpauschale(n)**, *f.*
well **gut; na ja**
well done **durch (Fleisch)**
well-known **bekannt**
what **was**
when **wann**
where **wo**
where from **woher**
where to **wohin**
which **welche/r/s**
whipped cream **Schlagsahne**, *f.*
white **weiß**
white cabbage **Weißkraut**, *n.*
white radish **Rettich(e)**, *m.*
Whitsun **Pfingsten(–)**, *n.*
who/m **wer/wem/wen**
whole **ganz**

why **warum**
wide awake **munter**
wife **(Ehe-) Frau(en)**, *f.*
win **gewinnen**
window **Fenster(–)**, *n.*
window seat **Fensterplatz(¨e)**, *m.*
wind up **aufziehen**
wine **Wein(e)**, *m.*
wine bar **Weinlokal(e)**, *n.*
winebottle **Weinflasche(n)**, *f.*
wine festival **Weinfest(e)**, *n.*
wine from Franconia **Frankenwein(e)**, *m.*
winner **Gewinner(–)**, *m.*
winter **Winter(–)**, *m.*
winter holiday **Winterferien**, *f.*
wireless **Radio(s)**, *n.*
wish **Wunsch(¨e)**, *m.*
withdraw **zurückziehen**
with it **dazu**
without exception **ausnahmslos**
with pleasure **gern**
wobble **wackeln**
woman **Frau(en)**, *f.*
women's magazine
  Frauenzeitschrift(en), *f.*
wonder **Wunder(–)**, *n.*

wonderful **wunderbar**
wood **Holz(¨er)**, *n.*, **Wald(¨er)**, *m.*
work **Werk(e)**, *n.*, **Arbeit(en)**, *f.*
work **arbeiten**
worker **Arbeiter(–)**, *m.*,
  Arbeiterin(nen), *f.*
working day **Arbeitstag(e)**, *m.*
world **Welt(en)**, *f.*
worry **Sorge(n)**, *f.*
worry **(sich) sorgen**
wound **Wunde(n)**, *f.*
wrapping **Verpackung(en)**, *f.*
wrinkle **Falte(n)**, *f.*
write **schreiben**
wrong **falsch**

year **Jahr(e)**, *n.*
yearly **jährlich**
yesterday **gestern**
yet **bisher**
you know **nämlich**
young **jung**
you see **nämlich**
youth **Jugendliche(n)**, *f.m.*
Yugoslavian **jugoslawisch**

Index

Breakthrough Language Packs
Complete self-study courses

Each Breakthrough Language Pack is designed as a complete self-study course using audio cassettes and a course book. Each Pack contains:

* Three 60- or 90-minute audio cassettes
* The course book

Breakthrough Language Packs available:

Breakthrough Arabic	ISBN 0–333–56692–0
Breakthrough French	ISBN 0–333–58511–9
Breakthrough German	ISBN 0–333–56730–7
Breakthrough Greek	ISBN 0–333–48714–1
Breakthrough Italian	ISBN 0–333–48179–8
Breakthrough Russian	ISBN 0–333–55726–3
Breakthrough Spanish	ISBN 0–333–57105–3
Breakthrough Further French	ISBN 0–333–48193–3
Breakthrough Further German	ISBN 0–333–48189–5
Breakthrough Further Spanish	ISBN 0–333–48185–2
Breakthrough Business French	ISBN 0–333–54398–X
Breakthrough Business German	ISBN 0–333–54401–3
Breakthrough Business Spanish	ISBN 0–333–54404–8

* CD Packs are also now available for:

Breakthrough French	ISBN 0–333–58513–5
Breakthrough German	ISBN 0–333–57870–8
Breakthrough Spanish	ISBN 0–333–57874–0

Companion Language Grammars

Companion French Grammar
Chris Beswick,
Head of Modern Languages,
Shena Simon Sixth Form College, Manchester
0-333-48079-1   144 pages

Companion German Grammar
Isabel Willshaw, formerly lecturer in German,
Ealing College of Higher Education
0-333-48180-1   176 pages

Companion Spanish Grammar
Sandra Truscott,
Adult education tutor in Spanish
0-333-48181-X   128 pages

These basic pocket grammars, designed for easy reference by travellers and students on non-examination courses, cover the most important rules for speaking and understanding everyday French, German and Spanish.

Contents include:
* Clear explanations of grammatical points with examples of the use of each item in common situations
* 'Try it yourself' and 'learn by heart' sections with a range of activities to test the most important points
* A grammar glossary to familiarize the reader with terms such as pronouns, direct objects, auxiliary verbs etc
* Verb tables
* An index referring the user to an explanation of the particular grammatical point.